Bridging Discourses
in the ESL Classroom

Bridging Discourses in the ESL Classroom

Students, Teachers and Researchers

By Pauline Gibbons

continuum
LONDON • NEW YORK

Continuum

The Tower Building	80 Maiden Lane
11 York Road	Suite 704
London	New York
SE1 7NX	NY 10038

British Library Cataloguing-in-Publication Data
A catalogue record for this book is available from the British Library.

ISBN: HB: 0-8264-5536-0
         PB: 0-8264-5537-9

Typeset by Servis Filmsetting Ltd, Manchester
Printed and bound in Great Britain by Biddles Ltd, King's Lynn, Norfolk

Contents

Chapter 1   'Bridging Discourses' in the ESL classroom:
an introduction   1

Part 1   **Language, learning and learners: perspectives across disciplines**   13

Chapter 2   A sociocultural view of language and learning   15

Chapter 3   Second language learning and teaching   43

Part 2   **Inside two classrooms**   71

Chapter 4   Researching the classroom   73

Chapter 5   Teaching and learning in two classrooms   95

Part 3   **Discourse contexts for second language development**   121

Chapter 6   Teachers and learners: constructing new meanings   123

Chapter 7   The teachers: teaching as mediation   173

Chapter 8   The learners: affordances for learning   235

Glossary of systemic functional linguistic terms   275

Appendix: Episode summaries   277

References   301

Index   319

1 'Bridging discourses' in the ESL classroom: an introduction

Introduction

This book is centrally concerned with the nature of talk in multilingual classrooms where students are learning in and through English as a second language, and on the ways in which such talk can support both the curriculum learning and language development of students. Within this broad context, the title of the book reflects three perspectives which relate to the topic, the research process and the purposes of the research.

First, 'bridging discourses' refers to the *process* of teacher-student interaction and thus to the most critical means by which teaching and learning occurs (or perhaps fails to occur). The following chapters illustrate how, in their co-constructed discourse, the talk of teachers and students draws together – or bridges – the 'everyday' language of students learning through English as a second language, and the language associated with the academic registers of school which they must learn to control. Through this process knowledge is constructed and new language is learned. At the same time, in describing how teacher-student discourse can construct bridges between learner and curriculum, the text that this produces is itself examined. In particular I focus on those features of this 'bridging discourse' which appear to be enabling of second language development and of ESL learners' participation in the activities of the classroom.

The book's title also reflects the interdisciplinary nature of the study. The analysis of the discourse crosses interdisciplinary boundaries, drawing on systemic functional linguistics; the work of Vygotsky and other educators who have developed sociocultural approaches to teaching and learning based on his work; second language acquisition (henceforth SLA) research; and broader educational studies of minority groups. The book thus continues in the tradition of other recent work in applied linguistics (see, for example, Williams and Lukin 2003) in illustrating how educational researchers from different discipline backgrounds can themselves develop 'bridging discourses', and through this process develop tools to view classroom talk through a more powerful lens than might otherwise be possible.

Finally, the notion of 'bridging discourses' is reflected in the approach taken to the study. The research is situated at the theory-praxis nexus, with the classroom itself as research site. I argue that if educational practice is to avoid the risk of an ever-growing gap between the realms of 'theory' and 'practice', and to the ever-decreasing validity given to the voices of those most closely associated with education – teachers – it is to this nexus, where theory becomes a reflexive dimension of practice, that we should look for the development of theory about teaching and learning.

Each of these themes emerges at different points throughout the book, and is briefly discussed here.

Bridging discourses in the classroom: teachers and students

'I can say what I want but not for school work or strangers.'
(Year 6 ESL student, responding to the question *How good is your English?* McKay *et al* 1997, p. 247)

These words were from a student in her final year of primary school. English was her second language and had been the medium of instruction for her years of primary schooling. Her response to the question *How good is your English?* encapsulates the issue with which this book is concerned: while she is fluent in most everyday contexts, she does not yet feel that she controls the more academic and 'written-like' language associated with classroom learning or with more formal interactional contexts.

In countries such as Australia, Canada, the UK and US, where there has been large-scale and increasing immigration, it is common to find in most schools numbers of students who are both learning English as a second language and learning in it as well (henceforth ESL students). In Australia approximately one quarter of all school-aged students come from a language background other than English, and in many schools in the larger cities the percentage is very much higher, with up to 95 per cent of children from a non-English-speaking background and with often more than twenty different languages spoken within the school. These learners come from a variety of linguistic, cultural, socio-economic and educational backgrounds. Some are highly literate in their first language, some are literate only in English, others are literate in both, some in neither. They may have arrived in their new country as refugees, having experienced personal trauma and interrupted periods of schooling. They may have arrived as first-generation migrants already literate in their first language and with cognitive and conceptual development appropriate to their grade level. Or they may be second-generation migrants, but have entered the first year of school speaking little or no English, having had all their conceptual development in their first language up to that point (a resource which tragically, for both the individual student and the society in which they live, few educational systems now systematically build on).

For all of these students who are in English medium schools, English is both an aim and the medium of education: that is, they are not only learning English as a school curriculum subject and as a new language, but they are learning in it and through it as well. Since the early 1980s a number of studies have shown that despite rapid growth in conversational fluency, a far longer time frame may be required for ESL students to develop the more academic registers associated with school learning at a level equivalent to that of their native-English-speaking peers, and this is especially likely to be the case for those students who have not had opportunities to develop first language and literacy skills (see, for example, Collier 1989; Cummins 1984, 1996, 2000; Hakuta *et al* 2000; McKay *et al* 1997).

Typically ESL learners in school rapidly become fluent in the day-to-day, face-to-face contexts of interpersonal communication, such as the school playground, which tend to be less cognitively demanding and are often typified by language contextualized within the immediate situation. Without explicit support however, these same learners may not necessarily be able to control the more academic registers associated with the classroom, even after five or six years in mainstream classes. For while English-speaking students are building on the foundations of their first language to develop the registers associated with academic learning, ESL learners in English medium schools are not. And ironically, the conversational fluency in English of many ESL students actually serves to mask their real English language needs, such needs being perceived by teachers and schools as 'remedial' or ability- or behaviour-related.

English language support is therefore needed far beyond the early period of arrival or the first years of schooling. Although specialist ESL classes exist in some schools, they cater largely for newly arrived children, or for children with obvious communication difficulties in English. In many other countries, government funding for ESL teaching has gradually reduced and been subsumed under broader and less targeted 'literacy' programmes, while at the same time there has been a philosophical and pedagogical shift away from the notion of separate 'withdrawal' classes. Thus for political and idealogical reasons, most ESL learners now spend all their school day in a mainstream classroom (that is, a regular classroom which has not been constituted for the purposes of ESL teaching), and increasingly mainstream or subject-based teachers carry the sole responsibility for their students' curriculum and language development. For most ESL learners, then, the mainstream classroom and curriculum must allow for the construction of curriculum knowledge to progress hand in hand with the development of their second language (L2). And so the notion of second language development must also be inclusive of the increasing language and literacy demands embedded within and constructed through the school curriculum.

These curriculum-based language and literacy demands are related to the academic language required in school across the entire curriculum. The registers associated with academic learning traditionally code knowledge in ways that are linguistically unfamiliar to many students. In relation to science discourse, for example, Martin (1990) points out that 'it codes an alternative perspective on reality to commonsense, a perspective accumulated over centuries of scientific enquiry' (p. 86). Literacy in science has to be considered both from the point of view of the knowledge being constructed and the genres and registers that, in Martin's terms, 'package' that knowledge. Similarly, development of literacy within any subject in the school curriculum involves learning to control the registers – the specific technical language and grammatical patterns – and generic structures particular to that subject. Linguists working within systemic functional linguistics have described many of the genres of school subjects (see, for example, Butt *et al* 2000; Derewianka 1990; Painter 2001; Sharpe (at press)) and the registers and macrogenres of teaching (Christie 1994; Derewianka 2003a, 2003b; Hammond 1990; Unsworth 2000) in ways which make clear that curriculum subjects construct meanings in specific subject-related ways, a point to which I will return later.

These school-related registers typically involve more 'written-like' discourse, which tends to be less personal, more abstract, more lexically dense, and more structured than the face-to-face everyday language with which students are likely to be familiar. While more conversational texts tend to have higher personal involvement, low explicitness of meaning and interactive features, most academic texts require a high explicitness of lexical content but allow for little interaction or personal involvement (Biber 1986). These registers play a primary role in the development of literacy skills, especially in relation to lexical knowledge, metalinguistic awareness and the processing of written language.

Vygotsky, whose work is discussed in more detail in the following chapter, offers another perspective on academic language learning, drawing a distinction between spontaneous and scientific concepts (1978, 1986). Vygotsky argues that spontaneous concepts emerge from a child's everyday experiences. While they may be rich they are embedded within specific situational contexts and instances and are therefore not systematic, thus they will vary from learner to learner. Scientific concepts, on the other hand, are located within the structured and specialized discourse of the subject, are relatively more fixed and are systematically and logically organized and related (Kozulin 1998). Gallimore and Tharp (1990) suggest that the written language of schooling 'enforces an experience of language as system. This systemacity – self-contained and self-sufficient – is what allows language to be unhooked from the sensory world, to be taken in hand by the thinker, to be used as a tool for thought' (Gallimore and Tharp 1990, p. 194). Cummins (2000) points to other related theoretical distinctions between what can be thought of as 'everyday' and 'academic' language made by a number of writers, among them Bruner (1975), Olson (1977), Donaldson (1978), Canale (1983) and Mohan (1986, 2002).

One pedagogical response to a situation where large groups of learners are learning in what is often their less well developed language is for a teacher to consciously simplify or modify the language of the classroom, by, for example, attempting to avoid all lexical or grammatical complexity that is beyond what she believes to be her learners' current understanding; a kind of 'simplified reader' approach to her own language use. While this strategy may help to make language comprehensible to learners in the short term, it does not take into account how the learner is to obtain new linguistic data in order to develop the kinds of academic registers and genres described above, and is therefore not likely to provide a basis for the ongoing development of a language-for-learning. A linguistically simplified, reductionist or 'alternative' curriculum is also likely to create lower academic expectations for both teachers and students which, as many studies have shown, impact negatively on students' educational outcomes. And once overall curriculum goals begin to be differentially selected for different groups of students, it is almost inevitable that differential outcomes will be the result.

Equally, merely exposing L2 learners to the mainstream classroom without language learning support is an inadequate response to their language development needs and 'cannot be assumed to provide optimal language learning opportunities as a matter of course' (Mohan 2002, p. 108). Most educationists, including teachers themselves, now recognize that in such contexts subject teaching must be planned in ways that provide the specific contexts needed for the development of academic English (see, as examples of such planning, Davison and Williams 2001). This book goes somewhat further in arguing that, while the planning of programmes that integrate language with curriculum knowledge is essential, we need also to consider how these programmes are played out in the day-to-day interactions of the classroom, for it is in this enacted curriculum that teaching and learning is actually situated. Or, as Edwards and Mercer powerfully express it, 'it is essentially in the discourse between teacher and pupils that education is done, or fails to be done' (Edwards and Mercer 1987, p. 101).

For all students who, for whatever reason, are unfamiliar with the academic ways of meaning of the school curriculum, this teaching-and-learning discourse must provide a linguistic bridge between the conversational and everyday language with which students are already familiar, and the specific and subject-related registers and genres associated with curriculum learning. There is a parallel here with Bernstein's notions of vertical and horizontal discourses. Boundaries are an important concept in his work: those between different social groups, between home and school or between different subject areas (Bourne 2003). Everyday or common-sense knowledge is context dependent, local and tacit, and is expressed in what he terms 'horizontal' discourse. Subject-specific knowledge is by contrast coherent, explicit and systematically principled, and is expressed through 'vertical' discourse (Bernstein 1996). Hasan's work (2000) demonstrates the way in which certain homes produce more or less specific orientations towards this more 'decontextualized' language, thus advantaging for some children when they enter school and disadvantaging others. She suggests that the best learning environments are those which show continuity between the familiar and the concrete, realized through horizontal discourse, and the unfamiliar and abstract, realized through vertical discourse. The challenge for teachers is how to provide bridges between horizontal and vertical discourse in ways that do not compromise the development of the latter, and how to relate students' current language knowledge and ways of meaning to the linguistic demands of the curriculum. How, in other words, to construct with students a 'bridging discourse'.

It is clearly important for reasons of social and educational equity that educators continue to develop the knowledge and skills to respond to linguistic and cultural diversity, and consider how the language of the classroom can best serve as a resource for language development. One implication of this is to examine how second language development can be better integrated with the 'content' of the curriculum. Thus the overall aim of the book is to identify patterns of discourse in classroom interaction that are enabling of second language development, but which at the same time support the learning of curriculum knowledge. Specifically, the book focuses on the learning of an academic register of school by young ESL learners who are already familiar with the English of day-to-day, face-to-face and situationally-embedded contexts. It seeks to address the question of how the development of these more academic registers can be facilitated, and what contexts for second language development can be constructed through classroom interactions in the course of mainstream curriculum subject teaching.

Bridging discourses across disciplines

This book does not claim to be a study 'in' linguistics, nor a full linguistic description of a second language pedagogy. Rather it aims to contribute more broadly to a theorization of pedagogy itself, viewing teaching as a domain of theory and practice in its own right. This broader pedagogical aim offers an opportunity to integrate methods and domains of knowledge that are sometimes artificially separated by knowledge boundaries and to bring together bodies of research which can yield complementary insights into the discourse of second language classrooms. The account of classroom practices throughout the book combines a recognition of the psycholinguistic processes of second language learning with a theory of language that is sufficiently complex and specific to detail the interactive processes by which classroom discourse itself can function as a mediating tool for second language learning. At the same time the account is informed by a view of learning which draws from sociocultural theory and critically conceived theories of pedagogy. Given the complexities of teaching and learning in the life of the classroom, this multidisciplinary perspective is especially relevant to a study which attempts to demonstrate how theory and practice in second language education can inform each other.

What is required for the purpose of such an investigation is the development of a way of exploring the discourse which is sufficiently precise to ground it within its immediate situational context but broad enough to locate it within the wider curriculum content and ongoing classroom processes in which it occurred. At the same time its significance for second language development needs to be considered. To this end I draw on insights from systemic functional linguistics, sociocultural approaches to learning and teaching, critically conceived pedagogical approaches to multicultural education, and second language acquisition studies.

Part 1 (Chapters 2 and 3) draws on research from this range of literature, in an attempt to theorize a pedagogy that is inclusive of minority learners and to take account of the highly complex and multifaceted phenomenon that constitutes pedagogy. Part 2 (Chapters 4 and 5) describes the context of the two classrooms that provided the data for the study, including the school community, the teachers and the children. Part 2 also discusses some of the issues around classroom research and identifies the major themes that emerged from the study of the two classrooms. Part 3 (Chapters 6, 7 and 8) explores in depth the discourse of the classrooms. Reflecting the range of theoretical interests in Part 1, three perspectives are taken on the discourse of the classrooms. The first of these perspectives focuses on how teacher and students jointly construct meanings through their discourse, and how the teacher-talk gradually recontextualizes students' 'everyday' ways of meaning in the process of the development of the more formal registers of school. This perspective on the discourse uses systemic functional linguistics as the tool for analysis and is developed in Chapter 6. The second perspective on the discourse draws more broadly on sociocultural theory to examine the role and mediation of the teacher in students' second language and curriculum learning, and is developed in Chapter 7. The third perspective examines the data from the standpoint of the learner, and suggests the kinds of discourse contexts, and the affordances for learning, that appeared enabling of second language development. This is developed in Chapter 8.

These differing perspectives allow the classroom to be viewed from more than one angle, illuminating different aspects of the topic and providing some theoretical triangulation on the data. The three perspectives address the key issues for the book: the nature of the talk that occurred in the classrooms; the role of the teacher in this talk; and the kinds of contexts and opportunities for second language development constructed as a result.

In relation to 'eclectic' approaches such as this, Edwards and Westgate comment:

> [Research which reflects a single perspective] is more likely to gain from its consistency the appearance of rigour; a more eclectic approach may be more realistic where the phenomena being studied are highly complex and many-faceted.
> (Edwards and Westgate 1994, p. 59)

And in relation to the SLA field, van Lier writes that judicious combinations 'can illuminate a particular field of study much more than some canonized scientific procedure can do' (van Lier 1994, p. 333).

Eclecticism, of course, does not imply using approaches that are incompatible within a single study, but rather, a 'bringing together [of] concepts and methods which can yield complementary insights into the 'same' phenomena, or can bring into view different aspects of classroom talk and its organization' (Edwards and Westgate 1994, p. 59). While this book draws on aspects of the work of a range of classroom researchers, linguists and cognitive psychologists who are each working within different traditions, there remains a consistent view of interaction as central to the meaning-making process of the classroom and as centrally involved in social action. The guiding principle underlying the book (which Davis (1995) refers to as a 'grand theory' and Ernst-Slavit

(1997) as a 'theoretical anchor') is the notion that language development interacts dynamically with the sociocultural contexts in which it occurs and cannot be analysed or understood apart from its situational and cultural contexts.

Bridging discourses: the teacher and the researcher

My own experience of the relationship between teachers and researchers, both as a consultant and as a researcher, suggests three ways in which it may be constructed. Teachers may view the researcher as someone who holds the key to good practice, who 'knows the answers', and so defer in their own judgements about classroom practices to the supposed authority of the 'expert'. (Some researchers too may suffer from this delusion.) Teachers often have little power in how such a relationship is constructed; that power tends to rest with the researchers since they are generally the ones who get into print. Clarke (1994, 1995) characterizes the typical power relationship between teaching and research in this way:

> I do not dispute the assertion that individuals who conduct research on language learning and teaching can provide information and insight for teachers, but I believe that the relationship in the profession is unnecessarily hierarchical, and that experts are generally accorded a disproportionate amount of time and space to accord their views.
>
> (Clarke 1995)

A similar point is made by Kumaravadivelu who argues that 'theorizers have traditionally occupied the power center of language pedagogy while the practitioners of classroom teaching have been relegated to the disempowered periphery' (Kumaravadivelu 1994, p. 29).

A second way in which the teacher-researcher relationship is constructed, and perhaps in reality a more likely one, is that teachers view research (and researchers) as irrelevant to the real business of the classroom, dealing with theoretical issues of no consequence to the practicalities of everyday teaching. As Shulman has remarked, practitioners tend to be more often 'missing in action' than 'lost in thought' (Shulman 1987, cited in van Lier 1996).

There is, however, a third alternative to the researcher-teacher relationship, and this alternative is bound up with a view of theory construction which has praxis as its focus and which does not 'set up a pecking order between practice-less theory and theory-less practice' (van Lier 1994, p. 337). In the field of L2 teaching, a number of researchers and scholars have argued for experience-based theory building (see, for

9

example, Block 1996; Clarke 1994; Kumaravadivelu 1994; van Lier 1994; Prabhu 1990; Richards 1990; Widdowson 1990; and for a broader view of the literacy field, Graddol *et al* 1994). Rather than viewing the practice of teaching as simply informed by research, their arguments are based on the notion that pedagogy is itself a domain of theory and research. As Widdowson writes, language teachers are often represented as 'consumers of findings that are retailed by research . . . which denies the nature of teaching as a domain of theory and research in its own right' (Widdowson 1990, p. 47).

Ironically, because theorists are rarely teachers themselves, the theory-practice distinction creates strata of expertise in which, paradoxically, teachers are often constructed as less expert than theorists. As Clarke suggests, 'it stretches credulity to assert that the best theory building comes from individuals who are disconnected from daily contact with the schools' (Clarke 1995, p. 13). He concludes that 'the discourse [about teaching] will be of little use at best, and disabling, at worst, if the total experience of language learners and teachers is not included in the theory-building effort' (Clarke 1995, p. 16). Yet research in language acquisition itself has until recently generally contributed only a narrow range of insights to language teachers, and this is largely because the methodological approaches taken in earlier SLA research tended to exclude the classroom as research site and excise teaching from authentic contexts. In recent years however there have been important exceptions, largely among studies which have drawn on sociocultural theory and hence located the research within authentic sociocultural contexts (see, for example, Lantolf 2000a, b). As Block (1996) suggests, if the classroom is seen as a social context, the point of departure for researchers is not 'a quest for a theory of SLA for all of humanity', but 'a modest attempt to understand language teaching in situ'.

One of the reasons that we need theory is to help understand complexity, and to provide the basis for new ways of looking at a range of contexts (Schratz and Walker 1995). Taking their authority from the academy, conventional theories typically operate on the assumption that explanation requires us to consider two or three variables, and aim towards generalization. From this perspective we tend to look at theory as a form of abstract knowledge divorced from everyday practicalities. But as Schratz and Walker suggest in relation to teaching and learning, 'human interactions do not work with the predictability we sometimes like to assume' (Schratz and Walker 1995, p. 108). Research can also aim at 'making us look twice at things' (*op. cit.*, p. 105).

In arguing for the breaking down of the traditional barriers between theory and practice, van Lier (1994) likewise challenges the notion that theory is something that is constructed and then applied to practice, defining it instead as a 'reflexive dimension of practice', with practical activities being seen as a rich source of theoretically relevant data. Putting forward the case for classroom-based research, he urges linguists to 'put their energies into the service of real life concerns, and not just to pursue the Snark of academic respectability' (1994, p. 336). Suggesting a profitable combination of action research and classroom ethnography, he argues that 'the ever present danger of the widening gap . . . between research and practice can only be avoided if the concerns of teachers and learners themselves are kept on center stage' (van Lier 1988, p. 15). Such research involves researchers' participation in the practical affairs of the field, and the development of theory which is subsequently 'put back into the service of progress in practical affairs, and so on, in cyclical reflexive ways' (van Lier 1994, p. 338).

The value of *a priori* claims often made by qualitative interpretive research of this type is sometimes questioned on the basis that such claims are in one sense telling us only what is already known. However, this in itself may be one of the strengths of interpretive research in classrooms: as Mehan (cited in Edwards and Westgate 1994, p. 59) comments, the highest compliment that a piece of classroom research can elicit from practitioners is 'Ah yes, of course!' By relating the particular and observable to the general, the claims that such studies produce offer important and relevant kinds of knowledge and insights for educational research. Understanding the real importance of *a priori* claims means considering in more depth what it means to 'know' something. What we 'know' is often stored intuitively or implicitly learned. Thus a child may 'know', at a subconscious level, how to participate as a student in a classroom, or a teacher may 'know' what helps students learn language. But the child and the teacher may not necessarily be able to put this into words, because such knowledge is not necessarily stored in propositional form (Heap 1995). And unless such knowledge is propositionalized, through being articulated, it cannot be reflected on, or fed back into the classroom and into curriculum design. I suggest that this is a significant aspect of qualitative approaches for educational research: that they have the potential to recast teachers' innate understandings as educationally 'usable' propositions. As Schratz and Walker argue:

> Behind what we think of as 'practical' lie theories which support . . . practical knowledge. We may not always make such theories explicit, still less formulate them as expository statements and propositions but, to the degree that we have the capacity to act in different ways in the face of similar circumstances, so we hold, albeit tacitly, a complex web of theories, including explanations, predictions and generalizations.'
>
> (Schratz and Walker 1995, p. 105)

This book, then, takes the view that the in-context experience of teach-ers should be seen as essential for the development and application of pedagogical theories. It would seem to be more strengthening of the professional growth of teachers, and more potentially transforming of classroom practice, to consider what can be learned from instances of teaching, and then to consider how this learning can be used reflexively in new kinds of practice. This demands collaborative associations between teachers and researchers that can extend the research agenda in ways that also foreground teachers' own professional concerns. It is through this reflexive process at the theory-practice nexus that the dis-courses and agendas of teachers and researchers can meet and produce new ways of knowing about teaching.

PART 1
Language, learning and learners: perspectives across disciplines

> . . . no single explanation for learning, and no unitary view of the
> contributions of language learners, will account for what [teachers]
> have to grapple with on a daily basis.
> (Larsen-Freeman 1990, p. 269)

Implicitly or explicitly, any theorization of teaching and learning makes
assumptions about what constitutes 'effective' practice, yet this is a
problematic term unless it is made explicit how certain moments in
the classroom or particular aspects of practice are to be viewed as
significant. The classroom texts that are selected for analysis in Part 2
have been chosen because they represent something the researcher sees
as significant, yet what the observer 'sees' is coloured by certain assumptions and belief systems. These two chapters make explicit some of the
assumptions and beliefs – about language, learning and the position of
minority learners in a mainstream classroom – which helped determine
what was viewed as significant in the analysis of the data. In order to
construct a picture of the sort of linguistic practices that might be
expected to support both language and curriculum learning, these two
chapters draw on research from a range of theoretical positions. As suggested in Chapter 1, what this interdisciplinary approach offers is the
possibility of several 'takes' on the same events, and a way of examining, through a multifaceted lens, what Larsen-Freeman suggests is the
complexity of the day-to-day life of the classroom.

2 A sociocultural view of language and learning

Two approaches to learning

To fully appreciate what a sociocultural perspective can bring to the study of discourse in a second language programme, and how it may allow for a more productive theorization of classroom learning than previous positions, it is helpful to backtrack to look at two other approaches to learning which dominated educational thinking in the twentieth century. In particular, I will consider the significance of the role of language in each of these approaches. For although usually seen as the result of influences within the field of psychology and beliefs about the nature of learning, approaches to teaching and learning have been implicitly influenced by particular models of language (or in some cases their absence).

While philosophical approaches are not discrete – they do not simply begin and end, but continue to leave traces beyond the epoch in which they influenced initial changes – it is possible to define two major orientations to teaching and learning (Wells 1999a). Although in many ways these two orientations claim very different images of the teacher and views of the learner, they share two major assumptions, although neither of these assumptions is made explicit within the theory. First, there is the assumption that learning is an individual phenomenon and psychological in origin, and second, that a theory of language is discrete from a theory of learning. Beyond being a 'conveyor' or vehicle for ideas and knowledge, language as it occurs between individuals has not been a focus for educational debate in either approach, and in neither is there an acknowledgement of the collaborative nature of learning and meaning-making. These two views, and the views of language they encapsulate, are briefly summarized below.

Knowledge as commodity, language as conduit

During most of the twentieth century, mainstream education was dominated by two related views: of knowledge as a commodity to be transmitted to learners, and of language as a 'conduit' by which this process of transmission occurred. Variously described by terms such as teacher-dominated, transmission-based, or, by Freire (1983) as 'banking education', the teacher's role is seen as a purveyor of knowledge who deposits information and skills into the empty memory banks of students, who are assigned the role of passive recipients. Significant in this view is that essentially 'learning' and 'development' are seen as identical: the social environment provides ready-made concepts which are absorbed by children. In such classrooms teaching is generally characterized by high teacher management, and learning viewed as a matter of building up skills from simple to complex, progressing through a sequence of teacher-controlled steps. The pedagogy typically relies largely on memorization and repetition and is in part influenced by behaviourist notions of learning, involving minimal negotiation between teacher and student (Webster *et al* 1996, p. 39). There is an implicit view of knowledge which this view espouses: the assumption that it is a fixed and immutable body of authoritatively given explanation and practice, in which the teacher is expert. Thus teaching is oriented to the acquisition of facts and depends largely on teacher-structured materials.

One explanation for the dominance of this model during the twentieth century can be found in part in the underpinning model of communication, which sees communication as a matter of information transfer and language as the vehicle for transferring thoughts and ideas from one person to another. Language in this model of teaching and learning functions like a conduit, by means of which 'content' or 'information' is conveyed (Christie 1990; Reddy 1970; Wells 1992). Since it implies a separation of language and content, it results in distinctions being made between form and content, or product and process (Christie 1990). As I will argue later, this is a particularly problematic separation in an ESL context where the target language is also the medium of teaching and learning in the curriculum.

Methodologies for teaching language within this model operate within the limitations of the communication framework it embodies. The univocal view of text suggested by the conduit metaphor sees any difference between the 'sender's' message input and the 'receiver's' message reception as a defect in the channel of communication, hence the concern with the importance of encoding, decoding and the 'transmission' of ideas. In language teaching this has tended to lead to teaching the component parts of language separately, beginning with elements seen as 'simple', and progressing to more complex forms; for example, phonics instruction as a prerequisite for reading, and spelling and grammar as a prerequisite for writing. In the second language classroom, this approach is paralleled by teaching sequences where a focus on specific grammar and vocabulary precedes language use, and more tightly controlled language exercises precede language tasks which allow broader choices of language on the part of the students. Inherent in this view of second language teaching is the assumption that language must first be 'learned' before it can be 'used'. This is a particularly problematic view in a context where students are learning through the medium of the target language. For as Mohan points out, 'we cannot delay academic instruction until students have mastered L2 skills . . . we cannot place . . . students' academic development on hold during this period' (Mohan 2001, p. 108).

Typically in traditional language instruction the teacher presents a task and explains a grammatical 'rule', learners then memorize the rule and practise applying it in 'typical' tasks. Because rules tend to be presented one by one and explanation reduced to a few examples, such a curriculum does not encourage holistic understanding, and many of the rules and regularities implicitly understood by fluent speakers remain hidden from the learners. As a result grammatical systems may be perceived as a meaningless collection of isolated examples rather than as a coherent system of relationships, so that learners may be unable to meaningfully generalize their learning to other contexts (Stetsenko and Arievitch 2002).

Ironically, teaching approaches typically based on 'conduit' models of language, and the teacher-controlled discourse they encourage, have tended to dominate the education of so-called 'disadvantaged' students, among whom those in the process of developing a second language are often included. Implicitly, responses to such students have assumed their prior learning to be deficient, with one aim of education being to 'replace' it with more appropriate language and cognitive skills. Because such learners are sometimes believed to be incapable of benefiting from a more challenging curriculum, and to require yet more control and structure from the teacher, compensatory programmes have also tended to focus on drilling children in low-level language and numeracy skills (Cummins 1996). (For an in-depth study of how assumptions of deficit serve to reinforce inequalities within a school at a structural level, see Oakes 1985.) And although few educationists, linguists or cognitive psychologists would now endorse the assumptions of a transmission approach to pedagogy, it is significant that calls for 'back-to-basics' instruction still regularly occur at times of public dissatisfaction with education, or as a result of broader social and economic anxieties. At such times, Cummins argues, 'skills-oriented approaches to instruction have submerged the fragile rhetoric of the need for higher-order thinking and critical literacy' adding that, with reference to some inner city districts in the US, 'teacher-proof' scripted phonics programmes that reduce the teacher's instructional role to 'parroting the one-size-fits-all script' have been presented as a quick-fix solution to improve students' reading and overall academic progress (Cummins in Gibbons 2002, vi).

Teaching as 'facilitation'

Since the 1970s there have been increasing changes in educational practice and challenges to teacher-dominant approaches. In part this has been the result of the influence of the much earlier work of John Dewey (see, for example, Dewey 1902, 1916), the significance of which lay in his assertion that learning is a constructive activity. It has also been influenced by the work of Piaget who saw new learning as crucially dependent on what the learner already knows; learning is seen as occurring when learners make changes to their existing understandings or model of the world, reshaping old knowledge in the light of new ways of seeing things. Education is therefore viewed not as a matter of habit formation or conditioning or the receiving of information, but of intelligent enquiry and thought. In contrast with earlier views, progressive pedagogy emphasizes active student enquiry in the construction of knowledge through the integration of new information with prior experience, and is concerned with the learner's struggle to understand, and thus with individual cognitive and personal development (Barnes *et al* 1986). Unlike traditional approaches, 'development' is viewed as separate from 'learning'; a learner's biological development is the dominant process and learning follows, refining already-developed structures. Learning is thus seen to develop naturally and spontaneously, proceeding along a defined set of biologically determined stages. Not surprisingly, therefore, Piaget saw language as an outcome rather than a cause of development, a secondary phenomenon which was the result of the sensorimotor activity involved in a young child's exploration of the physical world.

Thus while the processes of development 'may be utilized and accelerated by education at home or in the school, *they are not derived from that education* and, on the contrary, *constitute the preliminary and necessary condition* of efficacity in any form of instruction' (Piaget 1971, p. 36, italics added). Since it is the child's own developmental processes in interaction with their environment which provides the timing and motivation for change, one reading of Piaget's work in relation to pedagogical practice has been that social facilitation (that is, intervention by the teacher) is only effective when the child is 'ready' to move forward. From interpretations of Piaget's work (although not directly from Piaget himself) comes the notion of 'readiness', which, in the school context, and in particular in early childhood education, has led to the belief that the learning content of the curriculum needs to be matched to the developmental level of the child if learning is to occur. McNally (1973), for example, writing at the time when progressive education was beginning to influence primary education in Australia, states: 'the most fundamental of Piaget's insights for education is that the child literally builds his own intelligence, that he is in fact the architect of his own growth'. Piaget himself argues that 'each time one prematurely teaches a child something he could have discovered for himself, the child is kept from inventing it and consequently from understanding it completely' (Piaget in Mussen 1970, p. 715). Thus discovery and first-hand experiences are emphasized, with the student constructed as a self-motivated individual who behaves as a mini-scientist, mini-historian, mini-writer and so on. Consequently the teaching role in such learning has frequently been interpreted as one of 'facilitation', with the teacher's main job being to foster a spirit of enquiry and to provide a wealth of materials to create an environment which stimulates a learner's own curiosity and interest.

These progressive approaches imply the learner is an individual lone organism, largely responsible for their own learning if provided with a supportive learning environment. One of the results of such a view, as Feez (1995) and Bourne (2003) point out, is that educational failure is also then individualized, and seen as due to the 'natural' facility and 'innate' abilities of the learner. While progressive educators do not explicitly espouse this view, it is a likely consequence of a perspective on learning which in many respects minimizes the active role played by educators in the teaching and learning process. Feez writes:

> progressive approaches have reinforced the inequalities of access which are characteristic of older, traditional pedagogies. It is simply that in progressive pedagogies, the way these inequalities are perpetuated becomes invisible. Learners' individuality and freedom may be more highly valued in progressive classrooms, but during and at the end of their courses of study learners are still assessed against the standards of the dominant culture . . . although classrooms are more pleasant, what is actually expected of learners in order for them to be successful is not made explicit . . . progressive classrooms tend to reinforce existing social inequalities of opportunity because it seems that it is the learner rather than the educational institution, who is to be blamed for failure in such benevolent and rich learning environments.
>
> (Feez 1995, p. 9)

Arguing along very similar lines, Bourne (2003) draws attention to the fact that while the progressive classroom *appears* to operate with a weak classification of subjects in an 'integrated' curriculum, and a weak classification of the boundaries between teacher as transmitter of knowledge and students as acquirers of knowledge, the reality is that the teacher maintains the role of assessor and the child's progress continues to be judged against fixed norms.

However, within these more child-centred approaches the role of language in learning, and spoken language in particular, was certainly acknowledged. In the late 1960s and 1970s, especially in Britain with the publication of the Plowden Report, the importance of discourse to the development of understanding in the classroom began to be recognized; the work of Wilkinson (1965), Britton (1970), Barnes (1976) and Tough (1977) brought to attention the role and importance of spoken language across all areas of the school curriculum, which until that time had given prestige almost exclusively to the written form. Attitudes to student talk in the classroom changed from 'something to be forbidden to something to be encouraged at all costs' (Phillips 1985, p. 59). Where earlier approaches had given prestige almost exclusively to the written form, the importance of language in education was now seen as relevant not only to language as 'object' but to language as 'medium'; that is, not only to language as a subject but to its role in all areas of the curriculum (for example, Wilkinson 1965 and his notion of 'oracy'; Tough 1977; and the UK Bullock Report, *A Language for Life*, 1975). Among the basic tenets of this work are the belief that language develops through purposeful use, that it occurs through talk and writing and that it contributes to cognitive growth.

However, as in earlier teaching models, language within the progressive classroom is still primarily seen as a vehicle for representing already-existent 'meanings', rather than itself constructing meaning. Tough wrote at the time progressive approaches were first gaining currency: 'language provides us with a system for representing our inner meanings, our thinking, and for interpreting the meanings others express through the use of language' (Tough 1979, p. 5). And what was generally not part of this approach was a language model that allowed teachers and other educators to scrutinize language itself, and thereby reflect on how it was being used in teaching and learning processes, assess students' language and literacy learning and explicitly plan for its development.

A sociocultural view of learning

More recently the particular role of classroom discourse in students' learning has been more critically examined. Much of this work has been located within the socio-cognitive psychological frame developed out of the work of Vygotsky (see, for examples, Cazden 1988; Edwards and Mercer 1987; Hammond and Gibbons 2005; Hall 1998; Lee and Smagorinsky 2000; Mercer 1995; Moll 1994; Tharp and Gallimore 1988; Wells 1999b, 2000; Wells and Chang-Wells 1992; Wells and Claxton 2002). Vygotsky proposed that there is a close relationship between the use of language as a cultural tool in social interaction and the use of language as a psychological tool providing the resources for individual thinking. Language is therefore accorded central place in the development of a theory of human development, the means by which cognitive strategies develop via the social to the psychological plane. Unlike the two approaches discussed above, learning (including the learning of language) is seen as *leading* development, rather than either separate, or identical, to it.

A sociocultural view of learning sees as central the relationship between learning and the social situations in which it occurs. Rather than the acquisition of propositional knowledge, learning is seen as situated within certain forms of social co-participation (Lave and Wenger 1991). Drawing on examples of learning as diverse as studies of Yucatec midwives, Vai and Gola tailors and the apprenticeship of meat cutters, Lang and Wenger demonstrate how the individual learner does not gain a discrete body of abstract knowledge which is then transferred and reapplied to 'real' contexts, but acquires skills to perform by actually engaging and participating in the socially embedded practices of an 'expert'. This participation is initially limited, with the 'expert' taking major responsibility for the completion of a particular task, and the 'novice' participating to a limited degree, but taking increasing responsibility as they become more proficient. Learning thus occurs in the context of actual social practices, under the conditions of what Lang and Wenger refer to as 'legitimate peripheral participation'. In the classroom context, this situated view of learning challenges educators to shift the traditional concern with the kinds of cognitive processes and conceptual structures involved in learning towards a concern with the kinds of social engagements that provide the most effective and appropriate context for curriculum learning to take place.

The work of Vygotsky

Vygotsky's writings encapsulate three overall themes (Wertsch 1985; Wertsch and Toma 1991). First, there is the notion of genetic or developmental method, which asserts that it is only possible to understand mental functioning if its origin and developments are understood. Second, and related to this, there is the claim that an individual's higher mental functioning has a social origin. Third, there is the claim that

21

human activities are mediated by material or symbolic tools or signs; one such tool, and the most extensive, is language.

Vygotsky's developmental method

First, Vygotsky's theory asserts that it is only possible to understand aspects of mental functioning if one first understands their origin and the transitions that they have undergone: attempting to understand mental processes simply by analysing only the products of development may be misleading. He argues that an understanding of this development is crucial to understanding both the individual and the cultural and social activities in which the individual is involved. This can be applied to four different levels of human development: the development of the human species through evolution (phylogenesis); the development of humans throughout history; the development of the individual (ontogenesis) and the development of competence at a single task or activity by a learner (microgenesis) (Berk and Winsler 1995). Of the four domains it is the last which is most relevant to this study: the way in which development, and in particular the learning of a second language, results from specific interactions within a particular socio-cultural setting.

The social origin of 'inner speech'

The second theme in Vygotsky's work, and related to the notion of genetic orientation, is his assertion that mental functioning has its origins in social processes and remains quasi-social in nature. In their own private sphere, human beings retain the functions of social interaction. The interactions that young children engage in with more expert others later become internalized, constructing the resources for individual thinking, or 'inner speech'. As Vygotsky puts it in this well-known text:

> Any function in the child's cultural development appears twice, on two planes. First it appears on the social plane, and then on the psychological plane. First it appears between people as an interpsychological category, and then within the child as an intrapsychological category . . . Social relations or relations among people genetically underlie all higher relations and their relationships.
>
> (Vygotsky 1981, p. 163)

Vygotsky's formulation of the notion of inner speech suggests how the intermental and intramental perspectives are related and how the psychological perspectives on learning, which focus solely on the individual and which have played such a significant role in western education, can be addressed from a sociocultural perspective. These differing perspectives are reflected in Piaget's and Vygotsky's discussions of the phenomenon of young children engaging in 'private' or egocentric speech. Private or egocentric speech refers to the way in which children reflect on what they are currently doing or how they are solving a problem, sometimes in interaction with an adult but often when the child is alone. Whereas Piaget argues that this private speech 'withers away' as the child matures and as they develop 'social' speech, Vygotsky (1978) argues that the social speech and mental activities made evident in this talk are at a later point internalized to become inner thought. In other words they become a resource for self-directed mental activity, such as problem-solving and reflection. Thus in Vygotsky's framework the child internalizes the mental processes made evident in social activities and moves from the social to the mental plane, so that their mental processes mirror the social environment from which they are derived. For Vygotsky, therefore, talk is not simply a mirror on a child's inner thought processes, but actually constructs and shapes thinking. In the process of developing conceptual thinking, children move from a dependence on the linguistic context to a focus on the sign-sign relation of the adult. Higher mental functions do not develop simply as a result of intellectual maturation or an individual's interaction with their environment, but depend upon the use of the culturally created semiotic tools which occur in joint activity with more experienced members of the culture (Wells 2000).

Thus the clear-cut boundaries between individual and social that characterize much western thought are not part of Vygotsky's approach (Wertsch and Toma 1991). Rather, the processes and structures of the two planes of functioning are inherently linked. A sociocultural intepretation of the teaching and learning process encapsulates both the cultural reproduction of transmissive approaches and the concern with individual development and creativity, since 'these two goals, far from being in conflict, are seen to be both equally necessary and dialectically inter-related' (Wells 1999b, p. 242).

Vygotsky's view of language as the root of learning, rather than as a by-product of intellectual development, suggests that any examination of teaching and learning in the classroom will treat interactions between teacher and learner as crucial, since these same interactions will not simply shape young learners' talk, but help to construct processes of cognition. As Wells points out, as younger or less experienced people get things done together as they share in cultural activities, so they are inducted into ways of knowing and appropriate as their own the values, skills and knowledge that are enacted (Wells 2002). Within the social institution of the school, children's learning is explicitly based on the mastery of the language, behaviour, attitudes and thought as defined by the social practices of the school. Teaching and learning in school can be interpreted as the cognitive and linguistic socialization of students; education involves the process of initiation of students by their teachers into the common knowledge which comprises educational discourse and the disciplines that make up the curriculum (Edwards and Mercer 1987; Mercer 1995; Stierer and Maybin 1994; Webster *et al* 1996). Within sociocultural theory, education can be seen as a process of induction through dialogue into new ways of meaning and thinking. Knowledge is seen as jointly constructed through this discourse to become shared common knowledge, and learning is viewed as an interactive and communicative activity occurring *between* individuals, not simply *within* a single individual (Edwards and Mercer 1987; Mercer 1995; Webster *et al* 1996). As Wells suggests, the theory leads to a particular view of knowledge and understanding: 'understanding . . . comes into existence through participation in a particular activity . . . by contributing to joint meaning-making with and for others, one also makes meaning for oneself and, in the process, extends one's own understanding' (Wells 1999b, p. 108).

If, as Vygotsky suggests, the talk between teacher and students is of major significance in determining the nature and shaping of what will later become students' inner thinking, then we would expect that differences in teachers' interactional styles with students and the patterns of classroom talk they set up might influence students' later intramental functioning differentially. Recent studies by Mercer (2000 and 2002) on the 'talk curriculum' show very persuasively that this is in fact the case. Thus educators involved with school-aged second language learners need to consider not only how far the interactions in which students are involved are likely to impact on possibilities for language learning per se, but also how far they are likely to constrain or extend students' intellectual potential in all areas of the curriculum. If students are to learn to analyse and explain experience, solve problems and develop and challenge ideas, then sociocultural theory would suggest that what is needed is a critical examination of how far the discourse of the classroom, and in particular the interactions between teacher and students, is likely to develop these modes of thinking. We need to discover the ways in which a teacher's regulation of a classroom can be more than a means of control to become what Mercer refers to as an apprenticeship in thinking (Mercer 2000, 2002).

The notion of mediation

The third theme from Vygotsky's work which is relevant here is his notion of mediation and his assertion that human activities and human mental functioning are mediated and facilitated by 'tools'; that is, cultural practices and artefacts. Artefacts include both material tools, such as writing instruments, clocks or wheels, and semiotic modes of representation such as diagrams, mathematical systems, writing systems and language itself. Of these semiotic systems, the most extensive is natural language, of which the language of the school is a unique and institutional example.

Language functions not only as a mediator of social activity by enabling participants to plan, coordinate and review their actions, but is also the tool that mediates the related mental activities in the internal discourse of inner speech. It is this notion of cultural mediation that Wertsch and Cole (1996) argue constitutes the greatest distinction between Vygotsky and Piaget, and thus, by extension, between the two related educational approaches[1]. They suggest that there is no counterpart in Piaget to this focus on the importance of cultural artefacts in human mental processes. For Piaget, social transmission influences primarily the 'content' of knowledge; for Vygotsky it constructs the very nature of the thinking process.

Drawing on the analogy of apprentices learning to use material tools to construct an artefact, Wells suggests that through social interaction with others who are more skilled, children learn to use 'the language toolkit' – the genres of the culture – in order to achieve specific social purposes (Wells 1996). In the school context:

> . . . spoken discourse has an essential role to play in mediating the pupil's apprenticeship into a discipline, both as a medium in which to respond to and prepare for work on written texts, and . . . as an opportunity for 'talking their way in' to ways of making sense of new information . . . in forms that, with the assistance provided by the teacher, gradually incorporate the essential features of the discourse of the particular discipline.
>
> (Wells 1992, p. 291)

Martin has similarly argued that the technicality and abstraction that are integral to the specific subject discourses of school should be seen as 'tools', through which the subjects can be explored and understood (Martin 1990, 1993b). Later chapters illustrate some of the ways in which teachers begin to introduce students to some of the technicality and abstractions of the science curriculum and, more specifically, how they link this with students' existing knowledge and language use.

The zone of proximal development

Central to a view of learning as a mode of apprenticeship is Vygotsky's notion of the 'zone of proximal development' (ZPD), which refers to the 'cognitive gap' that exists between what an individual can do alone and what they can do jointly and in coordination with a more skilled other: 'the distance between the actual developmental level as determined by independent problem-solving and the level of potential development as determined through problem-solving under adult guidance or in collaboration with more able peers' (Vygotsky 1978, p. 86). Drawing on the example of a practical apprenticeship, Vygotsky argues that a learner learns through the joint participation with an 'expert' how to use material tools to create a concrete artefact. Successful coordination with the partner leads to the novice reaching beyond what they are currently able to achieve alone, to enter into new situations, to participate in new tasks, to learn new skills or, as is the focus of this book, to learn new ways of using language. Bruner suggests that the ZPD 'has to do with the manner in which we arrange the environment such that the child can reach higher or more abstract ground from which to reflect, ground on which he (*sic*) is enabled to be more conscious', a view of the ZPD which has clear implications for teaching (Bruner 1985, p. 24). Newman, Griffin and Cole, referring to the ZPD as the 'construction zone', define it as 'the changes that take place in socially mediated instructions' (Newman *et al* 1989, p. 2). It is worth noting that within the SLA area, although from very different theoretical standpoints, related notions to that of the zone of proximal development have also been put forward, for example, Krashen's 'input hypothesis' and the notion of I plus 1 (Krashen 1985), Prabhu's 'reasonable challenge' (Prabhu 1987) and Swain's 'pushed language' (Swain 1985).

However, as Mercer points out, while the empirical research on which Vygotskian theory is based has concerned itself with the supportive intervention of adults in the learning of *individual* students, the development of the key concepts of the theory has only recently begun to address the realities of the classroom, where, in most cases, one adult is responsible for the learning of large *groups* of students. While much work has been done on the application of the theory to the classroom, it is not unproblematic to directly apply many of the ideas that stem from a sociocultural perspective to a large group classroom context. One response to this issue is Mercer's notion of an 'intermental development zone' (Mercer 2000, p. 143). Building on the notion of the ZPD, Mercer proposes the 'intermental development zone', or IDZ, by which he refers to the shared understanding that teachers and students create together in educational activity. This shared understanding, or IDZ, is 'a continuing, contextualizing framework for joint activity' which is being constantly reconstituted as the dialogue continues (Mercer 2002, p. 143), and as the 'long conversation' between teacher and student develops throughout a topic or unit of work:

> A good primary teacher is not simply the instructor or facilitator of the learning of a large and disparate set of individuals, but rather the creator of a particular quality of intermental environment . . . in which students can take active and reflective roles in the development of their own understanding.
>
> (Mercer 2002, p. 145)

In the chapters that follow, a critical factor which emerges from the analysis is the significance of this shared understanding built up by teachers and students in the context of joint activity.

The ZPD and Mercer's notion of the IDZ have both theoretical and practical implications for education. Their theoretical significance lies in the fact that they represent a way of reconceptualizing the teaching/learning relationship in ways that move away from notions of 'teaching' and 'learning' as separate processes. Instead, teaching-and-learning (the hyphenation is suggested by Mercer) can be viewed as a single interactive process dependent on the active roles played by all participants in the learning activity. The pedagogical significance lies in the fact that the two constructs represent the potential for a student's intramental development which is created by the intermental interaction that takes place as the learner and teacher cooperate on the task. The theory therefore has room for teachers as well as learners, since a learner's achievement can never be seen as solely the result of their innate ability, but as a measure of the nature and success of the interaction between teacher and student. This has considerable implications for the teaching of minority students, which is discussed in the following chapter, and for the role of the teacher, which is explored in Chapter 6.

A social view of language

Perspectives on grammar

Broadly congruent with a sociocultural view of learning are the social-semiotic approaches to language development suggested by Halliday and other linguists working within the framework of systemic functional linguistics. While a full description of the theory is not possible here, some major principles relevant to this book are included here for the benefit of those less familiar with the theory.

If we accept that teaching and learning is about situated meaning-making, then a study of the discourse of teaching and learning needs likewise to be informed by a grammar which explains how language makes meaning. This study draws on systemic functional grammar (henceforth SFG), following the work of Halliday and other linguists who work within this tradition. The choice of this model of language is relevant for a number of reasons; primarily because of its concern with how meanings are made, and also because of its compatibility and complementarity with the social perspectives on learning and teaching discussed earlier: as in sociocultural theory, verbal meaning is viewed as the product of speakers' activities in a cultural and situational context, not as the 'content' of a particular linguistic form excised from this context. This section discusses those aspects of SFG that the study draws on, discussing the particular relevance of SFG to a study of this type.

The two traditions that together have led to the development of the study of language in context come from Malinowski and Firth, and from Sapir and Whorf (Halliday 1991). From the former comes the notion of the situation as the context for language as text, through which social relationships and social processes are enacted. From the latter comes the notion of culture as the context for language as system, where language is a form of reflection, a construal of experience into a model of reality. These two theoretical sources together create the foundations of a functional semantics or theory of meaning. Halliday argues that the entire construction of grammar is bound up with the situational and cultural contexts in which language has evolved:

> a theory of language in context is not just a theory about how people use language, important though that is. It is a theory about the nature and evolution of language, explaining why the system works the way it does; but with the explanation making reference to its use . . . It is a functional explanation, based on the social-semiotic interpretation of the relations and processes of meaning . . . I think this last point is fundamental in our language education work.
> (Halliday 1991, p. 6)

A full description of the grammar is beyond the scope of this chapter, which aims simply to identify and briefly describe those areas of the grammar which are of most significance to the discussion of the data. A fuller and more complete description can be found in a wide range of work based on the studies of Halliday and linguists and educationists who follow him (see, for example, Halliday 1975, 1978, 1984, 1985a, 1985b, 1993, 2001; Halliday and Hasan 1985; and also Butt *et al* 2000; Derewianka 1990, 2001, 2003a; Dufficy 2005; Eggins 2004; Hammond 1990; Gerot and Wignell 1994; Macken and Rothery 1991; Martin 1984, 1993; Painter 1984, 1988, 2001, 2004; Sharpe 2005; Unsworth 2000).

As readers will be aware, the dominant linguistic paradigm of the 1960s and 70s, Chomsky's transformational grammar, studies language as an idealized abstraction, in terms of the linguistic 'competence' underlying linguistic 'performance'. Thus it is seen as separate and in isolation from the contexts in which it is used and its real-life instantiations. Halliday, like Chomsky, defines as 'philosophical grammars' those grammars which represent the study of the linguistic code in isolation from behaviour, so that the system is explained without regard to its use. Central to the way that philosophical grammars are organized is the concept of the rule. The code is represented in terms of rules of grammar, which do not account for the ways in which language varies or is used in real-life contexts; philosophical grammars are thus essentially reductionist. Such grammars necessarily operate on the basis of a polarization between the 'ideal' and the 'actual': what people actually say represents a departure from the rules of the 'pure' language, (hence such distinctions as Chomsky's 'competence and performance', and Saussure's *'langue* and *parole'*).

Ethnographic or descriptive grammars, such as SFG, seek to close the gap between language as code and language as behaviour: the system is not dissociated from the instance. A systemic description attempts to interpret simultaneously both what language is and what people do with it, thus interpreting language in relation to its place in people's lives. It treats language simultaneously as both code and behaviour, as both system and resource, and aims to explain what kinds of meanings people make, and what linguistic resources they draw on to make meaning in a specific cultural situation. In terms of an examination of a classroom context, therefore, it offers a tool to do two critical things: first, to systematically link the kinds of curriculum-related meanings which students must learn to control with the lexicogrammatical patterns which realize them; and second, to show the grammatical relationships between students' everyday and familiar ways of meaning and the academic registers of the curriculum.

Transformational and systemic functional grammar also differ in another respect, which is of particular relevance here. Transformational grammar is informed by a mentalist account of language that suggests that children are born with a genetic blueprint enabling them to deduce the rules of the language. The talk they hear around them functions as a trigger for language acquisition and a testing ground for their developing hypotheses about how the language works. From this perspective, many of the major milestones of language, particularly spoken language, have already been passed by the time children start school and so the language of teachers and carers is not seen as of great significance in children's language development. In contrast to this, the functional and interactional theories of Halliday and other linguists present the view that children have to learn to use language for a range of purposes and in a range of cultural and situational contexts. Indeed, language development is a lifelong process, something we become aware of when faced with new literacy challenges even as adults. Rather than viewing language as a finite set of rules which must be 'acquired', systemic theorists view language as a semiotic system, as a set of choices from which speakers select according to the particular context they are in: a speaker makes a particular choice from a range of possible options. From the perspective of the grammar, each of these choices can be viewed against the possible choices that could have been selected, hence the notion of 'system', and language as a 'system of systems'. Every meaningful stretch of written or spoken language, referred to as a 'text', represents a particular instantiation of the resources of language. This semiotic interpretation of language, which views language as a set of resources rather than as a set of rules, makes it possible to consider the appropriateness or inappropriateness of language choices in a given context of use.

Register

SFG demonstrates that language use is influenced by three aspects of the immediate context of situation: the field of the discourse, the tenor of the discourse and the mode of the discourse, these features constituting the linguistic register of the text. The field of discourse is the cultural activity; what the language is being used to talk about. The field of much of the discourse with which this study is concerned is science, specifically the field of magnetism. There are also, however, two secondary fields, later to be identified as 'learning about language' and 'learning to be a student'. The tenor of discourse refers to the relationship between participants, between the speaker and the listener, or the writer and reader. The tenor of discourse can be influenced by a number of factors, including status (the relative status of the participants), affect (their affective relationships, including how they are feeling towards each other at the time) and contact (how well they know each other or how frequently they are in contact). In this study, the relationships which are foregrounded are those between teacher and students, with status and affect as significant dimensions of the tenor. The mode of the discourse is the channel of communication, whether it is spoken or written. Martin (1984) suggests that two kinds of distance are involved here: spatial distance between those interacting (for example, whether they are face to face) and experiential distance, or distance from the activities that are the focus of the discussion (for example, whether the language is accompanying action or reflecting on it). Because an analysis of mode is of particular importance to later chapters, it is discussed in more detail later in this chapter.

These three aspects of context make a difference to how speakers use language; that is, they each have linguistic consequences: 'text carries with it, as a part of it, aspects of the context in which it was produced' (Eggins 1994, p. 7). The three register variables correspond to the three metafunctions of language, which allow three kinds of meaning to be made using the lexico-grammatical resources of the language. There is therefore a systematic relationship between the categories of register and the structure of language. Halliday describes these three kinds of meanings as ideational (comprising experiential and logical meaning), interpersonal and textual. Experiential meaning is concerned with representing and making sense of the 'real world', and with reflecting on and understanding the environment and the world of ideas. Interpersonal meaning is concerned with participating in the world, enabling people to act on their surroundings through their interactions with others. This strand of meaning enacts personal relationships; it expresses the role relationship between speaker and listener, and the speaker's attitudes to the subject matter itself. Textual meaning is concerned with shaping and organizing different kinds of texts. Each of these strands of meaning is needed in order for people to make sense of each other and the world: 'language is as it is because of what it does' (Halliday 1991, p. 6).

Given a certain field, choices are made from within the resources of the experiential function of language; given a certain tenor, choices are made from within the interpersonal resources of the language system, and given a certain mode of communication, choices are made from within the textual resources of the language system. Because of this systematic relationship within the language between meanings and contexts, it becomes possible to predict how a given context will determine choices from the language system, and also how the language system itself constructs context. Eggins comments on the evidence of this two-way relationship:

> Our ability to deduce context from text is one way in which language and context are interrelated. Our equally highly developed ability to predict language from context provides further evidence of the language/context relationship.
>
> (Eggins 1994, p. 7)

Halliday expresses it thus: 'the context plays a part in determining what we say; and what we say has a part in determining the context' (Halliday 1978, p. 3).

Since language reflects the use to which it is put, and because it varies systematically according to the situation in which it occurs, there will be certain recurring predictable features that occur each time a particular situation occurs. It is this relationship between meaning and context, and between context and language, that underpins much of the analysis in this book: most importantly it enables the relationship between different discourse registers and specific teaching and learning situations to be made explicit.

A significant aspect of the metafunctional principle, and one which again sets SFG apart from formal grammars, is the claim that any text simultaneously makes three kinds of meaning by drawing on the lexico-grammatical resources of each of the three metafunctions. The metafunctional principle is significant for learning theory, since 'it is the combination of the experiential and the interpersonal that constitutes an act of meaning. All meaning – and hence all learning – is at once both action and reflection' (Halliday 1993, p. 101). Cummins (2000) has argued that all teaching and learning involves the construction of particular kinds of interpersonal relationships between teacher and taught, and that how these are realized is particularly significant for minority groups. The capacity of SFG to analyse interpersonal meaning simultaneously with experiential meaning is therefore of significance in a study concerned with the education of minority groups. Halliday states:

> [People] do more than understand each other, in the sense of exchanging information and goods-and-services through the dynamic interplay of speech roles. By their everyday acts of meaning, people act out the social structure, affirming their own statuses and roles, and establishing and transmitting the shared systems of value and knowledge.
>
> (Halliday 1978, p. 2)

The discussion so far has focused on the notion of register, which explains and describes the relationship between a text and its situational context, and on the related metafunctions of language. SFG also takes into account the cultural context in which the text was produced, in particular the purpose of the text, and therefore its 'genre'. Genres represent different ways of organizing human experience and knowledge, and are thus goal-directed. A genre has been defined as a purposeful, staged, cultural activity (Martin 1984; Martin *et al* 1987), and includes both spoken and written activities. It is characterized by a distinctive schematic structure, a distinctive purpose and a distinctive set of probable lexico-grammatical choices. While this study draws mainly on register theory, the construct of genre (as a curriculum macrogenre) is useful in theorizing the stages of the major teaching and learning sequence that characterize the classroom programmes.

The mode continuum

The broadest distinction that may be made in relation to mode is between spoken and written language. The linguistic differences between these two modes have been discussed many times (for example, Butt *et al* 2000; Christie 1992b; Derewianka 1990; Hammond 1990; Eggins 1994; Martin 1984). In summarizing the characteristic features of spoken and written language, Eggins notes that spoken language typically involves turn taking; is context dependent and dynamic in structure; is characterized by 'spontaneity phenomena' such as false starts, incomplete clauses and hesitations; uses everyday lexis and non-standard grammar; and is grammatically intricate and lexically sparse. Written language, on the other hand, typically has a monologic organization; is context independent and synoptic in structure; is 'polished' rather than spontaneous; uses 'prestige' lexis and standard grammar; and is grammatically simple and lexically dense (Eggins 1994, p. 57).

In reality, however, and if the effect mode has on language choices is to be fully recognized, then this distinction between spoken and written language is more accurately viewed as a scale or continuum. Martin (1984) suggests the ways in which aural and visual contact affect language choice: a telephone conversation for example, removes visual contact and hence requires different sorts of language choices from those made in a face-to-face conversation, whereas radio removes the possibility of both visual contact and aural feedback. Consideration of these factors makes it possible to set up a scale beginning with face-to-face dialogue; then, along the scale, for example, to telephone conversations, to TV and radio and to writing. Martin argues that mode is also affected by the distance dimension between language and what is being talked about, a dimension which opposes language in action to language as reflection. At one end of this scale might be talk among players in a game of cricket and at the other, a philosophical treatise on sport. Between these two poles, Martin suggests a number of hypothetical situations, each further distanced from the original event: a commentary on the game on TV, a commentary on the same game on radio, an interview with the players after the match and a report of the game in the paper the following day. Broadly these can be viewed as *language in action* (the game), *commentary* on action (TV or radio 'play by play'), *reconstruction* of action (interview, report or review) and *construction* (book or treatise on cricket).

> What is happening along this scale is that language is getting further and further removed from what it is actually talking about, not simply in terms of temporal distance (distance from the scene of the crime, as it were), but eventually in terms of abstraction as well. Abstract writing is not really about anything you can touch, taste, hear, see or smell, though of course, in the end, if what we write is in any sense empirical, it must connect with observable facts of some kind or other.
>
> (Martin 1984, p. 26)

33

Thus although spoken and written language have distinctive characteristics, it is also clear that there is no absolute boundary between them. Modern technology increases this blurring: sending an email, although it is in the written mode, often produces the kind of informal language that has much in common with speech. The current practice of using ideographs within emails to represent how the writer is feeling – or express affect – reinforces the speech-like quality of these texts. Similarly, leaving a lengthy message on an answering machine may be quite linguistically demanding, since it is a relatively context-reduced task which requires us to 'speak aloud' the kind of language that would more usually be written. Rather than referring to language as 'spoken' or 'written' therefore, it is more descriptive of actual situations to use the terms adopted by Derewianka (1990) who refers to texts at different points along the continuum as 'more spoken-*like*' or 'more written-*like*.'

The following four texts indicate the sorts of language changes that occur as a result of this spatial and temporal distancing, and are illustrative of the notion of a 'mode continuum', a construct which this study explores in some detail in the context of the classroom. The four texts show how certain linguistic features change, in predictable ways, as language becomes increasingly more written-like, or context-reduced, and closer to a written form. The texts were collected in a classroom of ten-year-old students.

Text 1
(spoken by three ten-year-old students and accompanying action)
this . . no it doesn't go . . . it doesn't move . . .
try that . . .
yes it does . . . . a bit . . . that won't . . .
won't work it's not metal . . .
these are the best . . . going really fast

Text 2
(spoken by one student about the action, after the event)
we tried a pin . . . a pencil sharpener . . . some iron filings and a piece of plastic . the magnet didn't attract the pin but it did attract the pencil sharpener and the iron filings . . it didn't attract the plastic

Text 3
(written by the same student)
Our experiment was to find out what a magnet attracted. We discovered that a magnet attracts some kinds of metal. It attracted the iron filings, but not the pin. It also did not attract things that were not metal.

Text 4
(taken from a child's encyclopedia)
A magnet is a piece of metal which is surrounded by an invisible field of force which affects any magnetic material within it. It is able to pick up, or attract, a piece of steel or iron because its magnetic field flows into the magnet, turning it into a temporary magnet. Magnetic attraction occurs only between ferrous materials.

Text 1 is typical of the context-embedded language produced in face-to-face contexts. There is a use of exophoric reference (*this, these, that*), since the visual context obviates the need to name the referent and, as a result, there is a relatively low lexical density. In text 2 the changes in language are the result of a change in context. The original experience is now distanced in both time (the text occurred later) and space (the student no longer has the science equipment in front of her). The speaker reconstructs the experience through language, and so makes explicit the participants (realized through nouns and pronouns: *we, pen, pencil, pencil sharpener, piece of plastic*) and processes (realized through verbs: *tried, attract*). Text 3, a written text, is further distanced from the original event, since the audience is now unseen; written texts cannot rely on shared assumptions and a writer must recreate experience through language alone. Here, for example, an orientation is needed to provide the context for what follows: *Our experiment was to . . .* There is also the inclusion of a generalization – *a magnet attracts some metals*. In text 4 the major participant (*a magnet*) is generic: its properties are those of all magnets. There is a further increase in lexical density and the text includes a nominalization, the coding of a process term as a noun (*attraction*) which is typical of much written text, and increased numbers of circumstances, which give details about where, when and how processes occur: *within it, into the magnet, between ferrous materials*.

These four texts illustrate what Martin refers to as 'the general concept of contextual dependency' (Martin 1984, p. 27), referring to the ways in which text meanings need to become increasingly explicit as less can be taken as shared between speaker and listener or reader and writer:

> The more speakers are doing things together and engaging in dialogue, the more they can take for granted. As language moves away from the events it describes, and the possibility of feedback is removed, more and more of the meanings a text is making must be made explicit in that text if they are to be recovered by the reader, no matter how well informed.
>
> (Martin 1984, p. 27)

35

Using Martin's categories, text 1 represents 'language as action', texts 2 and 3 represent 'language as reconstruction', and text 4 represents 'language as construction'. In text 3 there is also some evidence that the writer is beginning to move away from reconstructing personal experience towards constructing a new interpretation of the events in which she has taken part (the generalization *a magnet attracts metals*).

The notion of contextual dependency is an important one in this study. As discussed earlier, language development is partly realized by the degree to which learners are able to produce explicit text; the language of the 'here and now' develops long before a child learns to reconstruct their experiences through language alone, or to express generalizations (see Halliday 1975, 1993). It is the ability to produce the increasingly more explicit text in academic contexts – text that is independent of the immediate situation the writer is in – which learners may not always master in their second language. The construct of the mode continuum offers considerable potential for exploring this issue in the school context.

At a more macro level, the continuum reflects the process of formal education itself, as students are required to make shifts within an increasing number of fields, and to move from personal everyday ways of making meanings towards the socially shared discourses of specific disciplines. Clearly a second language learner is likely to have fewer difficulties with producing a language-as-action text, where the visual context itself provides meanings, and where they do not need great linguistic resources, than with more context-reduced texts, where there is a greater demand placed on the learner's lexico-grammatical resources. In the classroom, an oral 'reporting' stage (like text 2 in the set of four texts examined above) is, surprisingly, often not given much attention, and while infant and primary classrooms are rich in the provision of experiential learning activities, children are frequently expected to write simply on the basis of these personal experiences, which represents a very large linguistic step (as can be seen by comparing texts 1 and 3 above), and one which is beyond the linguistic resources of many young second language learners. In this study, a major focus is given to the way in which students can be supported in the development of spoken but more context-reduced language as a way into gaining control of the more formal, and often written, registers of the curriculum. The analysis of how this occurs draws largely on the notion of mode and the mode continuum.

Types of exchanges

There is a further aspect of the grammar that should be commented on here, which concerns the analysis of dialogue. In speech act theory (see

Austin 1962), a class of speech acts is treated as a structure or described as a set of rules which speaker and listener must share. In systemic linguistics, the process of dialogue itself is seen as a shared potential and described in terms of the network of choices made by speakers, so that the exchange of meanings is an ongoing process of contextualized choice (Halliday 1991).

Halliday (1985b) interprets dialogue as a process of exchange involving two variables: the nature of what it is that is being exchanged and the roles defined by the exchange process. What is exchanged may be 'goods and services' or information. Goods and services involve non-verbal commodities, for example, the request for action in *Can you pass me that book?* Language is used to bring about the exchange but is distinct from what is being exchanged. In contrast, information is only brought into being through language (or other semiotic systems), as in *It's ten o'clock.* Here language actually constitutes the exchange; it is both the means and the manifestation of the exchange. The second variable in the exchange is the role of the speaker, which may be one of giving or receiving, and simultaneously assigns an equivalent role to the listener. If A is giving something, B is receiving it; if A is demanding something, B is called on to give. Thus if a speaker asks: *What time is it?* (demanding information) the listener is obliged to reply: *It's ten o'clock* (giving information). There are therefore exchange-initiating roles and responding roles, and these will be reversed as the addressee in turn becomes speaker.

In children's language development, the ability to exchange information develops much later than the ability to exchange goods and services. Halliday describes the emergence of information in the child's developing language system as the ability to 'impart meanings which are not already known'. He writes:

> . . . when children are first using language to annotate and classify experience, the particular experience that is being construed in any utterance is one that the addressee is known to have shared. When the child says *green bus*, the context is 'that's a green bus; you saw it too (and can check my wording)'. What the child cannot do at this stage is to impart the experience to someone who has not shared it . . .
> As they approach the end of the transition [from protolanguage], children learn to create information: to use language not just as a rehearsal of shared experience but as a surrogate. They learn to tell people things they do not already know. This is a complex operation because it involves using language to 'give' a commodity that is itself made of language (as distinct from using language to make an offer, where what is being 'given' is a non-linguistic commodity . . . that is independent of the language that is being used to offer it).
>
> (Halliday 1993, p. 102)

It is clear from this that exchange-type also intersects with aspects of mode. Exchanging goods and services implies a here-and-now context, and hence an orientation to language-as-action. Exchanging information may not necessarily be context dependent, since what is being exchanged is language itself, and hence there is likely to be an orientation towards language as reflection. Exchanging information clearly demands greater linguistic resources than exchanging a commodity, illustrated by the sequence of development in the child's language. This aspect of the grammar becomes important in considering the nature of teaching and learning activities, and in predicting whether they are likely to create a context for the exchange of a commodity or the exchange of information. For teachers this is an important question, since a particular teaching and learning task may simply not provide the context for the kind of language that teachers expect students to use. For example, students (or indeed any other speaker) are unlikely to use a written-like register with field-specific lexis in an experiential task where there is face-to-face contact between participants, not because they are unable to, but because within the situational context it is inappropriate and unnecessary.

In exchange sequences, a further distinction has also been drawn between the roles of the speakers: between the 'primary knower', the speaker who 'knows' the information, and the 'secondary knower', the speaker to whom the information is imparted (Berry 1981). Taking into account these speaker roles suggests a number of implications for classroom talk, where typically teachers are the primary knowers but ask questions in the guise of being secondary knowers. Such exchanges are typically realized through a three-part interactional structure consisting of teacher initiation, student response, and teacher feedback or evaluation[2]. Berry refers to this structure as 'the delaying of the admission of knowledge in order to find out whether the secondary knower also knows the information'. The third move represents the 'consequent stamping of the information with primary knower's authority' (Berry 1981, p. 127). Once this has occurred, however, all further elements of the exchange are optional. (Thus it would be highly unlikely for a student to respond to a teacher who has said something like *yes that's right*). A consideration of speakers' roles and of the obligatory/optional distinction is particularly relevant in considering how teaching exchanges can be extended beyond the three-part exchange, something which needs to occur if collaborative dialogue of the sort described earlier is to be possible. Later chapters also discuss the potential for second language learning of the third move of this exchange.

Relevance of systemic functional linguistics to a sociocultural theory of learning

The previous discussion has suggested the relevance of SFG to a study where learning is seen as a sociocultural activity. From a classroom research perspective, other factors are also important.

First, if language is to be used as evidence of social processes and structures, it must be studied as a system, not as isolated items; it is otherwise difficult to see the direct relationship between isolated surface features of language and particular teaching strategies, between, for example, the number of closed questions a teacher uses and their teaching style. Coding utterances directly as pedagogical acts (such as *lectures, praises*) and taking these as evidence of a particular teaching style, ignores the inherent structural and systemic complexity of language, and as a consequence of focusing on the surface features of language, educationists may be missing a much richer source of information about learning and teaching (Stubbs 1986). Theories of language which ignore its social context of use are also of limited help to an analysis of educational talk. Rather, any discussion of features of classroom discourse needs to be related to general sociolinguistic principles of language behaviour which are drawn from observations of language in use in other settings. SFG provides such a tool.

Second, a study of classroom discourse needs to be underpinned by a text-based, rather than sentence-based model of language, since what is often of interest are the extended sequences of discourse that take place over a number of weeks in a classroom. This book is concerned with issues such as how students can be helped to accommodate new conceptual frames within the interactions of the classroom, how ongoing interactions can be analysed to identify shifts in students' conceptualizations towards more comprehensive frames of reference, and how teachers can maximize the potential of dialogue for language teaching purposes. It explores how classroom discourse is sequentially organized; how topics are introduced and ordered; how student contributions are reformulated; how some items of knowledge are valued over others and thus how teachers co-construct educational knowledge with their students over time. Mercer argues for classroom discourse to be viewed as a 'long conversation that lasts for the whole of their [teacher and students] relationship' (Mercer 1995, p. 70) and insists that any theory for explaining how talk is used to create knowledge must take into account the concepts of context and continuity. SFG provides a tool by which it becomes possible to examine holistically the total discourse of a unit of work, so that, for example, it is possible to examine differences between the exchange structures of teaching and learning activities at the beginning and end of topics, to explore the gradual movement in the discourse from an 'everyday' to a more scientific register, and to see how teachers gradually reduce the 'scaffolds' they provide for students.

Finally, as a social view of language and language development, SFG is both compatible with and complementary to the sociocultural views of learning and of the significance of interaction in the educational process. Like Vygotsky, Halliday views learning as social and interactionally based in origin, and hence views language as central to the developmental process. Halliday argues that children's language learning is not simply one type of learning among many, but the foundations of learning itself: 'the ontogenesis of language is at the same time the ontogenesis of learning' (Halliday 1993, p. 93). The child learns:

> . . . to construct the system of meanings that represents his own model of social reality. This process takes place inside his own head; it is a cognitive process. But it takes place in contexts of social interaction, and there is no way it can take place except in these contexts. As well as being a cognitive process, the learning of the mother tongue is also an interactive process. It takes the form of the continued exchange of meanings between self and others. The act of meaning is a social act.
>
> (Halliday 1975, p. 139)

Although there are some clear differences between the work of Halliday and Vygotsky, their claims are in some ways remarkably similar, especially given their divergent starting points and interests. And in both cases, the work that has probably had the greatest impact on the thinking of educators are their respective studies of language development, where both take a genetic approach (Wells 1994). Halliday's model of language is also particularly congruent with the way that Leont'ev (1981) discusses the centrality of tools within activity theory: 'the tool mediates activity and thus connects humans not only with the world of objects but also with other people' (Leont'ev 1981, p. 55). Halliday's model of language represents this linguistically, since, through the interpersonal and ideational functions of language, any act of meaning embodies both the world of humans and the world of objects.

As indicated earlier, one of the aims of the book is to explore the usefulness of bridging different fields of study to theorize pedagogy. Fields of study which do not always overlap may nevertheless have some common insights, if one is read in terms of another. SFG provides a tool for articulating, in linguistic terms, pedagogical insights from these other fields. Terms common within SLA literature (such as message redundancy, comprehensible input, or negotiation), or from sociocultural approaches to teaching (such as scaffolding, appropriation or contingency), provide important insights for teaching, and represent practices which many effective teachers carry out intuitively. However, if such practices are exemplified through instantiations in the classroom and can be analysed linguistically, then what constitutes these practices can be articulated more precisely. This 'propositionalizing' of intuitive behaviour, as has already been argued, is one of the strengths of ethnographic research, but when that research is concerned with linguistic issues, it also requires a model of language which is sensitive to the social context of that behaviour. Given the two-directional nature of language and context and the predictability that obtains between situational contexts and the texts that are constructed within them, a systemic model of language makes it possible to make some predictions about the kinds of affordances that specific teaching and learning activities offer for language use and development. And if we are able to define those genres and micro-interactions that prove to be enabling of second language development, then such a description of classroom discourse should ultimately provide a path towards more effective classroom action.

Notes

1 The most often presented distinction between the two theories is the individual/social, yet, as Cole and Wertsch point out, Piaget did not deny the role of the social world in the development of the individual intellect, and nor did Vygotsky ignore the centrality of the active construction of knowledge.
2 This well recognized pattern of classroom discourse was first noted by Bellack *et al* (1966) and later among others: Sinclair and Coulthard (1975); Barnes (1976); Mehan (1979); Edwards and Mercer (1987); Cazden (1988); Lemke (1990) and van Lier (1996).

3 Second language learning and teaching

Metaphors from SLA

Theories of second language acquisition (SLA) have until the last decade made few specific comments about classroom learning, either as relevant data or as relevant application. What perhaps underlies this reluctance to apply theory to practice is not only the lack of a commonly agreed theory, but also the extent to which mainstream SLA research has largely taken place in sites which are not themselves genuine classrooms, and the extent to which the research approach has been quantitative and experimental rather than qualitative and descriptive. Lantolf for example writes of the 'commitment to the rationalist epistemology and . . . the positivist legacy that continues to pervade SLA studies' (1996, p. 74). Clarke argues that research in language acquisition 'contributes only a narrow range of insights to L2 teachers, primarily because the classroom, which is the primary venue for SLA, is explicitly excluded from consideration' (Clarke 1994, p. 15). More recently, however, there has been a growing interest among teachers and researchers in understanding how second language development occurs through situated interaction in classrooms (Lantolf 2000a, b), and most current views of second language education are based on the assumption that social interaction plays a central role in learning. Recent work drawing on sociocultural theory has focused on examining the process of second language development as it occurs in the ongoing moment-by-moment interactions of learners in classroom contexts (see, for example, Donato 1994; Dufficy 2005; Gibbons 2003; Hall 1995; Hammond and Gibbons 2005; Lantolf and Alijaafreh 1995; van Lier 2000; Michell and Sharpe 2005; Ohta 1995, 2000; Swain 2000; Swain and Lapkin 1998). Recent work has also shown how learning and language acquisition are realized through a collaborative interactional process in which learners begin to appropriate the language of the interaction for their own purposes. Such work has challenged the notion that language learning is solely a mental process divorced from the social and cultural situatedness of language learning and use (Lantolf and Appel 1994; Hall 1995;

Kramsch 1993; Toohey 2000). A lot of this research has been concerned with the learning which results from peer-peer interactions rather than from between expert and novice (Swain and Lapkin 1995; Engeström and Middleton 1996; Ohta 1995, 1999, 2000; Swain 2000; Donato 1994, 2000; Wells 2000). Much of the dominant terminology – for example, terms such as *negotiation of meaning, co-construction, cooperative learning, responsive teaching, reciprocal teaching, collaborative dialogue* – illustrate the overall shift from 'laboratory-based notions of learning to human learning as it is situated in the every-day social world of the learner' (van Lier 2001, p. 90).

Taking a sociocultural perspective on second language learning requires challenging some of the central metaphors of mainstream SLA theory. First it challenges the notions of 'input' and 'output' (Swain 2000). A sociocultural perspective places its analytical focus on the notion of dialogue, and by implication therefore on the different kinds of social engagements in which interactions are embedded. However, in parts of this book I have chosen to retain the constructs of input and output for certain analytical purposes. Pulling apart the dialogue into its constituent parts of input and output becomes relevant when considering the pattern of participants' individual moves *within* dialogue: for example, when focusing on a teacher's pattern of feedback moves, or tracking an individual student's take-up of technical language during the course of an interaction. It must be recognized though that these are always embedded within situated social dialogue.

More fundamentally, a sociocultural approach with its emphasis on the collaborative notion of learning challenges the central metaphor of 'acquisition'. The notion of peripheral participation in fact supplies us with a more appropriate metaphor for second language learning. As Pavlenko and Lantolf (2000) point out, sociocultural theory requires as a starting point not an acquisition metaphor with its associated information processing models, but a participation metaphor which entails viewing second language learning as a process of becoming a member of a certain community, and learning to mean and to act according to the norms of that community. In relation to ESL academic learning in school, this means focusing on the ways that school-aged learners become members of particular discipline-related discourse communities, and learn to control the specific registers and genres of curriculum-related subjects. And so an exploration of ESL learning in school requires us to ask: what are the processes that allow for ESL students to become active participants in the cultures of school, and what opportunities are there (or could there be) for engagement in practice?

The remainder of this chapter summarizes a range of early and later studies in the SLA literature to respond to this question, and to

44

suggest the kinds of pedagogic practices, and in particular discourse practices, that might be found in a classroom that is a 'learning rich' environment for second language development.

Input

Early claims by Krashen that comprehensible input is the major factor in second language acquisition, and that all the necessary grammatical information is provided to the learner if there is sufficient input (Krashen 1985, 1988, 1989), has been consistently challenged. Most significant to the concerns of this book is Krashen's view of speaking as simply an outcome of learning, and not a contributing factor to learning. In contrast to this view, this book demonstrates the significance of talk for learning and language development, and will argue that collaborative talk is not simply an outcome of previous learning, but the process of learning itself.

Other aspects of Krashen's theory are perhaps less controversial, and certainly have a degree of face validity among teachers. In addition to being comprehensible, Krashen has argued that input needs to contain structures that are a little ahead of the learner's current level of competence, which he refers to as 'I plus 1'. Situations of stress and anxiety inhibit learning, and learners need to be in environments where they have many opportunities to practise language in personally rewarding situations.

While broadly accepting the notion of comprehensible input as significant in language acquisition, Long (1983) extended Krashen's notion of how it is provided by recognizing the importance of two-way interaction (and hence acknowledging a role for learner output within dialogue). This early work focused on the interactional modifications which occur as a result of lack of understanding between interactants (Ellis 1991; Long 1981; Pica 1987; Pica *et al* 1987). Pica *et al*'s study demonstrated the significance for comprehension of clarification requests, confirmation checks and the restructuring of contributions. Her study illustrates how interactionally modified input, where the initial input was unmodified but where learners were free to seek clarification from each other, appeared to lead to a greater degree of comprehension than input which had been premodified, and suggests that interactional modifications can maximize the potential of comprehensible input for language acquisition. Pica *et al* (1989) suggest that requests for clarification are more likely than simple confirmation checks to stretch learners to focus on how they have said something, since confirmation checks from the teacher tend to 'solve' the communication problem for the learner. Later studies (Pica 1994; Pica *et al* 1996) also suggest that when learners have opportunities to negotiate meaning, opportunities for language learning appear to be increased.

It has been suggested that modifications by the learner occur most often when native speakers signal an explicit need for clarification rather than provide a model utterance as confirmation (Pica 1988; Pica *et al* 1989). This may benefit second language learning in two ways: by providing clues to learners to assist them in actively noticing and modifying incorrect or inappropriate language, and thus revising their hypotheses about the new language; and by inviting student- rather than teacher-generated repair, which provides opportunities for learners to 'proceduralize' knowledge that they may have internalized about the language in declarative form (Swain 1995a, 1995b; Lyster and Ranta 1997).

In relation to the notion of comprehensible input then, a more important issue for pedagogical purposes is perhaps not whether it is necessary, but the forms it should take for the negotiation of mutual understanding and learning. It is likely that it is the quality rather than the quantity of interactional modifications which is significant for comprehension. Further discussion of the qualitative aspects of interaction follows later in the chapter.

While studies on input have been important in focusing on some significant qualitative features of interaction for second language learning, their focus has tended to be on specific and clause-level features within individual utterances, rather than on the communicative effect of the discourse as a whole. This may reflect both the earlier accuracy-driven view of language underpinning much mainstream SLA research, and the fact that discourse-based approaches are less amenable to quantitative analysis.

Learner output

Research into French immersion programmes in Canada has found that despite very great amounts of comprehensible input and a communicatively oriented classroom, students may not develop native-like proficiency in syntax and morphology (Allen *et al* 1990; Swain 1995a, 1995b). Swain suggests that what is missing in these classrooms is sufficient learner output, that is, the language that learners produce, and concludes that the limited opportunities that students had in the immersion classes for *extended* output (and thus for collaborative dialogue) which demanded linguistic accuracy, might be a factor in explaining lower proficiency levels than might have been predicted.

Swain argues that since the ability to decode the language is not the same as discovering and producing the linguistic systems that carry meaning, output encourages learners to process the language more deeply than comprehension alone may do: it 'stretches' or 'pushes' their interlanguage, by stimulating them to focus on form more than is necessary when listening. Output can thus be considered 'to represent the leading edge of a learner's interlanguage' (Swain 1995b, p. 12), a significant claim related to Vygotsky's notion of learning within the ZPD. Swain (1985) suggests that learners need opportunities to 'stretch' their interlanguage to meet communicative goals, thus arguing, unlike Krashen, that such production is in itself a source of learning, not simply an outcome of what has already been learned. The importance of interactions which are comprehensible to the learner is that, because they are understood by the learner, they match the learner's ongoing intentions and cognitions, leading to what Swain refers to as a 'communicative consensus' between interactants. This is a necessary first step to grammatical control: because the message is understood, the learner pays attention to form, thus 'paving the way' for future exchanges. While one-to-one conversations provide important opportunities for this, as well as meaningful use by the learner of their current linguistic resources, even more helpful for learning may be those occasions where communication breaks down and the learner, in response to negative feedback by the interlocutor, is 'pushed' to use alternative means of getting their message across. Since, however, this can occur with grammatically deviant or sociolinguistically inappropriate forms, Swain also argues that the notion of negotiating meaning should not merely imply that the learner has been able to get the message across, but should incorporate the notion of conveying meaning 'precisely, coherently and appropriately' (Swain 1985, p. 249).

Swain has posited three functions of output in second language acquisition (Swain 1995a). First it appears to promote 'noticing', by which Swain refers to the recognition by learners of a 'gap' in their linguistic system: that is, they consciously recognize something that is a linguistic problem for them, a gap between what they wish to say and what they are able to say. (Swain's use of 'noticing' in this way differs slightly from its use by some other researchers. Chaudron (1985) and Ellis (1994), for example, use the term 'noticing' to refer to the learner attending consciously to linguistic features in the *input*.) Second, output offers opportunities for learners to test hypotheses, for example, when feedback leads to learners modifying or reformulating their output. Third, output has a metalinguistic dimension, whereby a learner's reflection on their language use helps them to internalize linguistic knowledge. Using the example of 'dictogloss', a language teaching activity where small groups of students work collaboratively to reconstruct a text that they have heard read aloud, Swain shows how this procedure led students to talk *about* language in the context of *using* language, and was successful in getting them to notice the gap between their current language knowledge and what they needed to know. Many of the solutions worked out by the students through this reflective process were remembered a week or two later, leading Swain to conclude that contexts where students reflect on the language they are using appear to be supportive for second language learning. Other similar roles for output have also been posited by Ellis (1994), who has suggested that it is the mechanism that facilitates the integration of new language into the learner's developing system. Thus tasks that promote interaction and reflection, which in turn encourage the processes of noticing, comparison and integration, seem likely to support language learning.

As Swain suggests, there is an additional sense in which learners may benefit from being 'pushed', that is, when there is a need to communicate in more sociolinguistically appropriate ways. While some learners may have achieved a high level of grammatical accuracy, they may have in their linguistic repertoire only a restricted range of grammatical constructions and thus are unable to vary what they say according to contextual norms and requirements; that is, according to particular registral constraints. A functional perspective on language suggests that the result of this would be to limit learners' sociolinguistic competence, or the degree to which they are able to control the language appropriate to different social contexts and purposes. In the context of ESL learning in school, this includes the contextual demands and constraints of the curriculum and the spoken and written contexts of learning. Taking this into account requires consideration not only of the sentence level, but of the discourse level of language.

Discourse as learning

Discourse analysis has been on the SLA agenda for some time. In a seminal paper in 1978, Hatch wrote that 'the search for explanation [for second language acquisition] via discourse analysis is one of the more promising areas of research' (Hatch 1978, p. 402). In this paper she builds a case for discourse analysis as a methodology for the study of second language acquisition, suggesting that discourse analysis 'gives more revealing, if less formal and elegant, insights into the second language learning *process*' (p. 402). She argues that in talking about the importance of input and the frequency of forms found in that input, we have 'overlooked the most important factor of all, the link that explains *how* the child learns'. Discourse analysis offers one way to explore the interactions that take place within conversations to see how the interaction determines the development of language forms and functions. Hatch suggests that the importance of discourse in language development is that linear (grammatical and sentence level) structures arise out of the vertical constructions of discourse. Interaction serves to provide learners with opportunities to create these 'vertical constructions', where meaning is built up collaboratively over several turns. Vertical constructions provide the basis on which the learner is subsequently able to produce a meaning within one turn. Thus 'one learns how to do conversation, one learns how to interact verbally, and out of this interaction syntactic structures are developed' (Hatch 1978, p. 404), a claim similar to that made by Bruner who notes that the structure of language is a by-product of learning to use language in discourse (Bruner 1978). It is through this co-building of a conversation between learner and partner that children become what Wells refers to as apprentices in conversation, and learn both the language system and the cultural ways of making sense of experience (Wells 1992).

It has been argued by researchers both in first and second language learning that it is a particular quality of interaction – its responsiveness to the particular needs of the learner and the meanings they are attempting to construct – that is significant for language development (see, for example, the studies referred to earlier in this section, and also Ellis and Wells 1980; Snow 1986; van Lier 1996, 2001; Wells 1986). Wells has termed this quality 'contingent responsiveness', Snow has referred to it as 'semantically contingent speech' and van Lier characterizes it as speech which typically has links to previous utterances and to the shared world of the participants so that intersubjectivity is achieved and maintained. Such speech is more symmetrical than typical teacher-student classroom talk, in that both participants are accorded equivalent rights and responsibilities within the conversation. Among the features of contingently responsive speech with young children, Wells (1986) includes the following: experts check that they have understood children correctly; misunderstandings are negotiated; topics initiated by children are sustained; and children are given opportunities to contribute to the conversation. Contingent responsiveness appears to be a feature in the speech of parents whose children are seen as accelerated language learners (Wells 1985), and while the input of parents of fast-learning and slow-learning children does not differ significantly on linguistic features, it does differ in the number of interactional features such as expansions and acknowledgements (Ellis and Wells 1980). Wells argues that semantically contingent responsiveness is as important a feature of teachers' interactions in the classroom in facilitating the learning process of students in school, as it is in early first language development.

There are interesting parallels between mother tongue and SLA research on the types of interactional modifications believed to be most facilitative of second language learning. In a study of the second language development of two adolescent Punjabi speakers, Ellis (1994) examined whether and in what ways interactions with the teacher contributed to the children's acquisition of English. First it appeared that new items were more likely to be produced when the children were allowed to initiate the discourse topic; thus the children were able to establish intersubjectivity with the teacher without having to first understand what the teacher wanted them to talk about. Second, the teacher capitalized on learning opportunities by helping the children to 'stretch' their linguistic resources through providing models of new syntactic structures at the moment when the children needed them. The children could then incorporate these into their own speech, and were thus able to achieve a more complex coding than would have been possible alone. Third, the teacher's responses to the students' contributions frequently encapsulated expansions which supplied the missing parts of utterances that students had struggled to produce, or added new semantic information. Significantly Ellis concludes that comprehensible input is not simply the result of adjustments made by competent speakers, but is the result of the interactions themselves: both learner and native speaker adjust their speech in the light of feedback that they give each other. Simply noting native speaker adjustments does not therefore provide a full picture of how input is made comprehensible or how language develops. Rather, as functional linguists would argue (for example, Painter 1984, 1985), discourse occurs as a way of organizing and understanding experience as that experience takes place.

One type of semantically contingent speech is that involving reformulations or 'recasts'. Ellis, noting the significance of reformulation, comments that in such an exchange the learner's utterance is reformulated in the guise of a confirmation check, affording the learner overt comparisons between interlanguage and target language forms (Ellis 1994). Using the term 'recast' to describe a similar phenomenon, Long refers to 'utterances that rephrase a child's utterance by changing one or more sentence components . . . while still referring to its central meanings' (Long 1996, p. 434). Recent research in SLA has focused on the role of recasts in language learning as part of a broader concern with the role of negative evidence; that is, information given explicitly or implicitly to the learner about what is not allowable in a language. In the studies to date, however, recasts are defined in terms of grammatical acceptability rather than contextual appropriateness (see Morgan *et al* 1995 on parent-child dyads; Oliver 1995 on child native speaker-nonnative speaker dyads; and Lyster (1998) and Lyster and Ranta (1997) on teacher-student interaction in second language classrooms). Oliver (1995) offers evidence of the facilitative effect on language learning of semantically contingent feedback which occurs within discourse. Drawing on first language acquisition research and the work of Farrar (1990), Oliver defines recasts as utterances that correct the child's syntactic or semantic errors by a caregiver demonstrating the correct sentence after the child has produced an ungrammatical one. Oliver considers whether learners acquire a second language based purely on positive evidence (models of the correct form of the target language) or whether negative evidence (data that gives the learner information about what is not allowable) also plays a role, and argues that indirect and implicit feedback, such as recasts, negotiation strategies and forms of repetition need to be included in considering the role of negative feedback. Importantly, recasts are likely to be 'usable', or noticed by the learner, because they are salient and contingent on what the child has just said (Farrar 1990) and maintain his/her central meaning. Because the meaning is already clear, it is argued that learners are more likely to attend to and compare the differences in form between what they have said and the adult response.

However, 'implicit' recasts, those which simply reformulate all or part of the student's utterance with no additional meaning and without drawing the student's attention to the reformulation, have been described as 'remnants of audiolingualism that minimize the value of student utterances' (Calve 1992 in Lyster 1998, p. 55). There is evidence that implicit recasts lead to minimal uptake and do not lead to student-generated forms of repair (Lyster and Ranta 1997), perhaps because although they require the learner to acknowledge the response they do not require them to adjust what they have said. In Lyster and Ranta's study (1997), more than half of the teachers' corrective feedback moves involved recasts, but the majority of these (69 per cent) were followed by topic continuation in which students did not immediately repeat or incorporate the correct form. The researchers conclude that this is because recasts *provide* correct forms to learners, and so students are not required to generate their own repair. Allwright and Bailey (1991) also point out that simple repetition of the correct form by the student may be useless if the student is unable to differentiate between the model and their own utterance, and that time and opportunity needs to be given for self-repair. Van Lier (1988, 1996) likewise argues that teachers should delay correction until the learner has had opportunity to self-repair.

Lyster and Ranta (1997) suggest that in classrooms where the teacher is focusing on both content and language, as is the case in this study, a wider range of feedback strategies is required which explicitly focus on the negotiation of form, rather than simply on the overall meaning and substantive content of student contributions. These strategies include: elicitation (*how do we say that in French?*); metalinguistic clues (*we don't say it that way*); clarification requests (*I don't understand*); and repetition of student error as a question (*le girafe?*). Unlike the negotiation of meaning, the negotiation of form aims not only at comprehensibility of message but also for accuracy and precision in form, thus involving a more pedagogical and less conversational function of negotiation. Such strategies, involving focus on the negotiation of form as well as meaning and content, are used many times by the teachers in this study.

In a study which attempted to explore further how teachers use recasts naturalistically in meaning and content oriented classrooms, Lyster (1998) suggests that in the classrooms examined, the corrective function of recasts (i.e. in relation to grammatical form) appeared to be less salient than the discourse functions they served (i.e. in relation to the substantive subject content of the students' utterances). In addition, the intent of the recast from the students' perspective tended to be ambiguous, since teachers often used non-corrective repetition; that is, they repeated well formed as well as corrective utterances. It can be questioned how far learners (particularly young learners) are then able to distinguish one context from the other, and thus recognize those times when their utterances need repair. Such ambiguity makes it difficult for them both to test hypotheses about the target language, and to detect mismatches between input and output (Lyster 1998). Thus, though several studies support the role of negative evidence (for example, Carroll and Swain 1993; Lightbown and Spada 1990; Pica 1988; Pica *et al* 1989), none of these support the implicit use of recasts without some explicit attention being drawn to them by the teacher/native-speaker interactant (Lyster 1998). Some evidence exists however for the uptake by students of jointly constructed 'hybrid' discourse containing both students' contributions and teachers' more registrally appropiate recasts (Gibbons 1998 and this book, Chapter 6). Here too, however, teacher recasts were frequently accompanied by explicit comments by the teacher foregrounding the form of language (in this case the scientific register), for example, students were often reminded that they were 'learning to talk like scientists'.

In relation to the overall significance of recasts for second language learning, we may conclude that the jury is, thus far, still out. As Lyster points out, this presents a dilemma for teachers whose mandate is to teach both language and content, 'namely, how to reinforce the substantive content of student messages while giving [students] clear messages about language form' (Lyster 1998, p. 71). However, it appears likely that the usefulness of recasts is increased when they are accompanied by some explicit signalling to the learner, so that they are noticed. This signalling includes metalinguistic talk relating to the form of the recast item, and signs of non-comprehension by the listener which require the learner to take an active part in reformulating the utterance. Both these issues are taken up in following chapters.

Classroom-based issues

Participant and organizational structures

There have been relatively few studies on how classroom organization impacts on second language learning in multilingual mainstream (i.e. non-ESL specialist) contexts. This issue was specifically addressed in an early study by Wong-Fillmore (1985), where she examined possible reasons why some minority children learned a great deal more English in their first year of school than others. As it is one of the few studies on the effects of different kinds of classroom organization on young ESL learners' language development, it is discussed here in some detail.

Wong-Fillmore suggests that two sets of characteristics appear to distinguish classes that worked for language learning from those that did not, relating to the way the classes were organized, and the way language was used during instructional activities. Wong-Fillmore draws a distinction in her study between 'teacher-directed' or 'teacher-centred' classes, and 'open' or 'student-centred' classes. The first type was highly controlled by the teacher, and included a relatively greater number of whole-class or large-group instructional events. The second was 'coordinated' rather than 'directed' by the teacher, and included a relatively greater number of individual or small-group cooperative group learning activities. Wong-Fillmore concludes that the classrooms that were least successful for language learning were those which were more open in structure, while the most successful were those which made the greatest use of teacher-directed activities. While this book questions the naming of classrooms in generic ways (such as teacher-centred and student-centred), Wong-Fillmore's study is significant in relation to some of the hypotheses it advances, since it relates the success of students' language learning directly to the affordances for language learning offered within the classroom.

Wong-Fillmore advances a number of hypotheses to explain the relative lack of success of the more open classrooms in her study. First, it appears that how much practice students actually got with English was dependent on individual students: whether or not, for example, they had well developed social skills, and on who was in the class,

53

whether, for example, there were sufficient numbers of English speakers to support those with less English. In addition, much of the interaction in open classes was between teacher and individual student, and so the amount of actual exposure to English could (and did) vary considerably from student to student.

Three characteristics of lessons appeared to be significant for language learning. First, there were clear boundaries between 'subjects' or between individual and whole-class work. These boundaries were not only linguistic, but were marked in other ways such as a change in seating pattern or the teacher's voice quality or body language. It seems likely that such boundary markers served to 'frame' the lesson or activity (a point also made by Cazden 1988), thus indicating to the children when they should pay attention, what they should be listening for and the kind of talk that was appropriate.

The second structural characteristic of successful classes was the consistency of the overall lesson formats which resulted in students becoming familiar with teaching routines and thus being better able to play the roles expected of them as participants. They were able to follow the lesson without having to work out anew what was happening: they were 'ahead of the game in figuring out what they are supposed to be learning each day' (Wong-Fillmore 1985, p. 29). Thus, although the content may have been new, the regularity of the lesson routines, the routinized, consistent procedural language used by the teacher and the familiarity of the activities meant that the format in which new learning was presented was a familiar one. An important part of these familiar routines was the signalling devices used by teachers to orient and guide the learners, such as telling students what they were about to do and locating new learning in students' prior experiences.

The third structural characteristic of successful classes was related to turn allocation. Teachers tended to use a variety of procedures: at times students bid for turns, or they might be asked to recite in chorus, or they may be called on by teachers, but procedures for participation were always clear. In contrast, procedures in less successful classes were often unclear, with more aggressive students gaining more 'turns' and hence a greater share of the feedback. Quieter students in these classes got fewer turns to participate and consequently less individualized feedback from the teacher, and thus fewer affordances for learning.

Certain characteristics of teacher-talk also worked well as input. As many of these very young children had only been learning English for two years or less, it was difficult for teachers to teach anything that could not be easily demonstrated. How they communicated what was to be learned in the lessons not only impacted on how effectively curriculum content was learned, but also whether the language they used worked as language learning. The teacher-talk in successful classes shared a number of features. First, there was an emphasis on communicating meaning. Since English was the *medium* of education (unlike the situation where English is the *subject* of the lesson, such as in instructional ESL and EFL classes) ideas and concepts were often quite complex, and yet in the successful classes the lesson was at an appropriate conceptual level for the grade. Often the teacher used demonstration as a way of teaching concepts, for example by writing and working out maths problems while she was talking, and relating the words to known maths concepts, so that prior knowledge and experience provided the contexts for making sense of new material and possibly unknown language. Wong-Fillmore suggests that the presentation of the material in a variety of ways, such as talk, board work and demonstration 'added up to a *message redundancy* that gave the students *multiple access* to the materials that were taught in it' (Wong-Fillmore 1985, p. 38, italics added). In my own work, discussed later, I have referred to this multiplicity of meanings as 'message abundancy' (Gibbons 2003) and included within this construct the use of alternative semiotic systems such as graphs, mathematical systems and images.

Of particular significance in the teacher-talk in the successful classrooms was the fact that it was not only grammatical but registrally appropriate, more precise, more expository, and more highly propositionalized than ordinary talk. In addition, teacher-talk included the repeated use of patterns and routines that while they have the *appearance* of substitution drills, are used for the teaching of content, not merely for the rehearsal of language structures. As an example, she includes the following:

> What does an inventor do? They make things. New things. An inventor made the first TV. An inventor made the telephone, the first telephone. An inventor made the first electric light. An inventor makes things. He makes up new things for the first time.
>
> (Wong-Fillmore 1985, p. 39)

The repetition of key patterns and the 'message abundancy' in Wong-Fillmore's example offer the students more than one chance to understand what is being said, and to notice where and how forms can be substituted. The teacher's use of repetition gives students several opportunities to hear closely related meanings, and in this way, they can work out some of the substitution rules of English. Paraphrases were also common, again giving students several opportunities to understand a message and to learn alternative forms. (It is worth noting here that in a review of the effects of input modification on comprehension, Parker and Chaudron (1987) also note the facilitative effect of such factors, suggesting that simplified input may be less effective in facilitating comprehension than elaborations which contribute to redundancy, such as repetition, paraphrase or the use of synonyms.) In addition, teachers frequently repeated students' one-word answers to questions and expanded them into their full forms, an example of one type of recasting. Such patterns and moves are also evident in the examples included in Part 3.

Although she herself does not refer to the notion of explicitness, it is clear that the successful classrooms in Wong-Fillmore's study exhibited a high level of explicitness about both the content and the procedures of the lesson. Delpit (1988) also argues that this was a feature valued by the Afro-American school students of her study. Her work is discussed in more detail later in this chapter, but here it is worth noting the similarities between the pedagogy she favours and the more 'closed' classrooms to which Wong-Fillmore refers.

Teacher questions

With the concern for communication in language classrooms, there has been an interest in the nature of the questions that teachers ask, with many studies pointing to the fact that teachers ask many more 'display' questions, where the information is already known by the teacher, than they do referential questions, where the information is unknown. In a survey of research on teacher-student interaction, Chaudron (1988) suggests that while modifications of questions may help a learner, multiple questions do not, on their own, serve to make language comprehensible. He concludes that questions that negotiate comprehension and sharing of information are the most potentially useful to the learner. It also appears that the ratio of display to referential questions increases in contexts where there are non-native speakers. Early (1985) found that while the ratio used by teachers with ESL social studies students was almost 6 to 1, it was only 1.5 to 1 for native-speaker students, thus suggesting that display and referential questions are differentially distributed across ESL and non-ESL students. A more recent study by Jane Torr (1993) found similar results in primary classrooms. Her study involved two teachers, one with children from English-speaking backgrounds (ESB) and the other with children from non-English-speaking backgrounds (NESB), many of the latter group however being rated as fluent English speakers by their teacher. Torr suggests that the nature of the teacher-talk led to the NESB group playing different participant roles in the construction of the discourse compared with their English-speaking counterparts. The NESB teacher spoke more frequently, contributing more to the construction of the discourse, and asked fewer questions, with those questions requiring mainly display responses (such as the naming of people, things and processes). In the NESB classroom the teacher tended to be coded in the grammar as doing the 'thinking', 'knowing' and 'hoping'. By comparison, many of the questions asked by the ESB teacher required explanations of how or why something occurs, and it was the children who were coded in the grammar as 'knowers' and 'thinkers'. Relative to the ESB class, the NESB children spoke less frequently (thus limiting opportunities for interaction with the teacher), asked fewer questions and made fewer unsolicited observations. Consequently the classroom offered them fewer semantic options – and thus fewer affordances for language learning – than those available to the ESB students. Torr concludes that the two environments were 'significant in terms of the children's potential to gain access to society's resources' (Torr 1993, p. 52).

Group talk and group tasks

Much educational rhetoric espouses the value of group work. In relation to the second language context, advocates of group work argue that it offers students more opportunities to hear more complex language and in increased amounts, is likely to result in a wider range of rhetorical functions being used and promotes a positive affective environment. It has also been suggested that small-group work offers major benefits to students relating to three areas of theoretical importance for language learning: input, interaction and the contextualization of knowledge (McGroarty 1993). The process of asking questions, exchanging information and problem-solving provides a natural context for redundancy to occur. This may include the repetition of words, the rephrasing of ideas, the restatement of problems and the refining of meanings. This redundancy, when contextualized within the curriculum and driven by the communicative requirements of the interactants, seems likely to support comprehension. In addition, the need to get information or clarify meaning also increases the need for learners to ask questions which genuinely seek new information (in contrast to teacher display questions), and thus further input and practice in more authentic communication is provided.

There may be an additional reason why a heavily teacher-controlled classroom is insufficient for promoting language learning, and this has to do with the kinds of power relationships that are likely to be set up by such structures. The issue of social relationships in learning is one which was addressed by Vygotsky, who saw the affective domain as integrally related to cognitive learning (although interestingly this aspect of the ZPD has rarely been discussed in western interpretations of sociocultural theory). Within SLA theory, some work has been done on the impact of social relationships between participants. A study by Pica (1987) suggests that social relationships, in terms of the equality of the status of interactants, appear to be a factor in the extent to which interactional modifications take place, perhaps because of an increased need by both participants for mutual understanding. It appears important that participants see themselves as having equivalent status as conversational partners if interactional modifications are to be encouraged. Pica argues that this is more likely to occur in the process of a two-way information flow, when both participants have information which the other needs to share; each participant has both a right to request and an obligation to share. However in a classroom which is predominantly teacher-controlled, and therefore where there is likely to be an unequal distribution of participation rights, these conditions are less likely to be met. Within the traditional structure of classroom interaction, teachers tend to ask questions, students to respond, and teachers to evaluate the response (a triadic interactional structure, which is discussed in more detail in the following chapter). It is often unnecessary therefore for the student to restructure their interaction, since the discourse tends to be aimed at a one-way display from student to teacher, rather than a two-way flow of information. Teachers normally know beforehand the kind of things they want students to say and do: mutual comprehension does not have to be striven for but tends to be built into the discourse. Thus there are minimal opportunities for the restructuring of interaction: in fact many classroom activities are actually set up in such a way that students can opt out of interaction.

> When faced with ambiguous target or interlanguage material on a particular topic, classroom participants may be willing to suspend comprehension completely, or settle for less than total understanding, rather than interrupt the flow of classroom discourse to seek clarification.
>
> (Pica 1987, p. 12)

An implication for the classroom would appear to be that the teacher should avoid habitually taking responsibility for the immediate resolution of communication breakdown, and increase opportunities for students to share this responsibility.

The nature of the tasks in which learners are engaged also appears significant in how successful group work is in providing a language learning context. A number of studies have concluded that tasks which involve students in exchanging information (two-way tasks) lead to a higher frequency of interactional modifications and hence are more likely to promote negotiation of meaning than tasks which require only a one-way giving of information. Pica (1987) suggests that a critical factor in these more successful tasks was the fact that participants were exchanging information known only to them. This suggests that students are more likely to restructure their interactions, and work towards mutual comprehension, if the task *requires*, rather than simply invites them to do so. Pica concludes that talk must be necessary and integral to the task, not simply an accompaniment, and should emphasize collaboration and equality of responsibility. McGroarty (1993) likewise suggests that individual accountability should be built into group activities, so that the resulting interaction is more likely to lead to genuine collaboration and hence negotiation among participants, such as the kind of collaborative problem-solving language tasks described by Swain (2000).

Well structured peer group talk, then, would seem to be facilitative of language learning on two counts: it has the potential to offer many more and varied opportunities for language use, and it is more likely to produce the kind of social relations to which Pica refers. Studies have also shown that group work does not significantly compromise grammatical accuracy, and there is little difference in this aspect between teacher-fronted and group talk in the classroom (Long and Porter 1985; Porter 1986).

In one respect, student-student talk is likely to be inferior, however. Non-native speakers tend not to provide each other with sociolinguistically appropriate input and thus may be unable to develop aspects of sociolinguistic competence in a group-work context (Porter 1986). This is particularly significant in relation to the development of school-related registers. In the development of sociolinguistic competence, students will be dependent on other sources, such as the teacher, to provide access to the target language or register. How this explicit teaching may be achieved in more dialogic contexts is addressed in Chapters 6 and 7.

In summary, research studies present some tension between approaches that favour the teacher-centred or 'closed' classroom of the kind described in Wong-Fillmore's study, and those that argue for the value of small-group work. This issue is one that later chapters take up, where it is argued that the teacher takes a range of roles depending on the degree of 'peripherality' of the learner – their level of apprenticeship – in relation to a particular task.

Content-based language teaching

School-aged ESL learners are faced with the need to learn curriculum content through the medium of their second language, and teachers with the job of providing language teaching which is not at the cost of the development of curriculum knowledge. This section examines factors relating specifically to content-based language teaching in a school setting.

Language teaching methodologies have long accepted the notion that language teaching is more effective when learners are presented with meaningful language in context, and the integration of language and content teaching is now generally accepted as enabling of second language learning. In arguing for content-based teaching, Gibbons (2002) suggests five reasons for the integration of ESL learners into regular subject-based classrooms. First, the regular curriculum offers opportunities for the authentic exchange of meanings in a variety of contexts and for a variety of purposes. Second, because it may take five years or more for ESL students to match their English-speaking peers in learning to control the academic registers of school, concurrent teaching and learning of subject content and language is a way of responding to this developmental challenge. Third, an integrated programme supports both content and language learning in a reciprocal way, because it provides opportunities for an ongoing recycling of concepts and the academic language associated with those concepts. Fourth, separate instruction in language alone may be insufficient to enable ESL learners to effectively participate and learn mainstream curriculum content[1]. An integrated programme can provide a more systematic relationship between new language and subject content. Finally, there are benefits for all learners in a culturally and linguistically inclusive and explicit curriculum, which has the potential to model to students how to navigate difference and can encourage the development of dialogue across cultures.

Since language is being heard in the context of an academic activity that provides a conceptual structure for language redundancy, students are likely to remember more of what they hear, and since the focus is on meaning, correction is used in the service of understanding (McGroarty 1993). Likewise it has also been suggested that students learn language more effectively when their attention is focused on learning other things: interesting content provides a motivation to learn, and language becomes the means to this end, rather than an end in itself (Genesee 1987). In a model where linguistic structures are grouped around a contextual topic or theme, the content can be exploited and maximized for the explicit teaching of language. Since the topic is already given, teachers have no problem about the 'content' of the language lesson, something that may be a problem in a 'language' class where teaching may be done in the absence of a ready-made context. In content teaching, a focus on meaning rather than form is most likely;

communication takes place because the students are engaged in real, not just realistic, topics and activities.

However, although there is considerable support for content-based language teaching, there are still issues surrounding exactly what role 'content' should play in the language acquisition process and how the integration between the two should be accomplished (Davison and Williams 2001; Met 1994; Swain 1996). Often the relationship between 'content' and 'language' is not articulated, with language learning and content learning considered separately, an approach which is inadequate for students learning through the medium of a language in which they are not yet proficient (Met 1994; Mohan 1986). Mainstream classes into which minority students are placed without specific support or an 'ESL-aware' teacher are also likely to produce inappropriate contexts for language learning (Harklau 1994; Mohan 2001), since, as Mohan argues, 'mainstreaming of L2 learners . . . cannot be assumed to provide optimal language learning opportunities as a matter of course' (Mohan *et al* 2002, p. 109). An added consideration is also that programmes need to be cognitively appropriate for the chronological age and developmental level of the students (Cummins 1996; Met 1994).

Content-teaching within the immersion model used in bilingual Canadian schools involves English-speaking students being taught curriculum content through the medium of French, and here too the results are not straightforward. Although these programmes have been successful in developing students' knowledge of curriculum content as well as a high level of functional skills in the second language (Genesee 1987), students have not developed native-like competency in some aspects of grammar and syntax, and their language use tends to be sociolinguistically restricted (Swain and Lapkin 1990). Swain (1996) suggests that in the integration of language and content teaching, sufficient attention is not always paid to students' target language use, and that the input students receive from their teachers in immersion classes may not be as rich linguistically as might be expected. Her observations lead her to conclude that this input was restricted in a number of ways. Although grammar was taught, it was often isolated from meaningful contexts. Apart from context-specific meaning, there was little focus on vocabulary teaching. Extended discourse was rare among students, and their talk (mainly in response to teachers' questions) was rarely sustained longer than a clause, with only 14 per cent of student turns in teacher-fronted talk being utterances of this length. What Swain's study suggests is that the *potential* for content teaching as a context for language learning may not necessarily be realized in the enacted curriculum of the classroom.

Generally much less successful than the Canadian bilingual programmes has been immersion education for language minority children taught through the medium of their second language, an educational context that is familiar in Australia, the UK and North America. Since ESL students have not only to learn the second language, but also the subject content of the curriculum, the importance of curriculum content goes beyond simply providing a vehicle for language learning. As Mohan comments, 'it is all very well to use the math class as a resource for learning English, but the students' interests in [also] gaining an education in mathematics cannot be neglected' (Mohan 1986, p. 10). Arguing for an equal importance to be placed on language teaching, Mohan continues, 'unlike the deficiencies in other subjects, a deficiency in the language of instruction is a fundamental obstacle to education in all subjects'. While the curriculum must simultaneously promote language, cognition and content learning, it should not entail a 'dilution in the conceptual and academic content of the instruction, but the adoption of strategies that take account of students' background and that ensure comprehension of content' (Cummins 1994, p. 42), a point supported by others (Harklau 1994; Gibbons 1991, 2002; McKay *et al* 1997). Strategies as to how this might be achieved include: the use of the whole curriculum as a resource for language teaching in the context of a functional approach to language (Gibbons 1991, 2002); the use of multimodal information structures such as diagrams, graphs and timelines in making new information comprehensible (Mohan 1986; Early 1990); and more interactive approaches to students' vocabulary development (Zimmerman 1997).

Looking more broadly beyond the level of individual classroom strategies, a number of researchers argue for the significance of the social context and interaction for minority students' learning of both content and language (Edelsky *et al* 1991; Faltis and Hudelson 1994). As Faltis and Hudelson (1994) assert, 'the crux of learning occurs through social interaction in which content is being discussed and negotiated' (p. 458). Such a perspective represents an example of the shift away from cognitive ideas about second language acquisition towards a notion of language development as contextually situated in activities 'that must have one or more knowledgeable members who interact with learners in ways that invite them to "join the club"'. This socially based perspective, argue the researchers, 'more adequately depicts what happens in classrooms that invite students who are acquiring English to generate as well as gain knowledge and discourse from peers and the teacher' (Faltis and Hudelson 1994, p. 458).

It appears from this discussion that while many researchers would argue at a theoretical level for the potential value of the content classroom for language learning, and while strategies exist to make individual lessons more comprehensible, there remain complex issues embedded in how such programmes should be conceptualized, and how they can then be operationalized. Mohan's work (1986, 2002) is an example of a planned integrative model which seeks to respond to this issue by providing a framework that sequences knowledge and discourse from practical and implicit to theoretical and explicit, and is discussed again in Chapter 5.

So far the discussion in this chapter has centred on learners' academic achievements in terms of linguistic and cognitive perspectives. In recent years, however, the focus of much research around minority learners' academic achievement has been in terms of its relationship with sociopolitical, sociological and institutional factors. The following section briefly discusses some of this work.

Critical perspectives on the second language classroom

Discourse and identity

Along with a focus on discourse as a tool for learning has come a more critical perspective which focuses on how learners are positioned through the discourse of the classroom and how their identity is constructed through the interactions in which they are participants (Darder 1991; Nieto 1996, 1999; Toohey 2000; Walsh 1991). There is now considerable research that shows that not only the content but also the processes of student learning are embedded in the instructional practices realized through classroom interactions (Baker 1992; Cazden 1988; Delpit 1988; Green and Dixon 1993; Gutierrez and Larson 1994; Hall 1998; Lemke 1990; Lin 1993, 2001; Philips 1983. As Halliday's (1985) work in systemic functional grammar demonstrates, the experiential and the interpersonal metafunctions of language exist in any instance of language use at one and the same time. Language is not only the means by which experiential learning is constructed; through its interpersonal resources it also constructs the roles, relationships and identities of interactants in a particular situational context.

Much research has now been undertaken that links academic achievement not only to the pedagogical effectiveness of teaching programmes but also to the institutional and societal power relations in which classroom communication occurs (see, *inter alia*, Cummins 1986, 1996, 2000; Floriani 1993; Green and Dixon 1994; Gutierrez *et al* 1995a; Gutierrez *et al* 1995b; Gutierrez and Stone 2000; Kalantzis and Cope 1988; McLaren 1994; Toohey 2000; Walsh 1991). Such studies view the classroom as a historically and culturally specific context within a societally governed institution. Cummins argues that to educate learners in a culturally and linguistically diverse context it is necessary to nurture both intellect and identity equally in ways that challenge coercive power relations. Coercive relations of power include the expectation that minority groups deny their linguistic and cultural identity and work out of a narrow curriculum that results from approaches that take a reductionist approach to learning. Interactions represent the direct determinant of ESL learners' success or failure in school. They 'form an interpersonal space within which the acquisition of knowledge and formation of identity is negotiated' (Cummins 2000, p. 44), and so are never neutral. In the process of whatever instructional function they may be serving, interactions simultaneously construct how students are positioned as people and as learners, and are a powerful indicator to students about how they are viewed: 'children are aware, albeit not at the theoretic level, of when they are being treated as persons in an educational relationship and when as mere instructional objects' (Young 1992, p. 67). Creating opportunities to shape learning therefore depends not only on the kinds of instructional practices constructed through discourse but on the larger institutional forces by which learners' voices are shaped in the moment-by-moment interactions of the classroom:

> Our every use of language serves as a sociopolitical statement indicating our stance toward the particular interactive moment, our place in that interaction and our positioning toward the others involved.
>
> (Hall 1995, p. 214)

In a study that analyses the moment-by-moment interaction of one marginalized Latina student and her teacher, Gutierrez, Larson and Kreuter (1995a) show how the monologic and monocultural instruction in the classroom paralyses students and teachers and prevents the creation of a rich and vital classroom life, ultimately limiting affordances for learning. Gutierrez *et al* argue that in the classroom they observed participation in joint activity was so restricted that fundamental educational goals were subsumed within the goal of social order, producing an institution which valued social order over educational outcomes. A number of other studies based on a close analysis of interaction also illustrate how marginalized students may be offered differential opportunities for learning; through differential attention to their participation, students may be led along individual paths. Language learning thus does not depend only on students' abilities or motivation but is also tied to a teacher's motivation for and interest in providing learners with what Hall refers to as 'official participatory rights' to engage in opportunities for learning (Hall 1998, and see also Philips 1983; Gutierrez, Rhymes and Larson 1995b; Smagorinsky and O'Donnell-Allen 2000; Toohey 2000; Torr 1993). It is not simply students' participation patterns that are significant, but how students' contributions are responded to by the teacher and the consequence of such differential responses, which may result in 'primary' and 'secondary' groups of students. Differential responses include different rights to the floor and the roles participants are allowed to play: for example, certain students may not have their contributions responded to, or they may be less encouraged to bring in personal knowledge (see, for example, Bourne 2003). Such research suggests that the notion of the ZPD needs to be extended beyond the cognitive, to take account of affective development and the development of identity.

A discussion of how opportunities for academic language learning can be constructed in the classroom, then, must take account not simply of the experiential content of the discourse itself, but also the participation structures and responses constituted in educational practices, within which participants play out particular roles and relationships. From a more critical perspective on classroom discourse any set of interactions needs to be examined from at least two perspectives: the effectiveness of the instruction in fostering learning, and the impact of the instruction on the way students view themselves. In the words of Gutierrez and Stone (2000), learning contexts are 'complex social spaces that are inextricably related to what gets learned and how' (p. 157). Or as McDermott (in Chaiklin and Lave) puts it, 'the question of who is learning what and how much is essentially a question of what conversations they are part of, and this question is a subset of the more powerful question of what conversations are around to be had in a given culture' (Chaiklin and Lave 1993, p. 295).

The following section considers the ways in which minority learners have historically been defined, and the possibilities offered by a more critical redefinition of the roles of both learners and educators.

Redefining minority learners

For ESL students the classroom is simultaneously a site for the learning of a second language; a place where the learning of other curriculum knowledge takes place (usually through the medium of the second language) and a context for the playing out of power relations that will position learners in certain ways. As we have seen, these dimensions are not value-neutral. Particular views of the nature of language, language learning and literacy, and the social purposes for these, will influence how a second language is taught and assessed. Particular epistemologies, what kinds of knowledge are privileged and how it is

65

acquired, are reflected in the content and teaching processes of the curriculum. And the kinds of interpersonal relationships that are created between students, and between teacher and students, impact on how far students' identities and life experiences are negated or affirmed, and how far their school experiences, in Cummins' terms, 'construct' or 'constrict' possibilities for learning.

The discourse of deficit

Among attempts to discover the causes for the academic failure of minority groups have been those who place it at the personal individual level (see, for example, Dunn 1987). More commonly, 'cultural deprivation' theories lay the blame for educational failure within students' home experiences: students are seen to come to school behind their peers linguistically, cognitively and socially, with blame laid at the door of their bilingualism, perceived parent apathy, lack of cognitive stimulation or lack of home literacy. The individual learner, usually 'measured' in some way against factors considered important in the middle-class child, is thus found to be disadvantaged or deprived in terms of socialization practices and home environment (Eckerman 1994). Such theories are summarized by Oakes (1985):

> Most considerations of barriers to educational equality have focused on characteristics of students themselves as the source of the problem. Seen as products of disorganized and deteriorating homes and family structures, poor and minority students have been thought of as unmotivated, noncompetitive and culturally disadvantaged.
>
> (Oakes 1985, p. 4)

The ideology of deficit may be implicit in school discourse when teachers, albeit well-meaningly, speak of their students as having 'no experiences'. Eckermann, writing in the context of Australia, cites comments from interviews with teachers (who she claims were deeply committed to their students), which were 'firmly steeped in the philosophy of deprivation' (1994, p. 49). Among the teachers' comments, for example, were the following: '[the children] are not getting a lot of input from home'; 'socially some of the children are not very well adjusted . . . some of the children are not exposed to very much culture in their families'; 'the values of the school don't seem to be held by the parents'; 'there is a lot of poor language development around'. Implicitly, within such discourse, English-speakingness and middle-class values are normalized: as McLaren suggests, 'we naturalize whiteness as a cultural marker against which Otherness is defined' (McLaren 1994, p. 114).

Theories of cultural deprivation have been influential in producing large numbers of compensatory programmes, which aim to provide
those experiences seen as lacking. Although it could not be claimed that
such programmes have been without value, the assumption that underlies them is one that a more critically oriented approach to pedagogy
and to the education of minority students would reject: namely that
such children suffer from a deficit in skills which they bring to school,
and that the causes for this deficit lie in a lack of appropriate training
by parents and caregivers, and in the cultural experiences of the home.
Bernstein, whose critique of education lies in the unequal distribution
of students' participation rights, is highly critical of the concept of compensatory education, arguing that it detracts attention away from the
deficiencies in the internal organization and the educational context of
the school itself (Bernstein 1971). He argues that the speech variants
that children need to learn in school – 'the universalistic meanings of
public forms of thought' – that are less familiar to some children, do not
constitute *compensatory* education. Rather, these public forms of
thought *are* education itself.

One of the more invidious effects of locating a learning 'problem'
within the student, or within the student's home background, is that it
serves to legitimize existing school structures and approaches to curriculum and pedagogy, because it obscures any need for critical
reflection and change (Cummins 1996). We may add to these critiques
that not only are deficit approaches unhelpful in addressing the educational failure of students, a cultural deficit theory is also profoundly disempowering for teachers, since the problem of 'failing to learn' is
located outside the power of an individual teacher to address.

Challenging the pedagogy

Linguists have argued for many years that many of the difficulties that
minority children experience are not the result of 'deficit' but are in part
the result of sociolinguistic differences between the students and the
language and culture of the mainstream classroom (for an early example,
see Hymes 1971). These differences are compounded when educators
overlook often subtle differences in cultural capital and discourse strategies and are unaware of the result these differences may have on learning in school (Corson 1993). A number of studies carried out in the
UK, US, Canada, New Zealand and Australia have demonstrated that
minority students in mainstream classes, compared with their native
English-speaking peers, may have fewer opportunities for learning. For
example, they may have fewer opportunities for extended language use
with teachers (Au 1978; Cazden 1990; Biggs and Edwards 1991); receive

less feedback and participate less often in class discussion (Philips 1983; Jones 1987); are asked less cognitively demanding questions and generally have fewer opportunities to talk (Torr 1993); and use discourse structures which are evaluated less positively (Michaels 1981; Malcolm 1982; Heath 1982, 1983; Erickson 1984; Michaels and Cazden 1986). In her work on teacher interactions with students in primary classrooms, Bourne (2003) also shows convincingly how students perceived by the teacher as 'not very bright', take part in interactions with the teacher which systematically reduce their access to critical language tools and offer qualitatively different semantic orientations to the curriculum. These forms of rejection are usually unintentional but lead to educational inequality. It is also likely that when students' identities are devalued through their personal interactions with educators, academic effort is felt to be futile, and they may withdraw mentally and perhaps physically from the life of the school (Cummins 1996).

By comparison, a number of studies have reported on the positive effects on minority groups' educational outcomes, where there has been a conscious attempt by teachers to respond to minority learners by adapting their own pedagogy and discourse styles, simultaneously with maintaining a strong focus on the valued curriculum (see, for example, Ada 1988; Au and Mason 1983; Bourne 2003; Cazden 1989; Gibbons *et al* 1994; Vogt *et al* 1987). The educational responses documented in these studies have in common a perspective on minority learners which sees educational failure not as a factor of the learner or their background, but, broadly, as a reflection of a wider socio-historical context and, more narrowly, of a need for educators and institutions to reflect on and possibly adapt their own practices.

Vyogotsky's work offers an additional and particularly significant view on minority children's learning. The notion of the ZPD reminds us that learning needs to be geared to ESL children's potential learning, not simply their actual level of development (of English). For ESL students not yet fully in control of the language in which they are learning, this is a timely reminder. Vygotsky (1978) points out that more traditional forms of special education, where the pedagogical orientation is towards the use of concrete, look-and-say methods and where tasks involving more abstract thinking tend to be eliminated from the curriculum, actually deny students any chance of developing what is lacking in their own development. Equally we can assume that this is likely to occur in schools which have low expectations of ESL students' performance, and which, on the basis of students' perceived current abilities in English language, present a curriculum heavily weighted towards concrete learning and tasks that are reduced in cognitive demand. Vygotskian theory would suggest that it is precisely *because* students are less likely to have yet developed the academic registers of the classroom that the school must make every effort to support such development, rather than to opt for teaching a less demanding curriculum.

One clear implication of this thinking is that the educational curriculum must include explicit teaching to minority groups of those forms of language that will enable them to succeed in school and actively participate in the dominant community. In the context of Afro-American students' development of writing, Delpit draws on the notion of 'cultural capital' to argue the need for explicit teaching of the codes of school:

> Some children come to school with more accoutrements of the culture of power already in place – 'cultural capital' as some critical theorists refer to it – some with less. Many liberal educators hold that the primary goal for education is for children to become autonomous, to develop fully while they are in the classroom setting without having arbitrary, outside standards forced upon them. This is a very reasonable goal for people whose children are already participants in the culture of power and who have internalized its codes. But parents who don't function within that culture often want something else. It's not that they disagree with the former aim, it's just that they want something more. They want to ensure that the school provides their children with discourse patterns, interactional styles, and spoken and written language codes that will allow them success in the larger society.
>
> (Delpit 1988, p. 285)

Delpit points out that where educational standards are not accorded a high priority for minority students, then, no matter how friendly, egalitarian and caring the environment, classrooms may still operate to oppress students, albeit in a benign and less obvious way. Inexplicitness, whether it is about rules of conduct or forms of writing, often ensures ultimate failure for many students. As she puts it: 'pretending that gatekeeping points don't exist is to ensure that many students will not pass through them' (Delpit 1988, p. 292).

As Delpit points out, schooling is inherently biased towards reproducing the status quo and dominant culture. The ideology that is supported by this hegemony is usually invisible, and thus becomes the norm, the natural way of things in the classroom. The challenge for teachers is to recognize these undemocratic features of hegemonic control, such as the taken-for-granted interactional patterns of the classroom, and change them in ways which reposition minority learners. Such a change requires the recognition that the success or otherwise of students is a factor of the strengths of the cultural and linguistic frameworks that support their learning. Success or failure needs to be seen as resting not only within the individual, but in the interactional contributions of others in the educational process. These include both the way that students are spoken to, and the way they are spoken about. And what is significant for teachers about this view is that it acknowledges that individual educators have control over how they themselves define minority and culturally diverse students. The focus on teacher interaction defines individual teachers, rather than whole education systems, as change agents who are able to make a difference to the individual students they teach. As van Lier argues, 'the power of the status quo can only be broken by the power, minute in isolation but invincible in a purposeful project, of transformed interaction between educator and educated' (van Lier 1996, p. 158). This includes, in the case of schools where minority children enter school without control of the language of instruction, a more reflective and critical approach by teachers as to how language is used in their classroom. One example is illustrated in this book.

Notes

1 Saville-Troike (1984) also highlights some of the problems associated with separating ESL teaching from content teaching, citing the fact that the language focused on in structured ESL lessons was rarely carried over into other classroom contexts, accuracy in English morphology and syntax in spoken language did not appear to make any difference in academic achievement and the ability to interact socially with other children did not correlate with faster learning or with later academic achievement. Noting that some children's facility in answering teachers' questions (which often only required minimal language use) misled teachers into thinking that children were learning more English than was in fact the case, she concludes that emphasis on interpersonal communication does not of itself lead to academic achievement, and warns against the interpretation of 'communication' to apply only to social interaction.

PART 2
Inside two classrooms

Theorizers have traditionally occupied the power center of language pedagogy while the practitioners of classroom teaching have been relegated to the disempowered periphery.

(Kumaravadivelu 1994, p. 29)

As I argued in Chapter 1, the implicit knowledge of practitioners about teaching, and the processes of teaching and learning as they occur in real-life classrooms, should be seen as central to theory building. Chapters 4 and 5 address this issue by describing aspects of the research process. Chapter 4 describes the broader context of the two classrooms: the teachers, the learners and the school community. Chapter 5 discusses the approach to the initial analysis of the data, and presents a summary of the major themes that emerged.

4 Researching the classroom

The school context

The school community

The study was carried out in an inner-city school in a low socio-economic working class suburb in Australia. The school took children from kindergarten to year 6 and was a three-stream school, meaning that at each level there were three parallel (unstreamed) classes. At that time there were substantial numbers of Lebanese speakers in the suburb, although recent years have seen a steady influx of other migrants from South East Asia, China, Hong Kong and the Philippines. About 90 per cent of children at the school were and continue to be from migrant backgrounds, a mixture of first-generation migrants (born overseas) and second-generation (born in Australia). First-generation parents within the Lebanese community at the time tended to be from village communities, and had often had little formal schooling. Though highly supportive of education, they had not always felt competent or confident to take part in the life of the school, and many traditionally held a culturally-based view of parent and teacher roles whereby the school and the teachers were seen as entirely responsible for the education of the children. However, largely due to a dynamic headteacher committed to community involvement in the school, parent involvement had increased considerably over the eight years prior to the study and, at the time of the study, was an important feature of the life of the school.

Around one third of the children entered kindergarten with little or no English, and of the remainder, very few approached native-like proficiency in English. As Chapter 1 pointed out, such children typically become fluent in basic playground English very quickly, but remain below the English language levels of their native-speaker peers in the more academic registers of school. Most Lebanese children in the school were also unlikely to have had much exposure to standard written academic Arabic.

At the time of the study, the school had two specialist English as a Second Language (ESL) teachers, who withdrew some children for small intensive English classes but also worked mainly in the classroom alongside the mainstream teachers. The school had a transitional (Arabic) bilingual programme which operated in the first three years of school, with two Lebanese-Arabic speaking teachers. In general, the teaching programmes of these three groups of teachers (mainstream teachers, ESL and bilingual teachers) were closely integrated, with all teachers basing their teaching on a common curriculum in terms of the 'content' of what was taught. Thus, in the bilingual programme, children followed the same (content) curriculum as the other children, but learned through the medium of Arabic. Similarly, in withdrawal ESL classes, language teaching was based on the curriculum content of the mainstream classes. The school also had a special education teacher for children designated as eligible for special support, and a full-time librarian. Many parents also helped on a regular basis in the school, hearing children read, helping children in their mother tongue and working in teacher-aide type roles.

Despite these extra resources, the challenge to teachers in such a school is considerable. In addition to 90 per cent of the children being non-native speakers of English, a typical class might have two to three children who had arrived very recently in Australia, one or two emotionally disturbed children and one child with a significant health problem. All teachers at the school regarded themselves as 'ESL' teachers and saw themselves as providing the major resource for children's English language development. The notion of 'language across the curriculum' was firmly entrenched in the school, and most of the teachers had received some professional development in ESL education. In addition, there was a strong professional development ethos within the school, and using some release time, and a good deal of their own time, teachers regularly met to collaboratively plan teaching programmes, share problems, and discuss issues they had identified as their own professional development needs. Largely as a result of this strong professional development focus, the school had, over a number of years, redesigned the curriculum and the language programmes to better meet the needs of children from language backgrounds other than English and to make better use of the ESL specialist teachers. As a result of this ongoing professional climate, most teachers were reflective practitioners who were able to scan and select from a variety of educational theories those elements which best enabled them to meet the needs of the children in their classes. In relation to many other schools with similar student profiles it appeared to me that one aspect of the professional environment of the school was particularly significant: teachers held high expectations about what children could achieve if they were given appropriate kinds of support, and had very positive attitudes to the children's first language and culture.

While holistic and experiential work played an important part in the teaching programmes, teaching also included explicit and focused language work. This drew on a range of perspectives. At various times a teacher might include a notional/functional focus in their teaching programmes (such as *classifying* or *comparing*), aspects of grammar (such as the use of tenses or plurals) or the explicit teaching of genres (such as narratives, reports or discussions). Reading drew on a whole-language perspective, and within this included the teaching of phonics as part of the development of a range of reader strategies. Writing in a range of genres was explicitly modelled and guided. In short, the language programmes were the result of principled pragmatism, developed out of understandings of language and learner needs.

The effect of all these factors on the achievements of the children was considerable, and during the time of the data-gathering it became necessary for the teaching staff to rewrite much of the curriculum to meet the increasing achievements in reading and writing of the students.

The teachers

The two teachers in the study, Penny and Kath, (not their real names) were both personally known to me. Penny (classroom 1) had several years earlier been a school consultant for non-English-speaking children who were recent arrivals to Australia. She had many years teaching experience, held a Masters degree in Applied Linguistics, and had ESL specialist training. She held an executive position in the school. Kath (classroom 2) had been teaching in the school for nine years, and also held an executive position. She had taken part in a great deal of professional development at the school, and was familiar with the major issues in ESL education. Both teachers were familiar with the systemic model of functional linguistics which informs the study, although Penny's knowledge was much deeper as a result of her linguistics background.

Both Penny and Kath were approached to take part in the study because I considered them gifted teachers, and because our already established professional and collegial relationships meant that we would be at ease together in the classroom. This is an important requirement in studies involving teachers and researchers. Both teachers were aware that I was interested in the role of classroom discourse in second language development, and in the role of spoken language in the development of the more context-reduced registers of school. We agreed that while I was in the classroom, I would respond normally to children when they initiated interaction with me (which occurred frequently), but that I would not take an active part in teaching the lessons.

The teachers not only helped to collect data, but within the context of normal activities set up situations which might provide interesting data. For example, knowing that I was interested in children's explicit understanding of the processes of their own learning, Penny asked children several times during the course of the unit of work to write down what they had learned about what they were studying, and initiated whole-class discussions with them about what had helped them in their learning. The responses from the children proved to be an additional form of triangulation. Thus while responsibility for the research issues and development of methodology remained with the researcher, teachers were not merely passive informants or data providers. Their interest in working with me came out of their commitment to their students, a genuine interest in finding out possible ways to extend their own teaching skills, and ultimately to issues of social justice regarding their students. Much can be learned from the scrutiny of the professional practice of skilled practitioners, but collaboration between teachers and researcher rests on both parties recognizing and acknowledging the particular skills and strengths of the other, and acknowledging that each has knowledge which is legitimate. It is not an 'equal' relationship since what each brings is distinct, but if the potential of the researcher-teacher relationship is to be met it must be a relationship of equality.

The children

Both classes of children were 9–10-year-olds in their fifth year of school, and in both classes 90–95 per cent of the students came from a range of second language backgrounds.

In Penny's class there were 31 children, including two newly arrived children and two children on a special education programme. Two children came from English-speaking homes, the remainder from a range of language backgrounds but predominantly Lebanese. Typically most children's English in face-to-face informal situations was quite fluent, but more linguistically demanding and literacy-related classroom activities were often challenging for them. In group activities the groups were usually teacher-chosen, but varied from lesson to lesson.

In Kath's classroom, where there were 29 children, teacher-selected groups of children remained together for all group activities throughout the unit of work. I chose to focus on two groups: Julianne, Milad, Emily and Maroun; and Gabriella, Duncan and Andre. With the exception of

Emily and Gabriella, the teacher described the children as 'typical' second language speakers, meaning, as in Penny's class, that they had fluency in day-to-day aspects of English, but were much less able to use English in the less context-embedded registers of the classroom. Emily was an extremely capable and intelligent child, whose English approached native-speaker competence, and who excelled in music and sport as well as academic subjects. Gabriella had been in Australia for only three months at the time of the study. Milad, Maroun and Andre also received extra support from the ESL teacher in a withdrawal, small-group situation. All children spoke another language at home, and Emily attended a Chinese 'Saturday' school. The groups were teacher-chosen in this instance, and remained together for the duration of the unit, although this was not always the case in this classroom. In reality, the focus on specific children was only relevant during group work, since when a teacher is interacting with the class as a whole, a researcher has no control over who responds. Any whole-class recording thus included a wide range of children.

Before beginning the research both teachers explained to the children that I worked at a university and taught teachers. Since even very young participants in research have a right to be as well informed as possible, the children were told I was interested in finding out how children learn, especially what helps them to learn English. In an introductory session I elicited ideas from the children about how they thought I might do this; they offered a number of suggestions, including interviewing them, looking at what they wrote and listening to them talk. One child suggested a video recorder would be helpful, leading to a further suggestion to use an audio recorder. (With the exception of the video, to which unfortunately at that time I had no access, all of these suggestions were taken up.)

The teaching programme

Both teachers followed a similar programme for the units of work which form the basis of this study. A 'unit' of work comprises the study of a particular topic, and in these classrooms normally lasted between four and five weeks, with around three 45-minute classes per week. The unit of work in this case fell within the curriculum domain of Science and Technology and was on the topic of Magnetism.

All teaching programmes at the school were extremely detailed. This programme included a general overview under the four headings *topic*, *concepts and understandings*, *skills* (defined in functional-notional terms such as generalizing, classifying, predicting, etc.) and *values and attitudes*. This overview summarized the key learning expected over the unit of work as a whole. The summary was then detailed in terms of the objectives below under the headings 'knowledge' and 'skills':

Knowledge
For the children to:
identify what a magnet does
recognize that different types of magnets have different strengths
understand the difference between magnetic and non-magnetic

Skills
For the children to:
brainstorm their current knowledge of magnets
classify various magnetic and non-magnetic materials
make observations about polar attraction
predict the results of investigations
design and make a game using magnets
graph the results of an investigation

The programme then included a detailed plan of every lesson under the headings *objectives, learning activities, language, vocabulary, resources* and *evaluation*. In the *language* column, formal grammatical structures that are foregrounded in the unit have to do with the functions of generalizing, questioning and predicting. In the teachers' programmes, a language structure or function is named, and followed by a possible instance of the language that might be expected to occur. For example:

to generalize: *Magnets have . . . , All magnets . . . , Most metallic objects . . .*
to predict: *I predict that . . . , My prediction is . . .*

Although there was no evidence of the teachers in any way trying to restrict children to using these structures, this level of programme detail does suggest how thoroughly teaching had been planned, and how aware the teachers were of the kind of language that might be associated with particular topics and activities. The programmes indicate the degree to which 'content' and 'language' were integrated in the teachers' notions about what was involved in teaching a 'subject', a conclusion which is supported by many of the illustrative texts analysed in later chapters. This integration of language teaching and level of detail was apparent across the school in all curriculum areas.

During the course of the data collection, teachers followed the normal course of their programmes. Though I had little input into the planning stage, I suggested one modification to the planned programme. One activity was for all children, in small groups, to carry out four experiments designed to develop their understanding of magnetic attraction and repulsion, and then report back to the whole class about what they had learned. 'Reporting back' is a not uncommon strategy in primary classrooms, and one in which I already had some interest: I saw it as a context for children to use the more context-reduced language I was interested in. But if all children had done all experiments this would have reduced or removed any genuine communicative need for children to report back to the rest of the class, since in general they would simply have been telling their audience what they had already experienced for themselves. After discussion, it was decided that each group of children should do only one or two of the activities so that at the reporting back stage they had something to say that was new to most of their audience, and so that there was a genuine communicative 'press' on them to make clear to others what they had found out. This minor organizational change repositioned the students as 'primary knowers', vis-à-vis the rest of the class when they reported back, and the audience had a purpose for listening. As discussed in Chapter 3, the importance of an information gap is attested in the literature on second language learning, and this minor change of classroom management not only improved on the original teaching strategy, but probably also provided more interesting and relevant data.

The teaching programme itself followed a sequence of learning activities which required increasingly more 'explicit' discourse; that is, the early tasks elicited the kind of 'here-and-now' language associated with early stages of language learning, and later tasks required language in which less and less of the situational context could be assumed by the speaker or writer. The unit of work incorporated a number of three-stage cycles: the students first took part in hands-on experimental work in small groups, they then reported on what they had learned in what I have termed 'teacher-guided' reporting sessions, and finally they normally completed some written work based on these discussions. This sequence meant that students were required to use language in increasingly more subject-specific and explicit ways. As later chapters will show, teacher-guided reporting sessions were also the time for the teacher to guide students away from personal recounts of what they had done in small group experiments, towards general scientific principles and a more socio-linguistically appropriate register (an objective reflected above in the teachers' references in their teaching plan to *making generalizations*).

The underpinning of (and the major rationale for) this teaching sequence was the systemic functional view of language, and in particular the construct of a 'mode continuum', as described in Chapter 2.

A constructivist teaching sequence for the teaching of science developed by Driver and Oldham (1986) parallels this in its movement towards increasingly decontextualized language and in the importance they place on teacher guidance. Their sequence comprises four phases: orientation, elicitation, restructuring and application and review. As Driver points out, understandings and explanations do not necessarily spring clearly from children's data alone, and her framework gives importance to the teacher's role in guiding children's initial understandings towards scientific principles. The TGR episodes in this study played a very similar function:

> If we wish children to develop an understanding of the conventional concepts and principles of science, more is required than simply providing practical experiences. The theoretical models and scientific conventions will not be 'discovered' by children through their practical work. They need to be presented. *Guidance is then needed to help children assimilate their practical experiences into what is possibly a new way of thinking about them.*
>
> (Driver 1994, p. 47, italics added)

In its overall organization, the unit of work also resembles Wells' (1995) description of the 'inquiry-oriented curriculum' which follows the steps of launching the theme; research (often including observation and experimentation and based on empirical data); interpretation, which Wells describes as 'making sense' of the evidence; presentation (ideally made to an audience not already informed about the topic); and reflection, both on the content and the processes involved in the course of the enquiry. More broadly, the teaching activities that comprised the unit of work followed the sequence suggested by Mohan and discussed in Chapter 2: of less to more explicit discourse, of practical to theoretical learning and from experiential to expository learning (Mohan 1986).

Approaches to analysis

Interpreting the classroom

The methodological approach taken, and the procedures and methods used, depend on the objectives and purpose of the research, but are also implicitly or explicitly informed by the theories and assumptions held by the researcher (Simon and Dippo 1986; Norton Pierce 1995): 'all methods are ways of asking questions that presume an underlying set of assumptions' (Simon and Dippo 1986, p. 195). The theories and assumptions that impact on a study such as this include knowledge and belief systems about teaching and learning, and about language itself, and were the subject of Part 1. Also relevant is the way in which the endeavour of educational research itself is conceived, including the status and place of 'theory' and how such theory should be constructed; and how the relationship between researcher and researched is viewed, who the 'experts' are and the status of the 'knowledge' they hold.

Rather than the traditional distinctions made between qualitative and quantitative research, a more relevant question is around the question of what *kinds of knowledge* might be useful in order to investigate classroom second language development. Until recent years, much of the work in the SLA area has focused on what learners can say, rather than what they can do with language, with the SLA field often dominated by narrowly prescribed research methods (van Lier 1994). Many SLA researchers have tended to view SLA as a mental process, and adopted research approaches which are dominant in psychology, characterized by the perspectives of mentalism and individualism. These are based on positivist approaches, which seek 'objective', hard data and aim to produce replicable findings (Davis 1995), leading to what one researcher has described as 'science envy' (Block 1996). Such approaches commonly utilize experimental research designs and paradigms and draw on statistical analyses. This focus on cognitive factors has been challenged, not on the grounds that it is irrelevant, but because if there is an expectation that this is the dominant line of enquiry for the entire field, it may lead to a narrow view of what is a complex phenomenon, and to a further widening of the gap between researchers and practitioners (Block 1996; van Lier 1994)[1].

The major theoretical principle that underlies this book is that while mental processes are not unimportant, *language development interacts dynamically with the sociocultural contexts in which it occurs and cannot be analysed or understood apart from its situational and cultural contexts.* Research which seeks to address language in its situational and cultural context is best served by qualitative approaches which can offer 'an alternative to mainstream SLA research in viewing acquisition not only as a mental individualistic process, but one that is also embedded in the sociocultural contexts in which it occurs' (Davis 1995, p. 432). Although, as we have seen, a concern with the social and situational context is increasingly evident in more recent studies of minority groups and of second language development, there is still in general a dearth of socially situated SLA studies that are classroom-based and focus on young learners.

The approach taken here is primarily an interpretive and semiotic one: what is important is the immediate and local meanings of the actors (teachers and students) understood in terms of social purpose. Many of the questions of relevance to SLA research, at least those which are concerned with pedagogy, can be better addressed within this interpretive paradigm. Van Lier argues for:

> [a theory] that allows us to answer the questions . . . Does it [classroom development] make a difference? How effective is it? How can we improve it? What kind of world is the classroom? . . . How differently can it turn out in different circumstances?
>
> (van Lier 1988, p. 9)

In Chapter 1 it was suggested that ethnographic research can articulate the intuitive behaviour of teachers. Since such research is able to bring to consciousness previously unnoticed, unremarked and routinized behaviour, it provides the means for this behaviour to be questioned. In the classroom, what is usually routinized and goes unnoticed are the discourse patterns and responses that teachers commonly employ in their classrooms. As activity theory suggests (Wells 1996), a more conscious awareness of routinized operations has the potential to disrupt them, and in turn to change the nature of the activity within which they occur. Thus 'articulating the intuitive' has the potential to lead to educational change. As van Lier (1996) has argued, interactional change can lead to educational change.

The importance of particular instances of practice is that they may be a source for new theorizing. It is important, though, to draw a distinction between pedagogy and practice, and avoid treating pedagogy and teaching strategies synonymously. Instances of practice are not themselves theory: they are representations of the enacted curriculum via which new theorizing can occur. Yet it is probably fair to say that teachers are told what they should be doing and how they should do it, rather more often than they take part in discussion and critique of current pedagogical theories which build on the wealth of their own expertise, and out of which teachers themselves can generate a range of practices. This confusion between pedagogy and practice is not only profoundly disempowering for teachers; it is ultimately reductionist in its effect on teaching and learning, leading ultimately to theoretical reduction. In contrast, Kumaravadivelu (1994) describes what he refers to as the 'post-method' condition, which he defines as 'a search for an open-ended, coherent framework based on current theoretical, empirical and pedagogical insights that will enable teachers to theorize from practice and practice what they theorize' (1994, p. 27). This framework 'signifies a search for an alternative to method rather than an alternative method' (1994, p. 29). As Clarke also argues, 'we will have a much better success in understanding language instruction if we assume that teachers' decisions and behavior meet some criteria of rationality, what Prabhu (1990) calls a sense of plausibility, than if we attempt to fit observed behavior into a preconceived theoretical mould where linguistic or other criteria predominate' (Clarke 1994, p. 17).

From the perspective of the researcher, one of the compromises they must be prepared to make if they work in authentic sites is to remain aware that the research agenda is likely to be far less important, and certainly less immediate, to teachers than it is to researchers. Nevertheless, and despite considerable school pressures, the teachers with whom I worked regularly provided me with copies of their programmes, talked through with me what they planned to do, reflected on the course of events in a class, made photocopies of children's work and provided me with copies of any documentation they saw as relevant. An important principle in the teacher-researcher relationship is therefore that of reciprocity. Major insights that came from the research were shared with the two teachers and the school, through a series of professional development activities for the whole staff. Discussions with the two teachers involved in the study frequently indicated that the research process affirmed their practice. On being shown the positive effects on writing of her talk with an ESL student, for example, one teacher commented: 'I didn't realize I was doing that. I suppose you do it without thinking.' Comments like this were not uncommon, and lend support to Heap's claim that the value of *a priori* claims is in unfolding educational concepts and putting teachers' intuitive understandings into propositional form (Heap 1995). Returning to the same school a year after I had begun working there, I discovered that a particular practice on which I had focused and consequently talked to teachers about (which in the book I refer to as 'teacher-guided reporting') had been named as such and built into several teachers' programmes as a regular event across the curriculum. Such is the power of telling teachers what they already 'know'.

Documenting the classroom

One way to document what goes on in classrooms is to make use of an observation scheme, the purpose of which is to allow an observer to record systematically what they observe to be happening in the classroom, often by recording against predetermined categories defined by the researcher. While the early frameworks used in classrooms were relatively simple and unsophisticated, later studies have provided considerable insight into the frequency of particular linguistic behaviours, and have proved to be especially valuable in considering large amounts of data in broad macro-educational settings. Such studies have revealed, for example, the common and pervasive triadic IRF (initiation-response-feedback) interaction.

But while observation schemes may be an appropriate tool for mapping general patterns of classroom behaviour, there are a number of reasons why they were not used here. First, given a research paradigm in which research is viewed as an emergent process of exploration and is reflexive in nature, what will be of significance cannot necessarily be predetermined. Second, in systematic observation, the primary coding unit tends to focus on the single speech act rather than on the interaction as contextualized dialogue: it is difficult to see how a scheme could be devised which could adequately capture the progressive and cumulative nature of discourse which is largely the focus of this book. To do this, it is necessary to go beyond the alternation of turns, and beyond the flow of talk as it occurs moment to moment. Third, it is likely that any coding scheme may miss capturing the less obvious or the 'single occurrence' which might actually be of significance. The researcher may be blinded to aspects of interaction and discourse which are not captured by the scheme, yet which may be relevant and perhaps very significant to the understanding of the classroom under investigation (Nunan 1992). In addition, numerical codings of frequency cannot on their own adequately reconstruct interactions, or the course of lessons, or the ways in which knowledge is progressively constructed. Finally, because the observations are often made on the spot, researchers are necessarily restricted in their ability to adequately interpret, even moment to moment, what is happening within a broader context. This broader context is both 'spatial' (*what else is going on?*) and 'temporal' (*how does this fit into what happened last lesson and what will happen in the next?*).

The theoretical need to observe ongoing sequences of lessons has been argued by several researchers (Christie 1995; Brilliant-Mills 1993; Lin 1993; Heras 1994; Floriani 1993). Since a major area of interest in the study is on how knowledge of a topic gets constructed and how language learning occurs, whole units rather than single lessons have been chosen as the macro-unit of analysis. A single 'lesson' is in any case a somewhat arbitrary unit; it may represent a time frame within the school day rather than representing, from the students' perspectives, a coherent piece of learning. In addition, in any classroom, teacher and students will hear and produce what is said against an extensive background of accumulated meanings, which researchers are in danger of ignoring if the data are collected on single visits (Edwards and Westgate 1994). It was therefore necessary to examine the textual and knowledge relationships between individual teaching and learning activities in order to more fully understand the ongoing and changing roles played by teachers and students and the ongoing dialogue they constructed together. Thus,

> . . . if it is a main hazard in classroom observation that the meaning
> of utterance will often depend on past encounters which the observer
> has not shared, then there are good practical reasons for observing
> relationships [and we can add, curriculum knowledge itself] . . .
> *being talked into existence.*
> (Edwards and Westgate 1994, p. 103, italics and comment in
> brackets added)

If participants in an interaction draw on prior contexts as meaning
resources in their discourse, then an analysis of how knowledge is constructed needs to account for the range of contexts that have been constructed over time. Thus 'the analyst, like a group member, needs to
understand those past times, spaces and instances of being "with texts"
that members signal, through their talk, as being socially significant to
the meaning and content currently being constructed' (Floriani 1994,
p. 260).

A further argument for data to include a sequence of lessons is that
otherwise inaccurate conclusions may be reached. Some of the science
lessons observed consisted entirely of students carrying out experiments in small groups. In other lessons the teacher took a major role in
initiating talk: the IRF pattern was very much in evidence. Watching
one or other of these lessons might lead to a conclusion that this was a
'teacher-fronted' and 'teacher-directed' classroom, or conversely that it
was totally student-centred. Neither lesson alone would have provided
a sense of what the teacher was doing or how knowledge was being progressively built up.

For all of these reasons classroom observations took place over a
more sustained period of time and represented consecutive science
lessons. This made it possible to observe how a teacher handled all
stages of learning; for example, how the topic was introduced, if and
how children's prior learning was built on, how new learning was
developed through the discourse, and what evidence there was that this
was taken up by the students. In brief, observing an entire unit of work,
from opening to closure, allowed specific items of data to be more fully
contextualized and interpreted.

As Christie argues:

> in order to demonstrate how a pedagogic discourse works, it is
> necessary to study quite long-sustained sequences of lessons. This
> is because the various practices involved in the very complex
> process by which students enter into shared knowledge and under-
> standings, as well as demonstrate capacity to manipulate these
> things in reasonably independent ways, involve considerable time.
> (Christie 1995, p. 221)

The data

Sources of data

The data were collected in two classrooms over the course of the unit of work discussed above. They were not collected simultaneously, which would have been logistically difficult since the programmes usually ran in tandem in each of the parallel classes. As a result the two sets of data were collected a year apart, in each case in the final term of the year, first in Penny's class and then in Kath's. This proved to have a number of advantages. It allowed for data-gathering techniques to be refined, for example, and it allowed for research themes emerging from the first set of data to be re-examined using the second set, and thus for the reflexive and emergent nature of this type of research to be taken into account.

In both classrooms data were collected during one complete unit of work or topic, numbering between seven and eleven lessons of approximately 45 to 50 minutes each. To gain as complete a picture of the classrooms as possible, a range of data sources was used. Even so, no data set, however rich, comes near to capturing what occurs in the life of the classroom. A thick data set simply makes it easier to reconstruct something of what occurred, and a range of data types provides for some triangulation in interpretation. Figure 4.1 is a summary of the sources of data.

Figure 4.1 Sources of data

	Classroom 1 9–10-year-olds	Classroom 2 9–10-year-olds
Number of visits	Seven visits	Eleven visits
Audio-tapes of oral interactions (transcribed)	300 minutes	500 minutes
Language on display and environmental print around the classroom	Some record in field notes	Detailed record in field notes
Field notes	Observer's comments	Observer's comments
Student writing	29 pieces (one piece from each student)	40 pieces (taken over the course of unit, from focus children)

| Interviews with children | Information gained through whole-class discussion with teacher | Group of seven children with researcher |
| Interviews with teacher | During process and after, informal | During process and after, informal |

Transcribed interactions

All teacher to whole-class interactions were recorded, and selected groups of children, as identified earlier, were recorded in small group or pair interactions. It was helpful to give children time to get accustomed to being recorded before attempting to collect data, and so for several weeks prior to the start of the unit children were recorded in other lessons.

One of the difficulties of recording in genuine classrooms (as opposed to a group of students in a laboratory-type setting brought together solely for the purpose of research) is the almost inevitable background noise, which can make it difficult or impossible to decipher tapes. In Kath's classroom this was made especially difficult because of the school's building programme! However, the inevitability of indecipherable gaps was outweighed by the authenticity of the data, and in research that is concerned with praxis it is probably one of the compromises that researchers have to make. As van Lier comments:

> I have found, while working in extremely noisy conditions, with large classes and very vocal children, that no more than partial transcriptions even in those circumstances could reveal classroom and interaction patterns that observation checklists, interviews and training programmes could not. Especially, such analysis . . . allows us to describe what the learners actually and actively do during the lesson, as individuals and as groups.
>
> (van Lier 1988, p. 64)

Even when it was possible, it was not necessarily useful to rank obtaining a good recording ahead of this authenticity. On one occasion the classroom was particularly noisy because an extra ten children were in the room. The class were doing a dictogloss, which involves students in groups discussing and reconstructing a text, on the basis of key words and very brief notes which they have earlier noted down individually while the teacher is reading a text aloud at normal speed. As there was an empty classroom next door I took out one group of four children. I was unprepared, however, for the effect on the children of being in an empty silent classroom with a cassette recorder. The recorder, which they had always previously ignored, now became a focus. The discussion which is integral to a dictogloss did not eventuate. Instead children showed each other their notes, gestured silently, occasionally whispered and only spoke aloud, one at a time, when they had completed their text, which they then read aloud into the tape recorder. Clearly they saw this as some kind of performance and were not prepared to allow the process itself to be recorded.

Even a good recording is no more than a partial record of what has occurred. It does not show the extra-linguistic information which is part of the resources for meaning-making such as facial expressions, gestures, body positioning or glances. Neither does it capture what I often saw or felt – the sense of urgency of a child wanting to answer a teacher's question, the frustration of a child who could not find the words in English to express what they wanted to say or a shy student's inability to break into a conversation. While field notes help to fill out the context of talk, and while a video recording may have provided extra contextual information, no data can adequately capture the reality of the class as it is lived by the participants. Any account of a classroom is ultimately a story told by the researcher.

It is interesting to speculate how far the presence of the tape recorder itself actually influenced students' language, for at times it seemed the research itself became the curriculum. One notable example of this occurred early on in classroom 2. In general the students' interactive and interpersonal skills when they talked together were impressive, but at times, and as might be expected, there was a considerable amount of overlapping of turns, attempts to make a point by talking louder than anybody else, and a high level of background noise from other working groups. The children were keen to hear the tapes, but on the first occasion they commented with some disappointment that 'you can't hear what we're saying'. What follows is a summary of the conversation that then took place between the children and the teacher.

Teacher	Why can't you hear what you're saying?
Children	Because we're all talking at once.
Teacher	And what happens if you all talk at once?
Children	Mrs G. can't hear what we're saying so the tape won't be any good.
Teacher	Well yes, but why else isn't it a good idea?
Children	We can't hear what other people are saying?
Teacher	And why isn't that a good idea?
Children	It's rude to people.
Teacher	And why else?
Children	Because if we can't hear we won't hear other people's ideas.

Teacher	And so?
Children	We don't learn so much.
Teacher	So what must we remember to do when we're talking in groups . . . not just for the tape recorder but always.
Children	(*giving suggestions*) Take turns, listen to each other, not shout, don't all talk at once.

From then on, turning on the tape recorder usually became a signal for model group behaviour. Though it would be fair to point out that inter-personal group skills was something the teacher and children worked at in an ongoing way, the incident with the tape recorder illustrated to the children in a tangible way the importance of listening to each other and the need for collaboration. From this interchange involving the data, the teacher and themselves, the children learned some important lessons about how to work together successfully. Explicit teaching and learning of collaborative skills is a prerequisite for the kind of small-group work that many SLA researchers and teachers see as essential for language learning, and the development of these skills needs to be taken into account in classrooms where language development is a key focus. From a methodological standpoint, however, what is signi-ficant here is that it is hard to see where the research process ended or began; it becomes impossible to separate out the process of data-gathering, its effect on the participants and the reaction to it from chil-dren and teacher. From the process of recording grew new learning for the children which was in turn a new source of data for the researcher. It is an example of the complexity of the familiar observer-paradox, but at the same time, it is an example of the importance of acknowledging the relationship between the research process and the situational context of the research, and sometimes, in the classroom, of recogniz-ing the richness this relationship may offer in terms of its pedagogical value. Such instances suggest a notion of 'research as curriculum'. They exemplify the reflexive and open-ended nature of such research, and the value of a positive relationship between researcher and teacher.

Field notes

Field notes were made using a simple framework with the headings: *Activity, Discourse pattern and time; Description of activity; Language on display* (e.g. on the blackboard or on butcher's paper) and *Comments*. They documented the major features of each episode and provided situ-ational information to accompany the transcripts, helping to substanti-ate insights gained from the analysis.

Issues in transcription

What is perhaps more problematic than collecting authentic data is the question of how it is transcribed. Again we return to the impossibility of separating researcher from data. Transcribing involves conscious choices on the part of the transcriber, choices about what and how much to transcribe, what to leave out and how to represent the relationship between speech and writing. As Ochs (1979) points out, mechanical recording does not eliminate problems of selective observation, it merely delays them. Ultimately, the choices made relate to the purpose of the transcription. Equally, choices will be influenced by the transcriber's theory of language and, in a classroom context, what they count as important in learning. As Ochs comments, transcription is a 'selective process reflecting theoretical goals and definitions' (Ochs 1979, p. 44).

Rather than presenting the transcript as a linear 'script', participant columns are used in most of the illustrative texts. This was a deliberate choice in order to maintain a focus on the interactive nature of discourse, and the ways that teachers and students construct knowledge together. Pulling apart the turns, but at the same time presenting them as visually contingent, makes it possible to focus on both individual verbal behaviour and interactive behaviour. For example, by reading vertically down one column, it is possible to track students' developing field knowledge through their changing verbal behaviour, or to focus on the number and types of contributions of either students or teacher. But it is also possible, by reading across the columns, to see the process by which dialogue is achieved, for example by analysing the semantic relationship and discourse coherence between speakers. Ochs, writing of this convention, suggests:

> The assessment of pragmatic and semantic links becomes a more self-conscious process . . . the reader can see more easily the prior verbal behavior of the child. In interpreting an utterance of a child, the reader of the transcript can assess its place with respect to what the child has been saying or doing as well as with respect to the talk or behavior of the co-speaker.
>
> (Ochs 1979, p. 48)

Leftness in English script tends to be associated with control or prominence, and so we might tend to 'read' the speaker on the left as the dominant or initiating speaker. Since the study foregrounds learners' increasing control of language, and the role of teachers viewed from a sociocultural rather than a transmission-based perspective, it did not seem appropriate to place the teacher on the left, which could have suggested a different kind of teacher role. Choice of layout therefore evolves out of a theoretical frame of reference, and coming to decisions about how to transcribe should be seen as part of the analysis itself.

The layout of data also throws up insights, hence itself *develops* theory. The following example (Figure 4.2) exemplifies this point. The layout shown here came about because, as will be discussed in the following chapter, initial reflection on the data suggested that the teacher-talk encapsulated more than one field. The discourse was not only about science, but also involved talk about language, or metalinguistic talk. To show this more clearly the two fields have been pulled apart, and this is represented through the transcription. In terms of insights about language learning, this example indicates how talk about language can occur in the context of actual language use. In terms of methodology, it shows how the use of a particular theory of language, in particular register theory as discussed in Chapter 2, has coloured the way in which the raw data are 'heard'.

Figure 4.2 Two fields

In this example[2] teacher nominations are italicized to indicate they stand outside both fields.

Students	Teacher	Teacher
	Field – talk about language	Field – talk about magnets
		let's try this what if I try the north pole and the south pole . . of the magnet . . who can tell . .
	I want a sentence a nice sentence *Carol Ann?*	
C: the north pole and the south pole attract		
		good . . . what if I try the south pole of this magnet and the north pole of that magnet . . . *yes Francois*
	come on a sentence	

F: the south pole and the
north pole will attract

Decisions must also be made about how much information to include within a transcript. A guiding principle is to include whatever features are necessary for the researcher's purpose and to suit the depth of detail to the kind and depth of analysis intended. It is also of course important that the data is comprehensible to the reader. Among the transcription conventions significant in this study is the marking of pauses. It has been suggested that a major feature of classroom discourse is its very fast pace (Edwards and Westgate 1994), whereas a teacher's tolerance of hesitations and a longer 'wait time' for a student's response have been seen as a marker of more open and reflective learning (Rowe 1986; Dillon 1988; Cazden 1988). Initial reflection on the recordings indicated that extended wait time was a feature of both classrooms. Thus pauses have been marked.

No attempt has been made to indicate pronunciation and intonation, except as indicated below. Often children and teacher used very informal speech such as *yeah* or *gonna*, rather than standard pronunciation. However such features have not been transcribed since representing only the more obvious non-standard forms (and not others) risks possible stereotyping of certain students on the basis of dialectal features, while not differentiating others.

Figure 4.3 shows the notational conventions used in the transcription.

Figure 4.3 Transcription conventions

(.)	Represents a perceptible pause of less than one second.
(. .)	Represents a pause of approximately two seconds. Following this convention, each additional (.) represents an additional second.
/	Represents the end of a 'meaning' or 'sense' unit, and the start of another, often but not always corresponding to clause boundaries. Its sole function is to facilitate the reading of the transcription where there is no other indication (such as a pause or a question mark), which would indicate the boundaries of the unit meaning, e.g.

we predicted/ we predicted how many . paper clips we thought would make a chain/ what do you think I was . trying to find out/ why would I do an experiment like that . Fabiola?

| underlining | Used to indicate unusually marked stress or extra emphasis, e.g. |
| | |

we say magnets <u>repel</u> (*said with great emphasis*).

| = | Indicates an utterance from one speaker which continues after interruption, e.g. |

S1:   and then we put the magnet in it =
S2:   and then we got
S1:   = and then we got another magnet

| *** | Indicates unclear speech. Each (*) represents approximately one syllable. |
| [| Denotes two speakers speaking simultaneously. |

Names of students are usually indicated by their initial. Where it was unclear who is speaking, this is indicated by numbering speakers with S1, S2, S3, etc. Each speaker turn is numbered.

Since a transcription represents spoken language, sentence conventions have not been used. However, question marks have been included to indicate to the reader how to interpret particular utterances. Commentary has been included when needed to give details necessary for understanding the transcript, or to give a fuller representation of the situational context. This is indicated in italics, e.g.

it goes here (*indicating position on the blackboard graph*)

Telling the story of the classroom

Typically, the approach to researching the classroom presented in this chapter results in a major threefold challenge: how to find ways of initially handling and organizing the large amounts of data yielded, how to select the data of most relevance for discussion, and how to then weave these data into a coherent classroom story. To address these questions, the data were analysed at two levels.

The first level, the *episode summaries*, documents every teaching and learning activity in the two classrooms, and provides a holistic perspective on the data (see Appendix). This broad analysis indicates how each overall unit of work is organized, defines major patterns of discourse and provides a context for later more detailed analyses. From this broad analysis there emerge a number of themes which are taken up in the more detailed examinations of selected excerpts of discourse in Part 3. These excerpts were selected as representative of the regular occurrences and typical discourse patterns identified by the episode summaries. The episode summaries are the subject of the following chapter.

Notes

1 The extended debate and range of stances around the nature and purpose of research in the SLA field is illustrated in many papers in *Applied Linguistics* during 1993–1996.
2 The complete text is included and discussed in Chapter 7.

5 Teaching and learning in two classrooms

As suggested at the end of the previous chapter, one problematic issue in classroom-based research is the initial handling of large quantities of data. This chapter illustrates how that issue was addressed, and summarizes the overall themes that emerged from the corpus as a whole. This summary provides a context for the more detailed examination of the key texts in Part 3.

The data from each classroom are summarized in two episode summaries, described in this chapter. These provided a starting point for analysis and account at a macro level for all the data in each classroom.

The episode summaries: rationale and explanation of categories

I refer to an episode as a bonded unit which roughly correlates with a single teaching activity. Linguistically each new episode is marked by realizations of frames and markers, for example: *well, what we're going to do now is* . . . It is also marked by three non-linguistic features which define its opening and closing. First, each episode has a particular participant structure which is likely to change when a new episode starts, for example, students may work as individuals, pairs, groups or as a whole class. Second, and related to this, are the physical seating arrangements, which again frequently change with the start of each new episode, for example, students may be sitting in groups or pairs on the floor, sitting at individual desks or sitting together as a whole class on a mat in front of the teacher. Third, each episode has a particular purpose or function, for example, to carry out an experiment, to share findings with others or to write a journal entry. The term 'episode' as used here is similar to its use by Lemke (1990). Lemke includes the following in his criteria for defining the start of a new episode: signal words by the teacher, such as *OK* and *now*; structural or functional changes in the activity type (for example, from triadic dialogue to teacher-student debate); topic changes; or movements by students, such as a change of posture or putting down of pens. Each episode is thus a unit of discourse with a unifying topic and purpose.

Each lesson is made up of a number of episodes (see Lemke who describes lessons as 'basically episodic' (Lemke 1990, p. 50)), but unlike a lesson, episodes cannot be classified in units of time; functionally they are related to each other rather than to the larger unit of the lesson. In this sense they cut across lesson boundaries; there are, for example, clear intertextual relationships between the last episode of one lesson and the first of the next, both cognitively and in terms of linguistic features such as field and mode. For the purpose of the study, then, what is of interest is not a structural analysis of lessons, but an analysis of the kinds of meanings created within and across the episodes, and the intertextual relationships that exist between them. The term intertextuality is used here to refer to the ways in which the text produced in one episode echoes, contains traces of, and is interpreted on the basis of, previous texts. As later analysis will show, these relationships suggest ways in which, through the ongoing sequence of episodes, students and teacher 'relate discourse to context, and build through time a joint frame of reference' (Edwards and Mercer 1987, p. 65). It is therefore the 'episode', not the 'lesson', which serves as the basic unit for consideration of the data.

The episode summaries serve a threefold purpose. First, they illustrate the cumulative nature of classroom learning and classroom discourse, and indicate how curriculum understandings and language get built up across a complete unit of work or study of a topic, thus providing a tool for understanding how particular patterns of classroom interaction relate to learning. Second, they provide a contextual frame for examining and interpreting those excerpts chosen for in-depth analysis in Part 3. Third, they validate those excerpts as typical and recurring patterns within the data set as a whole, serving as a check on the representativeness of the selected texts in these chapters and making more explicit the criteria for the selection of particular illustrative examples in the later chapters. In the episode summaries, particular aspects of each episode are noted (see Appendix) as set out in Figure 5.1.

Figure 5.1 Format of episode summaries

Episode No.	HOW			WHAT		
	Teaching and learning processes	Dominant participant and interaction structures	Mode/ degree of context-embedding	Knowledge constructed about science	Knowledge constructed about language	Knowledge constructed about being a student

In Figure 5.1, the initial divisions within the table (headed HOW and WHAT) refer respectively to the classroom processes by which curriculum knowledge is constructed, and the fields or content of the knowledge constructed. The number of the episode, and the start of each new lesson, is also indicated. Individual episode summaries are referred to in the text and in the illustrative examples by the number of the class (1 or 2) followed by the number of the episode.

The 'how' and 'what' categories can be broadly related to the register theory described in Chapter 2. The 'how' category takes into account aspects of tenor (in that it describes the interactional patterns set up by the teacher, and mode (the vehicle, spoken or written, for the teaching activities themselves). The 'what' category takes into account aspects of the field (the kinds of experiential knowledge being constructed). These two major divisions are each broken down into three categories described below. These were not predetermined but emerged from the data as significant factors in the identification of language and curriculum learning opportunities for students.

Thus an initial analysis of the discourse revealed that the knowledge being constructed was not simply to do with science, the 'official' curriculum area with which the class was engaged. There was in addition considerable talk about language, and also about the teachers' expectations of students in terms of their socialization and identity as learners in the classroom. Hence the identification of the categories *language* and *being a student*. It was also clear that there was a great variation in patterns of interaction, from teacher monologue to student-student talk in groups. Hence the use of the category *participant structures*. In addition, teaching activities resulted in a constant shifting along the mode continuum between more and less context-embedded language; hence the category *mode of discourse*. The episode summaries thus make it possible to examine recurring patterns of relationships, for example, between the types of teaching processes and the interaction patterns most likely to be associated with them, or to examine how sequences of episodes result in mode 'shunting' along the spoken-written continuum.

It is never possible to reconstruct a lesson exhaustively in the way that it occurred, nor to fully represent the complexity of the context, but as far as possible data need to be contextualized sufficiently for a reader to have a feel for what being in the classroom was like: the sorts of things that were said and done. An additional purpose of the episode summaries is therefore to construct part of the story of the classroom, by describing the kinds of activities that went on. The choice of what is included in each section of the table, and how to note it, is therefore partly determined by what will help to give a richer representation of classroom life. For this reason, direct wordings taken from the transcripts are sometimes included (identified by the use of italics). For example, in 2.41 under *Knowledge constructed about language*, actual words taken from the transcript are included (*we're talking about the way the language is put together*). In other places, often where the sequence is a more extended interaction, it is simply noted that such talk occurred, e.g. T. models how to make a generalization. These conventions also apply to *Knowledge constructed about science* and *Knowledge constructed about how to be a student*.

An explanation of each section in the table follows.

Teaching/learning processes

This category describes the teaching processes and procedures of each episode. They correlate closely to what is glossed in the teacher's programme as *learning activities*, but were based on observations and field notes. The sequence of teaching processes, from episode to episode, represents the process by which curriculum knowledge was built up during the course of the unit.

It should be acknowledged that any attempt to name or describe classroom events and teaching processes is in itself problematic, and necessarily reflects a somewhat idealized version of events. The naming of an activity reflects the orientation of the teacher and researcher, that is, the reality of such an event is, up to a point, a teacher-constructed one. For example, at times it is evident that the students may not have shared the teacher's understanding about the purpose of the activity. Thus while an episode may be described in the analysis as *sharing of individual reflection* the discourse that actually occurred – the enacted curriculum – may not always have been what the teacher might have hoped for. In general, however, it is fair to state that the teacher's description of the activity remained close to what actually occurred (although see Chapter 8 for discussion of this).

Dominant participant and interaction structures

This category describes the participant organization of the episode (for example, teacher to whole class, groups, individual) and the interaction pattern that occurred (for example, IRF, teacher monologue). The entry in this category refers to the *dominant* pattern that occurred.

Mode/degree of context-embeddedness

Earlier discussion has indicated that the degree of context/situation-embeddedness is a factor in determining the comprehensibility of language for ESL learners, while reduction in embeddedness is a feature of the academic language they must learn to control. The mode of the episode, whether it is spoken or written, and the degree of context-embeddedness of the language demanded by the task are therefore significant factors in the description of each episode. An additional perspective offered by noting the degree of contextualization is the relationship *between* episodes; that is, how far they are distanced from each other along the mode continuum. This is important in examining the significance of the temporal sequence of activities.

The *mode* category thus describes the mode of the texts produced in the playing out of each episode. Where the mode is noted as *spoken*, an attempt is made, where relevant, to indicate the degree of context-embeddedness, for example, *language accompanying action, language used to reconstruct personal experience* (see the explanation of mode in Chapter 2). Also included here are notes about relevant environmental print, for example, what is written on the board while students are talking or writing.

Knowledge constructed about science

This describes the content of the episode in terms of what has been learned about science. Decisions about what to include here (given the impossibility of defining exactly what each student has learned) have been made on the basis of the transitivity resources evident in the transcripts from both teacher and students, and on the lesson objectives stated in the teacher's programme.

Knowledge constructed about language (talk about language)

As suggested earlier, talk about language emerged as a significant field within the discourse. Notes made in this category refer specifically to metalinguistic talk; that is, talk *about* language, not to language *use*. That is, the fact that students have *produced* a generalization (such as *all magnets have a north pole and a south pole*) is not noted here, whereas talk about how it might be written (*what word might we use to begin a generalization*) is recorded. While most talk about language is initiated by the teacher, there are exceptions to this. Where the talk is initiated by students it is glossed with S. Otherwise it may be assumed to be teacher-generated.

The purpose of this category is to indicate at what points in the unit, or in which types of episodes, talk about language most frequently occurs, and to indicate the nature of such talk. It also allows for an examination of any relationship between students' metalinguistic talk and uptake evident in their subsequent language use.

As in the previous category, notes are made in two ways, either by reference to the topic being talked about, or by direct quote from the transcripts.

Knowledge constructed about 'how to be a student'

This has been included because, like talk about language, it appeared to be a secondary field within the discourse. In discussion later in the chapter, it is argued that the knowledge being constructed here appears to be part of the instructional register itself rather than simply playing an enabling role. As in the previous two categories, the notes may include direct quotes from the transcripts.

Discussion of emergent themes

As described in the previous section, a view of the data set as a whole suggested a number of areas of potential significance, and these formed the basic framework for viewing the data: the 'how' and the 'what' already referred to. Out of this way of viewing the data there emerged major patterns of practice and discourse features which later chapters (Part 3) take up and explore further. These themes are briefly introduced here.

A recurring teaching/learning cycle: a curriculum macrogenre

One significant theme that emerges is the significance of the teaching sequence adopted by the teachers, and its existence as a distinct macrogenre.

It was earlier pointed out that each sequence of teaching and learning activities in the teachers' programmes could be described from three perspectives: as a social-constructivist teaching sequence (Driver and Oldham 1986); in terms of a mode continuum from implicit to explicit discourse; and in terms of a movement from experiential to more theoretical learning. Christie (1995) has referred to particular regular structured sequences of learning activities as 'curriculum genres'. She defines this in terms of the definition for other instances of genres in language, that is, as Chapter 2 describes, as a staged, goal-oriented social process. In the case of the classroom, however, the genre is one which has an explicit pedagogic purpose. In attempting to capture the notion of a *sequence* of curriculum genres by which students are apprenticed into particular behaviours, skills and forms of knowledge through the ongoing discourse, Christie adopts the term 'curriculum macrogenre':

> A curriculum macrogenre is so called because it refers to the overall sequence or cycle of lessons in which a unit of work is developed with a group of students: such a sequence will normally involve several genres, constituting the unit which is the macrogenre.
>
> (Christie 1995, p. 227)

Christie describes one particular macrogenre which her data suggest to be common in the primary schools in her study. Drawing on data from a social science unit, Christie identifies three genres which make up the macrogenre: curriculum initiation, curriculum negotiation and curriculum closure. Curriculum initiation establishes broad pedagogic goals, curriculum negotiation involves exploring aspects of the instructional field and the nature of the writing tasks and curriculum closure involves drafting and finalizing individual writing. Each of these genres involves a series of stages and includes specific elements, and has a functional significance in the overall structure and unfolding of the macrogenre. Christie points out that she does not claim this to be the only macrogenre within primary schools, and argues for the development of a taxonomy of curriculum macrogenres.

Within the current study, the episode summaries indicate another kind of recurring curriculum macrogenre, described below. This provides a framework for the organization of the analysis in Chapters 6 and 7.

An inspection of the category *teaching/learning processes* indicated that a set of stages occurred over the course of a number of episodes (between three and eight episodes), and that this set of stages was repeated several times over in the course of the unit of work. These stages can be identified as follows:

Stage 1   Review and orientation; (*whole-class activity*)
Stage 2   Setting up new task (in this data, usually an experiment); (*whole-class activity*)
Stage 3   Carrying out task; (*group activity*)
Stage 4   Reflection on task/'making sense' of what's been done; (*whole-class activity*)
Stage 5   (*optional stage*) Written work based on 4; (*individual or group activity*)

(for examples, see Appendix, Classroom 1: 5–7, 13–20; and Classroom 2: 12–17)

Each of these five stages is in itself a genre with predictable elements and sequence of stages (although it is outside the scope of this book to carry out a detailed analysis of the schematic structure and elements of each stage as Christie has done). At the same time each of the five genres represents the stages of a larger macrogenre; the labelling above indicates their functional significance within the macrogenre.

Stages 1–4 (that is, those stages primarily realized through spoken discourse) are those with which this study is primarily concerned. These stages are briefly discussed below in relation to how they were played out in the two classrooms.

Stages 1 and 2: review/recap and set up

At the beginning of a lesson, or at the beginning of a new sequence of episodes, teachers typically first reviewed or recapped with students the work they had done so far, focusing both on the information gained (what students had learned) and the processes used (what students had done). They then gave very explicit instructions for the next new task, which, in these units of work, was usually a scientific experiment. The *review* and *setting up* stages always occurred consecutively, with children remaining in the same position (sitting together in front of the teacher): they are closely related temporally and spatially. Such two-part episodes have a 'Janus' quality, directing students both back and forwards, and represent an explicit link between old and new learning. When one or other stage is extended, for example when the teacher spends time on giving extended instructions for new tasks, the *review* and *setting up* stages are treated as two separate episodes.

Stage 3: carrying out the task

Tasks were carried out in small groups. As described in Chapter 4, each group carried out slightly different tasks although each of the tasks demonstrated the same scientific concepts. The teacher visited each group in turn, but the students were responsible for carrying out the task by themselves, although they frequently had access to written instructions. This stage usually included some recording of the results by students within each group, either as brief notes, graphs or diagrams.

Stage 4: reflection on the task: 'making sense' of what's been done

As discussed in the previous chapter, Driver (1994) asserts that the simple carrying out of experiments is not in itself sufficient, arguing that heuristic 'discovery' methods are problematic in that they expect two 'possibly incompatible' outcomes: students are expected to explore a phenomenon and make inferences for themselves, but at the same time they are expected to develop standard scientific thinking. In developing scientific understandings, she argues, it is not simply the experience which is important, but what sense is made of it: 'guidance is then needed to help children assimilate their practical experiences into what is possibly a new way of thinking about them' (Driver 1994, p. 47).

In these classrooms the reflection stage provided this guidance, which typically took place over several episodes. In this stage most time was spent on teacher-guided reporting, but focus was also given to guided writing and language-based small-group activities, often with a focus on the students making generalizations about what they were learning. As later chapters will demonstrate, teacher-guided reporting episodes proved to be particularly significant in supporting language development. These episodes followed a predictable pattern. Teachers invited groups or individual children to share what they had learned in their groups. Typically each group came to the front of the class and reported to the remainder of the class who were seated on a rug. The teachers were seated either at the back of the class or to the side of the reporting group, so that the reporting group were always positioned spatially as the dominant participants, in control of the conversation. These individual reports were not student monologues however; teachers interacted with individual students, probed where meaning was not clear, and, as Chapter 6 shows, frequently recast a student's meaning into more registrally appropriate wording. At the same time, and as discussion in later chapters will show, teachers guided students to interpret their individual findings within broader understandings by locating students' personal recounts of what they had learned within the broader framework of established scientific understandings. The teacher-guided reporting episodes encapsulated the Vygotskian principle of assistance within the ZPD, hence their labelling as teacher-*guided* reporting. In relation to the mode continuum, teacher-guided reporting episodes, and the other episodes in the reflection stage, are significant in that they provided opportunities for the *reconstruction* of action (as the students recounted their experiences) and the *construction* of new knowledge (as they 'made sense' of these experiences in terms of broader scientific principles).

Stage 5: written work

This was an optional stage which did not occur with every cycle, although both classes made notes and other recordings while engaged in the experimental work. Individual pieces of writing were not extensive in this particular unit of work and took the form of science journal entries, and wall displays of the knowledge the children had developed.

The relative lack of writing within this unit was not typical of other subjects in the classrooms, nor of other units of science: a unit on 'Minibeasts' (insects), for example, produced extensive reports. Perhaps the relative lack of student writing here was because written texts did not provide the knowledge base for student learning as they had in other units of work. Rather, because of the experiential nature of much of the unit, the knowledge source was located primarily within these student activities, and the children's guided reflections with the teacher.

This curriculum cycle, or macrogenre, is of particular significance when considered in terms of the mode continuum. The doing/ reflecting/writing sequence represents a mode shift from language accompanying action to language as reflection, or a movement from more to less context and situation-dependent language. This plotting of teaching and learning activities along the mode continuum is the theme of the next chapter.

Three 'fields' within the discourse

A second area of significance is the existence of the three fields discussed earlier: knowledge is constructed about science, about language and about how to be a student.

Drawing on Bernstein and the notion of pedagogic discourse as incorporating the total social practices of the classroom, Christie (1995) shows how in the classrooms she studied pedagogic discourse is marked by the operation of two registers, each constituting a set of linguistic choices. She defines these as an *instructional* register, which transmits specialized knowledge (such as science) and is to do with the 'content' or field of knowledge being taught, and a *regulative* register, which creates the social order and kinds of relationships that determine the manner of realization of the instructional register, and also establishes and sequences the activities themselves. The instructional registers are realized largely through transitivity choices related to the instructional field. The regulative register is largely realized through textual themes, which shape the learning that is taking place and through choices that realize mood and modality and relate to the nature of the relationships between teacher and students.

Christie shows how one or other of these registers is foregrounded at different points in the sequence of lessons she analyses. At the initiation stage of the lesson, during which time the students were discussing *how* they should write a discussion genre, the discourse foregrounded the regulative register, but as students focused on *what* they should write, the instructional register became increasingly prominent. Christie points out that by this stage the work of the regulative register has been done: 'the measure of the success of this initiation is that the regulative register is no longer realized. Its work has been done and the students operate with competence and independence' (Christie 1995, p. 230).

In the study that is the focus of this book, the discourse can be interpreted in similar ways. Thus the instructional register is realized in talk about magnets, and the regulative register in what I have referred to as 'talk about language' and 'talk about being a student'. As Christie also suggests, there is a clear interplay between the instructional and regulative registers, with what could be defined as the regulative register fading away at certain points. For example, as the episode summaries indicate, talk about how collaborative group work should proceed occurred immediately before children carry out a group-work task, but rarely during the group work itself, since at this stage, in Christie's words, its 'work has been done'. Similarly, talk about language occurred most often before or during those activities when students are expected to shift into a more formal register, but not at those times when students were engaged in experiential work.

However, to interpret these aspects of the regulative register simply as serving an enabling function is, in these classrooms where there were large numbers of ESL learners, to underplay their significance in the discourse as a whole. Rather, what Christie refers to as regulative registers in her work appear in these classrooms to have the status of co-existing, or secondary, instructional registers. This interpretation is suggested not only by the classroom discourse, but also by interviews with the teachers and inspection of their teaching programmes. Teachers indicated that they considered these aspects of the classroom as important teaching objectives in their own right, a statement substantiated by their teaching programmes, which include specific reference to aspects of language and to the development of children's ability to work collaboratively. For example, under a heading *values and attitudes* there is reference to *working cooperatively in groups, valuing each other's work and responses* and *providing constructive criticism*. Talk about language and about being a student appeared to be not simply enabling of the task at hand, and not solely a function of immediate activity or immediate classroom discipline, but a matter of proactively teaching 'new' language and the social rules of the classroom culture to students unfamiliar with them. This concern with matters other than the immediate instructional register is in line with Delpit's argument (Delpit 1988, and see Chapter 3) that minority groups are supported in their learning of a new language and culture by being taught about it explicitly. It can be argued that learning how to be a student, and developing the language of instruction as a second language, (in other words, learning how to learn in the dominant culture), is *additional to* – as well as *enabling of* – the learning of specific field knowledge. Such learnings by students are presumably intended to be transferable to other classroom contexts. As Saville-Troike (1984) points out, the socialization process of school, though a part of all children's learning, takes on a greater significance for those less familiar with the dominant culture of the school.

The significance of the three fields is discussed below.

Science

The episode summaries suggest that, in terms of curriculum 'content', comparatively little science appears to have been taught or learned. This is in part a function of the summary itself (which is not intended to represent a detailed analysis of learning). However, as later chapters will show, a great deal of teaching and learning did in fact occur. What this suggests is the problematic nature of attempting to represent learning in terms of quantifiable items of knowledge, especially in documenting the learning of students who are learning through a second language. The additional achievements of these students in the learning of language and culture may often not be captured, which in turn has implications for the kinds of assessment used with second language learners.

There are also implications for the planning of curriculum for second language learners. While I have argued against the notion that minority learners should be given an alternative curriculum (where this implies a watered-down version of the standard curriculum), it is also unrealistic and equally inequitable to assume that the standard curriculum should be presented in the same ways to all students. What the teachers in this study appear to have done is to reduce the amount of content to be 'covered', but, as later chapters will show, to use this as the vehicle for an in-depth focus on language development and the processes of science learning. In Hawkins' words, they have put a greater focus on 'uncovering the subject' rather than on 'covering the curriculum' (Hawkins, cited in Duckworth 1987, p. 7).

Van Lier also points to the significance of more process-oriented approaches for minority groups:

> Education that is based on a specification of subject matter, on performance in tests, and on measurements of outcomes of one kind or another, is product oriented. Such education can work quite well for highly motivated students with strong, supportive home backgrounds, in other words the elites which have traditionally done well in school and for whom the school system was originally designed . . . However, in a system in which all children have the right to be educated, and in which there is a great diversity of

cultures and languages, a process-oriented approach is needed to engage the students and allow them to grow academically. A process-oriented approach must of necessity be conversational in character.

(van Lier 1996, p. 182)

Metalinguistic talk

The episode summaries indicate the degree to which talk about language was integrated with the learning of science. It can be argued of course that much of this talk, for example, talk which focused on the nature of generalizations or on the meaning of specific field lexis, is a part of learning science, since at a theoretical level it is impossible to separate 'content' from 'language'. Nevertheless, such talk in the context of the science lesson is probably not typical of many classrooms, and here reflects the focus on language development which appeared to inform many of the interactions between students and teacher. In classroom 1, for example, 7 out of 27 episodes included or consisted of extended talk about the language students were being expected to use. In classroom 2, 27 out of 37 episodes contain some metalinguistic talk, 20 of which include extended interactions.

Talk about language encompassed both learning *about* language and learning *to use* language. Both teachers included a focus on helping students understand certain metalinguistic notions. For example, the notion of register informed many of their interactions with students. Though the term *register* itself was not used, many interactions indicated that one of the teachers' objectives was to help children understand that there are particular ways of talking and writing in science which are different from everyday talk, as the following examples show:

> remember we're scientists and we need to use the proper words/ all of you told me and explained it very well/ now we're going to learn the proper scientific words for this (1:8)
> Gina we're trying to talk like scientists now (1:8)
> now let's start using our scientific language Michelle (1:18)
> I'm just going to give you another word/ and that is the word for what Joseph was trying to say/ one more <u>scientific</u> word (1:15)

Teachers also talked explicitly with students about the changes that take place between language which is situationally-embedded, and that which is more written-like and less context-dependent. Penny, for example, talked with students about some of the differences between talk and writing, and elicited from them some quite sophisticated meta-linguistic understandings:

S: when you're writing you have to make the people . . you have to let the people understand what you're writing and when you're doing something they could see what you're doing . . . what you mean . . (1:19)

S: when you're writing you need more detail than . . . when you're speaking (1:19)

Kath also spent considerable time helping students understand how speakers need to take account of their listeners' needs by being aware of what cannot be taken as shared assumptions, in this process helping them to understand some of the features of more written-like language. Being aware of listener needs was often referred to prior to the teacher-guided reporting sessions when small groups of students reported to the whole class about the results of their experiments:

Teacher: we all did different experiments so we don't know the results/ we only know the results of one experiment [*each group's own*]/ so the language you choose is going to be very clear and precise because people don't know what was going on/ remember this morning when I was talking to you about your novels/ it's all in your head/ all that information in your novel/ and your story is in your head/ your audience doesn't know so you've got to unpack that all for them/ and it's a bit like this/ people didn't do the activities that you did/ other children didn't do them (2:21).

Later, she reminds a small group who have been practising how they will report back:

you've remembered that your language has got to be really precise because the other children have got to try and get a picture in their mind of what you did (2:21).

As well as evaluating students' contributions to the discourse in terms of science knowledge (*right, good, so you're saying they attracted*), both teachers also evaluated students' contributions in terms of their language use, positively acknowledging appropriate wording or clear explanations:

I think that was very well told/ very well told (1:16)
well done/ well done for fixing up the language straight away (*student self-corrects a generalization he has just read out*) (2:25)

In the following example, the teacher comments on the student's use of *whereas*, thereby both providing a grammatical label for the term, and describing its function:

Student 1	the north pole and the south pole attract whereas the north pole and the north pole repels
Teacher	well done/ that's exactly what happened/ you joined those two together/ whereas/ some people used different sentences
Student 2	*repeats similar response, again using 'whereas'*
Teacher	well done/ that's exactly what happens/ you used *whereas*/ the same connective there/ well done

(2:25)

Teachers also focused on specific aspects of language use. Both teachers, for example, spent time discussing the nature of generalizations:

so I would like two ideas that we get from this/ two general ideas/ what we call generalizations/ who can give me something that happens all the time/ not what just happened to us today
(1:17)

In Kath's class, students were often asked to predict the results of experiments prior to carrying them out. Before they did this, the teacher several times brainstormed with the students what she referred to as *the language of prediction*. Students gave a range of expressions, including *maybe; I think; I suppose; this might* (2:12). Chapter 6 includes further examples and indicates where there is some evidence of uptake.

Teachers were also careful to indicate the function of conventions; language usage was not presented as a set of arbitrary rules. Thus when children were asked to work on producing four generalizations, and to check the language they were using, the teacher reminded them that this was because the writing was to be 'public':

you must agree on the language/ then they can go onto the cardboard so that they're public.
(2:37)

There were also many examples of teachers checking that students were familiar with the meanings of words, and explicitly teaching new lexis:

now we're going to learn the proper scientific words for this/ what happens is that magnets attract (*great emphasis*) certain things and so rather than say that it grabs it or it sticks to it/ what we say is magnets attract/ and that

means this kind of thing (*demonstrating*) so if I am a magnet and I attract
Carol Ann I <u>bring her to</u> me (*demonstrating*) <u>attract</u>/ so I'd like for us to
think of other things that the magnet <u>attracted</u>
(1:8)

what does that mean/ 'negotiating'?
(2:40)

What these examples suggest is the degree of explicitness that characterized teachers' talk with students about language, both in terms of
helping students develop certain metalinguistic understandings, and in
making explicit the meanings of linguistic items and grammatical forms
which they predicted students would be likely to need to use in subsequent activities. Significantly, talk about language and the teaching of
new language occurred in the context of actual language use, so that
children had opportunities to develop both science knowledge and
language simultaneously.

Talk about 'being a student'

Along with the development of both science and language, students are
socialized into the life of the classroom, and expectations about
behaviour are built up. Again the discourse is characterized by the kind
of explicitness that Delpit has referred to (Delpit 1988). Effective participation, which in most classrooms involves taking initiative, can only
occur when the learners know the rules of classroom discourse (Mehan
1979). Some researchers have argued that classroom realities may be so
demanding that teachers are preoccupied with issues such as keeping
order, organizing movement, giving out resources or maintaining
behaviour and that when order and cooperation are high priorities, the
nature of learning and the quality of the engagement between teacher
and students become secondary issues (Webster *et al* 1996). In the classrooms in this study, little time was wasted on disciplinary directives,
and it can be suggested that this was partly a result of the time spent
making explicit the expectations of what it meant to 'be a student'. This
foregrounding of the social 'rules' for interpersonal behaviour meant
that teachers at other times spent time managing learning rather than
managing learners and their behaviour: the regulative register, in terms
of overt control, was rarely foregrounded. This is an important point,
given the significance attached to group work and talk-oriented activities in language teaching, since if learners are unable to work collaboratively, even the best designed teaching activities are unlikely to be
successful. The kind of dialogic and participatory classroom talk which

much current educational thinking espouses is only possible given shared expectations of social behaviour.

Talk about being a student is clearly value-laden. Referring to the establishment of teacher-student relationships in the study mentioned above, Christie (1995) writes:

> At issue is her [the teacher's] very strong expectation and require-ment that students cooperate. A value is at work here, to do both with establishing respect for the teacher and with the value of students respecting each other and learning to work together har-moniously. Such a value is constantly affirmed through the regula-tive register. It has consequences for the building of the pedagogic subject, and by extension, of the institutionalized subject who will not only continue to function in school for some years yet, but who will also enter the workforce and the wider community.
>
> (Christie 1995, p. 231)

In these classrooms, and probably in most primary classrooms, the kind of values to which Christie refers are likewise made very explicit. Talk about being a student includes several extended discussions about the interpersonal aspects of group behaviour. Usually ideas about 'model' behaviour are elicited from students, suggesting that they are familiar, at least theoretically, with what is expected. Issues discussed include taking turns, listening to each other (1:6); listening behaviour (2:9); being patient; being cooperative; using quiet voices (2:18); negotiating (2:40); sharing ideas; communicating with the group; making sugges-tions rather than demands; not being stubborn and completing the task in the best way rather than insisting on individual ideas (2:42).

Teachers frequently respond positively to students who demon-strate 'appropriate' behaviour, for example:

> that was packing up with the minimum of fuss and bother/ thank you that was very well done (2:14)
> now Milad/ good to see that you're listening (2:36)

Talk about appropriate and inappropriate behaviour is usually accom-panied by some explanation as to why or why not such behaviour is desirable:

> excuse me Francis/ if you talk <u>I can't hear</u> (1:7)
> what's the rule when we sit on the floor Pierre and someone is speaking/ you don't speak <u>because it interrupts others</u> (2:11)
> can you put this down/ <u>just to help your concentration</u>
> can you put that in the bin/ <u>it will distract you</u> (2:23)

Often mention is also made of the effect of inappropriate behaviour on others. The rules for social behaviour are presented, then, not as a set of institutional and arbitrary 'rules', but as a code of behaviour based on showing respect to peers as well as to teachers.

On one occasion, Tufik, who was often in trouble for various forms of antisocial behaviour, was involved in an argument with several peers. The argument was conducted in whispers during a teacher-guided reporting session, and became quite heated, at which point the teacher intervened. Even on this occasion she favoured an indirect method of control, explaining to Tufik that 'this stuff' prevents not only his own, but others' learning too:

> sorry/ I really (7-*second pause, looking at Tufik*) is there a problem down here/ is there Tufik/ is there something I need to know because that's about the third time I've been interrupted? can you/ can we <u>forget</u> about that for the moment/ OK there's children who are trying to learn and this stuff gets in the way/ I will talk about this <u>after</u> the science lesson so I want you to wipe it out from your mind/ . . . Tufik/ here/ down in front of me please/ it will be easier for you to concentrate/ you need to try/ I know it's difficult/ you need to try and put that out of your mind and concentrate on what's going on at the moment/ OK/ otherwise you're not going to be able to do your work when it comes time to do the next step
> (2:23)

Though listing the comments on social behaviour in this way may give the impression that such talk was unduly prioritized, the overall effect was of a well-ordered classroom, where students were clear about behavioural boundaries and in general were willing to cooperate with each other and with the teacher. Because of these shared understandings about the social aspects of being a student, including a shared expectation of what constitutes appropriate behaviour, there were very few direct and extended admonishments such as the one above, with the result that the teachers were able to use more indirect means to maintain order and working relationships, and to direct activities. Direct imperatives are therefore rare; the more indirect means of control are typically realized by the use of modality (including what Halliday (1985b) refers to as interpersonal metaphors such as *I want you to*):

> (*to class who are engaged in group work and are becoming noisy*)
> excuse me <u>can I remind you</u> that <u>we should be using</u> quiet group voices/ if I want to be with a group of children I shouldn't know what's going on at the front of the room (2:37)

Given that students from ESL backgrounds may not be familiar, in English, with aspects of register relating to politeness forms, there is a risk that this unfamiliarity may result in their being viewed as impolite or aggressive by their teachers and peers. It is significant, then, that both teachers spent time modelling specific wording for situations in which students might find themselves in the course of the group work. In reviewing an activity in which students had to share, in turn, a generalization they had each written, and then collaboratively write three generalizations as a group, the teacher reminded children of how such negotiation might proceed:

> so someone might have said <u>oh no, I don't agree with that</u>/ and you had to say <u>well this might be a better way of saying it</u> (2:40)

Similarly, working collaboratively with others was included in the instructions for a later group-work activity, when children were asked to design a game that used magnets; the same teacher again focused on the nature of collaborative activity. Taking up a student's suggestion that this involved *communicating with your group*, she discussed with students what this might mean, and provided models of specific wordings which students might need to use in order to come to a jointly shared decision about the design of their game (see example 7.5).

Interactional patterns

The episode summaries indicate that a wide range of interactional patterns occurred. The major interactional patterns are briefly discussed here; their significance to the study as a whole is discussed in detail in later chapters. Four major types have been identified. The purpose of this coding of classroom interaction is to characterize the manner in which meaning is constructed in relation to the activity being undertaken; thus the coding is not at the level of a move-by-move analysis, but a summary coding at the level of the episode. The aim is not to provide a rigid system of classification but to give an indication of the kinds of choices teachers made about how talk would be constructed in their classrooms. And as van Lier (1996) points out, many pedagogical activities are 'hybrid' ones, in which aspects of several types of patterns are interwoven (for example, in the current study a teacher may join the discussion of a small group, momentarily taking control of the discourse by virtue of her status, and so subtly altering the discourse by her presence).

The episode summaries indicate that when these interactional choices are mapped onto the activities themselves (see *Teaching/learning processes*), then each of the interactional patterns can be seen as being used fairly systematically for specific educational purposes. It will be suggested at several points in this book that linking interactional types to their *function* within the unit of work appears to offer greater potential in the description of pedagogical practices and teaching style than describing them more generically as 'open' or 'closed' or as 'teacher-centred' or 'learner-centred', and making subsequent claims about the 'effectiveness' of each type. A more relevant issue is how appropriate the relationship is between a particular pedagogical interactional type and the educational purpose it is trying to achieve at that point in the unit of work.

The four major interactional types that have been identified in the data are discussed below. They are listed along a cline from least to most participatory, from the point of view of the students; that is, from inter-actions which are the most asymmetrical in terms of the rights of participants, and where information is essentially one-way (such as teacher monologues), to interactions which are most self-determined and symmetrical (such as small-group work, or discursive conversations with the teacher). The four types also represent a movement from most to least teacher-centred, and in terms of participant roles, from least to most equality.

This classification of interactional types as a cline towards participation draws on van Lier (1996), although there are some differences in the terminology used to describe each type. Van Lier distinguishes four types of pedagogical interaction, which he describes not as a clear-cut system of categories but as a 'map of pedagogical options' (van Lier 1996, p. 180). These he defines as *transmission*, which in classrooms is realized by the typical monologic lecture format, drills, and commands; *IRF questioning*, where most commonly the direction of the discourse is determined by and familiar to the questioner; *trans-action*, where information is exchanged by means of a two-way process, as in group discussions, information exchange tasks and other cooperative learning tasks; and *transformation*, which is jointly managed talk where the agenda is shaped by all participants so that meaning and events are genuinely co-constructed.

The four types of pedagogical interactions identified in this study are described below.

Teacher monologue

Teacher monologues refer to those points in the discourse where the teacher holds the floor without interruption. In these classrooms they are normally very short, varying between one and two minutes, and represent a one-way transmission of information and directives[1]. They refer to those times when the teacher did not seek to elicit verbal responses from the students. The episode summaries indicate that they are used mainly for setting up tasks and giving instructions (see, for example, episodes 1:5; 1:9; 2:10; 2:11; 2:15; 2:18); introducing new language items (1:8; 1:12) and occasionally for disciplinary purposes (2:23).

IRF

The IRF pattern was described in Chapter 3, and in most classrooms is commonly the dominant form of interactional exchange. Although the IRF exchange can be considerably modified towards more democratic and contingent discourse in the ways suggested by van Lier (1996), the term 'IRF' in this book refers to its more restricted realizations, where the teacher is clearly 'primary knower' and is looking for a particular response from the students. (More participatory patterns of discourse are described below, but are distinguished in their labelling from IRF.)

As the episode summaries indicate, IRF interactions occur most frequently at two points in the macrogenre. They occur in the giving of instructions (the setting up stage), often after a teacher monologue when teachers check that students have understood the task (see, for example, episodes 1:5; 1:9; 1:17; 2:4; 2:6; 2:10). They also occur very commonly at the end of the 'reflection' stage, thus at the end of each macrogenre when teachers are checking that the knowledge that has been built up is now shared (see, for example, episodes 1:8; 1:17). A similar point is made by Edwards and Mercer (1987) in their discussion of teachers' use of speech in unison. Thus sometimes the IRF interaction, especially at the end of the macrogenre, is a cued elicitation, when teachers provide most of the propositional content and students are required to provide a single key term (see 2:27; 2:32). IRF interactions are also used when the teacher is focusing on a specific linguistic structure or grammatical accuracy (see 1:8; 1:15 and discussion of text 7.5). Again this occurs towards the end of the macrogenre, when the students have already developed some understandings of the topic and built up field knowledge. IRF patterns are much less commonly used at other times.

Dialogic exchanges

Dialogic is used here to refer to the kind of transactional exchanges in which the discourse is determined through the contributions of both participants. It remains, in one sense, IRF-*like*, in that there is an external agenda imposed by the teacher, and the process of the discourse continues to be controlled and maintained by the teacher. For these reasons the discourse cannot be said to be symmetrical. Nevertheless it represents an important variation of the more restricted IRF pattern, in that it allows the voices of students considerably more freedom, and often leads to extended sequences of discourse between students and teacher.

Dialogic interactions occur most commonly in teacher-guided reporting episodes, where although the teachers maintain the overall thematic development of the discourse as a whole, students very frequently initiate the topic of individual exchanges. These interactions are discussed more fully in the following chapters, and their significance for second language learners suggested. Here an example is included.

> T: Maroun/ something that you can tell me that you found out last lesson
> S: Miss I thought that all metal can stick on magnets but when I tried it some of them didn't stick
> T: OK so you thought that no matter what object/ if it was a metal object/ it would be attracted to the magnet
> (2:15)

While this interaction retains many of the characteristics of the IRF pattern (the teacher, for example, has the first and last word) it differs significantly in two ways, both of which relate to an increase in what has been referred to as the *contingent responsiveness* of the teacher.

Firstly the teacher's question that opens the exchange is a genuine one. As described earlier, teacher-guided reporting sessions followed those episodes where groups of students were carrying out different experiments, and hence when they reported back the results, they were reporting what was unknown information to most of the audience (including, in terms of the detailed events, the teacher). Although of course the teacher has knowledge of the experiments and the likely results, it is left open to the student to decide what aspect of the topic they will talk about. The degree to which the student is allowed to initiate the topic of the individual exchange, therefore, represents a departure from the teacher-prescribed responses associated with the IRF structure. In many TGR sessions, teachers did not repeat their first move once the session had begun, simply nominating children to contribute to the discussion, creating discourse with a more conversational feel.

The second and related way in which dialogic interactions differ from IRF interactions lies in the nature of the teacher's response. The teacher frequently recasts what the student has said: student meaning is recast or reformulated into more registrally appropriate wording (note the teacher's recast of *stick* to *attract*). Thus the modelling the teacher provides occurs after, and on the basis of, what the student has contributed: it is semantically contingent upon it. The teacher, in comparison with her role in the IRF structure, 'leads from behind' in a way that parallels a caregiver's response in early first language learning (described in Halliday 1975; Painter 1984; Wells 1986 and discussed in Part 1). Unlike the IRF sequence, which frequently closes off the exchange and sandwiches the student's contribution between the two controlling moves by the teacher, dialogic interactions have the potential to build up to a discourse sequence and hence to open up the discourse in ways which, as later chapters will argue, are likely to be enabling of second language development.

It can be seen that the use of the term 'dialogic' in this way is essentially a textual one, and differs from the ideological and moral interpretation it has for some critical theorists; for Freire, for example, dialogic discourse represents an instrument of liberation which is transformative in its goal of working against societal injustices. The use of the term in this study is closer to the textual definition of Bakhtin (1981), which emphasizes the relatedness and interplay between the utterances of different speakers. Nevertheless, it can be argued that dialogic interactions do have an ideological interpretation in that they create opportunities for students' voices to be heard. Chapter 7 characterizes the role of the teacher in such interactions as one of mediation rather than transmission: she mediates between the personal ideas and everyday language of the student and the subject knowledge and 'public' discourse of the curriculum area.

Participatory exchanges

Although all the discourse in the classroom is participatory in one sense (even if students are only required to listen), I use the term here to refer specifically to talk in which the agenda is shaped by all participants, and is thus truly co-constructed. It is characterized by symmetry of participation rights and self-determined contributions to the discourse, and relates to Lemke's description of 'true dialogue' and 'cross-discussion', which he describes as the two rarest activity types (Lemke 1990, p. 55) and to van Lier's description of 'transformation' (van Lier 1996). 'True dialogue' occurs when teachers ask questions to which they do not presume to already know the answer, and 'cross-discussion' is dialogue directly between students, with the teacher playing only a moderating role or having equal standing with the students (Lemke 1990a).

Although truly participatory talk is probably rare in most classrooms, some of its characteristics can be found in small-group work. In Penny and Kath's classrooms, for example, group activities are participatory in the sense that participants have equal participation rights.

117

However, even here the overall agenda has been set by the teacher, not by the students. Nevertheless, within the constraint of an externally imposed agenda, students' contributions within the group are self-determined, and participation rights are shared equally.

Much more rare in this corpus is truly participatory and discursive talk between teacher and students. Participatory talk is by its nature democratic with regard to participation rights. Yet by virtue of her authority and knowledge, it is unlikely that in a classroom context teacher and students will have equal power and knowledge status within the discourse. Power differences bias the tenor away from a free discussion of issues between equals. Such a situation is not impossible, however, and can occur when students are in a position of expertise or where expertise (or in some cases, non-expertise!) is shared equally. The early days of computer use in the classroom, for example, created many situations when students had a greater expertise than their teachers. In this study, given the nature of the topic, there are few examples of such student expertise. However, classroom 1 provides evidence that when a genuine problem or disagreement arises, more participatory talk between teacher and student may occur. The following text exemplifies this.

On one occasion, two students (George and Ramond) disagreed with the teacher's explanation that the reason for a screw being non-magnetic was that it was made of non-magnetic material. They both argued that this could be the result of galvanization and the teacher, although still maintaining her argument, was (on her own admittance) unsure of the correct interpretation, and the discussion continued for some minutes. In this text, following the use of this technique by Edwards and Westgate (1994), the contributors are not named, so that the teacher is less obviously conspicuous. Here the address terms are also omitted. With these markers removed, and although it is still possible to identify the teacher, the nature of the discourse means that it is less obvious which contributions are hers, since all contributors initiate ideas.

> magnets only stick to some kinds of metals
> only some metal
> yes
> only some
> I think I know why the magnet got to steel on top of the wood but not to the/ stuck to the other stuff/ cos maybe its chemicals are too strong/ too strong for the magnet
> you mean than this
> what do you think?
> on this

yes maybe what they put on it is too strong for the magnet
I don't think so/ I think that the reason is what Rana and the other people
    thought that this is a different kind of metal
it is
so that magnets don't attract all metals/ right one more thing before we start
I think it/ it/ it's the same colour but when they dipped it/ dipped it in/ in
    different things
it's the same colour/ you mean it's the same metal?
the same/ I think it <u>was</u> the same but they dipped it in something else
well that's what George was saying/ and I think that we're arguing that it/
    no/ that it is another metal
(1:11)

The teacher's control of the discourse is clearly suggested at one point, when the regulative register is foregrounded: *one more thing before we start*, and also by the fact that she exercises her right to say what other participants said or meant. However, it is more difficult to identify the teacher simply from the amount that she contributes or from any other realizations of the regulative register. This text thus comes close to 'participatory' discourse between teacher and students.

It is perhaps unrealistic to expect that truly participatory discourse can regularly occur within a whole class situation (nor, it is later argued, would it always be desirable). A coherent 'conversation' among 30 people is a virtual impossibility and hence many teachers' reliance on small-group work in the classroom to extend participation rights. However, these two texts illustrate that even when the teacher continues to maintain some control of the discourse, it is possible to approach some symmetry of participation. Students are here free to express individual thinking, and to interpret the situation according to their world view and experiences. No one is the 'primary knower', all ideas are accepted as valid and are listened to and treated with respect. (The seriousness with which this teacher treated all contributions, even in more structured discourse, was a feature of all her interactions with students.)

As the episode summaries indicate, teachers are able to extend the range of discourse roles within educational talk, even within the social and institutional constraints of the classroom. There are regular and extended opportunities for students to participate more fully than traditional classroom talk typically allows.

Mode shifting in the second language classroom

Since mode shifting is the theme of the following chapter, only brief comments are included here.

While mode shifting was in a general sense deliberately planned into the teaching programme (see previous chapter), what emerges from the episode summaries is the systematic nature of the relationship between the different teaching and learning activities and the degree of context-embeddedness of the language. Of note too is the strong relationship between mode shift and particular interactional structures, with instances of mode shift often involving the teacher taking on the role of 'mediator' between students' local and personal knowledge and the public language and knowledge of the subject.

The themes identified and introduced in this chapter have been drawn from the summary represented by the two episode summaries. These themes are now taken up in the following three chapters.

Notes

1 It can be argued that even 'monologic' discourse is never truly so, since there will always remain traces of previous talk (see Bakhtin 1981; Maybin 1994).

PART 3
Discourse contexts for second language development

It is essentially in the discourse between teacher and pupil that education is done, or fails to be done.

(Edwards and Mercer 1987, p. 101)

Drawing on the theoretical constructs presented in Chapters 2 and 3, this final section of the book examines, in depth, examples of the discourse that appeared to be enabling of second language development. Central to this is the discussion throughout the three chapters of the relationship between the talk, the contexts in which the talk occurred and the pedagogical purposes of the talk. Chapter 6 draws on systemic linguistics to illustrate how over the course of a number of lessons, teachers and students together co-constructed new ways of using language, building on students' everyday language and shared experiences. Chapter 7 examines the data through the lens of sociocultural theory, and conceptualizes teaching as a mediational process. Chapter 8, the final chapter, takes the perspective of the learner, and discusses the affordances for second language development offered by specific discourse contexts.

6 Teachers and learners: constructing new meanings

Introduction

Earlier chapters have suggested that the degree to which language is embedded in the 'here and now', in contexts where meaning can be partly retrieved from the immediate situation, is an important factor in determining its comprehensibility for ESL learners. However, it has also been pointed out that a decrease in situation-embeddedness is typically a feature of the academic registers which they must learn to control in the school context. Teaching programmes must therefore aim in part to 'progressively [free] the system from a dependence on situational constraints' (Halliday 1975, p. 142). Within the ESL context Mohan suggests:

> While context-dependent discourse is important for the early stages of language learning, competence in processing relatively context-independent theoretical discourse is necessary for academic achievement and is a major aim of schooling.
>
> (Mohan 1986, p. 101)

Addressing this issue, Mohan (1986, 2002) has described a planned integrative approach which relates language learning and content. This teaching model is developed around a 'knowledge framework' for the sequencing and development of structures of knowledge across the curriculum and is related to sequencing principles of discourse. Mohan's knowledge framework is sequenced from practical to theoretical content: that is, from specific practical activity to theory which may require students to classify, define principles and evaluate. In parallel, the discourse framework is sequenced from 'implicit' to 'explicit' discourse: that is, from practical discourse of here-and-now action situations to theoretical academic discourse, in which theoretical knowledge is made explicit and conveyed through language alone. These two frameworks are underpinned by a sequencing principle for learning itself, from experiential to expository learning.

In the classroom one way to provide for a gradual development towards theoretical discourse is to arrange teaching from practical to theoretical, with teachers building on the transition between the experiential and the expository, for example, following experiments and simulations with discussions and reports which reflect on the experience. Mohan describes this as an 'expanding environments design': learners understand increasingly more distant environments and develop the ability to handle increasingly less situationally dependent discourse, so that ultimately unfamiliar content can be learned through language alone. A critical issue within such a model is the management of the transition from experiential to expository learning, which teachers must achieve while taking into account both the development of curriculum understanding and the development of discourse. Drawing on the notion of the mode continuum described in Chapter 2, and reflecting Mohan's implicit-to-explicit discourse principle, this chapter illustrates how two teachers managed a transition from practical to theoretical learning. It explores how such mode shifts were actualized in the classroom and how the teachers developed new registers with their students. By tracking the activities and organizational structures through which the texts were produced, which broadly shifted from experiential to expository learning, it also illustrates how the notion of the mode continuum can be operationalized as an integrated framework for language teaching purposes in the content classroom.

In the first part of the chapter, teacher-student talk is examined in relation to what I have termed the 'micro-discourse' context. 'Micro-discourse' is used to refer to the exchanges that occur between teacher and students in the course of a single conversation *within* one particular episode. In the second part of the chapter, I examine what I refer to as the 'macro-discourse' context, by which I refer to the mode shifting which occurs *across a sequence* of episodes. These sequences of talk are examined to show how the discourse of an episode as a whole develops out of the discourse of a previous episode and how it also provides a shared frame of reference for the discourse of the following episode. In this way it is possible to track how a sequence of episodes is structured in such a way as to lead to the use of increasingly more written-like language. However, although the distinction being made here between micro and macro mode shifts is a useful way of exploring the data, such a distinction is considerably less obvious in the reality of the classroom. Indeed it will become clear that the examples examined as examples of micro-mode shift (for example, texts taken from the teacher-guided reporting where the teacher recasts student wording) contain many 'traces' of previously shared experiences and earlier discourses. For talk is not produced and heard in a vacuum, simply in the immediate context of the discourse in which we are engaged, but, at least in successful interaction, is located within larger understandings shared by interactants. And it is precisely this building up of shared understanding and shared discourse which is a particular feature of the classroom talk of the two classrooms.

Many of the texts that follow have a hybrid quality. To use Bernstein's terms, the 'horizontal' discourses used by the students are meshed with the 'vertical' discourse of education. It is in these texts that the everyday and familiar language of the students and the technical and subject-related language of school come together to create a pedagogic 'bridging' discourse.

Micro-mode shifting

In this section I have represented the most common pedagogical functions of mode shifts that occurred in the data.

Recasting by the teacher

A common context for mode shifting was teacher-guided reporting. In these interactions teachers frequently responded to students' meaning through recasting their contributions into a more scientific register, often involving a field shift from everyday to more specialized lexis. As discussed in Chapter 5, a significant factor in this discourse context is that the students initiate the topic of the exchange, and so teacher recasting is a response to student-initiated meaning. This occurs frequently in teacher-guided reporting. Examples 6.1 and 6.2 exemplify these contexts, and are glossed as *Recasting by the teacher*.

Talking about the talk: making the new register explicit

Both teachers also used metalanguage with the students to make explicit the fact that they were learning to use a new register; for example they frequently referred to 'talking like scientists'. Though not in itself an actual instantiation of mode shift, this use of metalanguage brings to students' notice, and gives them access to, the kinds of linguistic resources they need in order to *use* the register. Examples 6.3–6.5 illustrate this, glossed as *Talking about the talk*.

Reminding and handing over

Often, rather than recasting student wording, teachers simply prompted students to reformulate what they had said themselves; in Vygotskian terms, they promoted handover. These situations occurred at the point where teachers saw students as able to take a more active role as participants in the discourse. Frequently this prompting drew on the metalinguistic knowledge that the teacher had built up with the students and the students were frequently able to produce the new wording alone. Examples 6.6–6.8 are examples of this, glossed as *Reminding and handing over*.

Unpacking written language

Mode shifting also occurred in a reverse direction, as a move towards *less* written-like language, when for example the teacher 'unpacked' written instructions. Text 6.9 is an illustration of this, and provides an example of how written (and linguistically more complex) input is made comprehensible to learners. This section is glossed as *Unpacking written language*.

Recasting by the teacher

The notion of recasting was introduced in Chapter 3, where it was used with its more usual meaning to refer to morphological or syntactic change within a clause. I am using the term here more broadly to refer to rewording by the teacher at a discourse level. Examples 6.1 and 6.2 illustrate how a student's contribution is recast by the teacher into more register-appropriate wording, or what Lemke refers to as a 'foreign "register" within English' (Lemke 1990, p. 172).

Example 6.1 *You thought it would be attracted*

2:15
This text occurred during a teacher-guided reporting session, following small-group work in which the students had experimented with magnetic and non-magnetic materials.

	STUDENTS	TEACHER
1		Maroun/ something that you can tell me that you found out last lesson
2	Ma: Miss I thought that all metal can stick on magnets but . . when I tried it some of them they didn't stick	
3		OK so you thought that no matter what object/ if it was a

metal object it would be
attracted to the magnet/
interesting .

Example 6.2 You felt the magnets attract and stick together

2:23
Like the previous text, this also occurred during a teacher-guided
reporting session, this time following small-group experiments
designed to show that like poles repel and unlike attract.

	STUDENTS	TEACHER
1		what were your results?
2	when we put it on one pole . . em faces the other one it doesn't stick but when we turned the other one around . it sticks together	
3		OK can I just clarify something? you've got two magnets? they're in line/ when you put . the two together
4	yes Miss	
5		like that (*demonstrating*) they attracted to each other/ they stuck to each other/ is that right?
6	(*nods*)	OK can you then tell me what you had to do next . ?
7	when we had em the things the first one like if you put it up in the air like that . the magnets you can feel . feel the em . that they're not pushing?	
8		when you turn the magnet around? you felt that
9	pushing and if we use the other side we can't feel pushing	
10		OK so when . . they were facing one way . . they/ you felt the

> magnets attract and stick
> together/ when you turn one of
> the magnets around you felt it .
> repelling .. or pushing away ..
> OK thank you well done
> Charbel

In both examples the teacher recodes students' everyday wordings. By responding to the meaning of what students are saying, she allows for communication to proceed, while at the same time her response recasts these meanings – for example as *attract* and *repel* – and so gives the learner access to new ways of meaning. This recasting and extension of student-initiated meaning depends on the adult's contribution being closely related to, and thus following, the student's contribution. While following the learner's lead and accepting as a valid contribution the information given, the teacher at the same time provides alternative linguistic forms to encode the learner's meaning in more context-appropriate ways. In this process new meanings are collaboratively developed. The teacher's responses suggest the Vygotskian notion of the ZPD: she takes as a starting point what the student is able to contribute, but scaffolds the language they will later be expected to use. Focusing on the role of the adult in early first language development, and reflecting the earlier discussion on contingency, Wells (1981) points out that adult contributions to discourse must be modified in timing, form and content to the child's receptive capacities, but at the same time they must provide the means for the child to increase their linguistic resources and, through these resources, their understanding of the content of the communication. These examples show how the same process occurs in classroom interactions.

Such interactions seem more likely to occur when the initial move by the teacher does not require a prescribed answer and where the learner has a chance to enter the discourse on his or her own terms. In both the examples, the students are the 'primary knowers' (Berry 1981) in that they possess specific information (what happened in their group work) that the teacher does not have. Although of course it is the teacher who is in control of the knowledge associated with the overall thematic development of the unit of work, and who controls the overall structure of the discourse, such initiating moves temporarily locate that control in the student: they are the initiators of the specific topic of the exchange.

Example 6.2 is a particularly interesting example of the linguistic complexity of this seemingly simple recasting strategy and is worthy of a closer look.

The teacher's recast version is thematically related to the students' version, even though different thematic items are used: *stick/ attract*; *lift up/repel*; *not pushing/repelling*). The same semantic relations are constructed within the same thematic pattern: *they stick together/ they attracted each other; you can feel they're not pushing/ you felt it repelling.* In describing one of the ways in which science teachers build up basic semantic relationships for thematic development, Lemke refers to 'local equivalence', whereby two expressions are marked as equivalent within the thematic pattern being built up (Lemke 1990). The strongest parallelism occurs when, as in this example, the words and expressions to be marked as equivalent occupy the same or corresponding 'slots' in a similar grammatical construction. (Later in the sequence of lessons however, as the second part of this chapter shows (see 'Mode shifting across episodes', p. 142), teachers recontextualize students' contributions to the discourse somewhat differently, by using different wordings and grammar.)

The teacher's questions lead to an opportunity for her to model both *attract* and *repel* in turn. She begins by asking about the results of the experiment, which the student then describes in a single turn. The teacher responds with *can I just clarify something* (3) even though the information that Charbel has given is apparently adequate as a response to her initial question. She appears to want him to describe each step in turn, asking *can you tell me what you had to do next* (6). As he responds by retelling each part of the experiment, describing how he held the magnet first one way and then another, an opportunity is provided for the teacher to focus first on *attract* (5) and then *repel* (10). It is worth noting, however, that the shift between the everyday and technical is not a simple linear progression. If we focus simply on the teacher's contributions, it can be seen that they include instances of three distinct 'points' along the mode continuum, representing in each case what is essentially the same propositional content. In Figure 6.1, I have characterized these points as 'formal' to refer to the use of the standard lexico-grammar of school science; 'everyday' to refer to the informal spoken language familiar to the children and 'situation-embedded' to refer to those parts of the discourse that contain exophoric reference and are bound up with and rely on the immediate and visual context. I have earlier used the term 'message abundancy' (see Chapter 3) to refer to the way that meaning is constructed within the particular interplay of different language modes (spoken and written, 'everyday' and technical); alternative semiotic systems; and mediational texts and artefacts. As Figure 6.1 illustrates, there is considerable message abundancy here as a result of these mode shifts and use of artefacts.

Figure 6.1 Mode shifting

STUDENT	TEACHER (Situation-embedded)	TEACHER (Everyday)	TEACHER (Formal)
it sticks together			
	like that (*demonstrates using magnets*)		
			they attracted to each other
		they stuck to each other	
you can feel . . . that they're not pushing . . . if we use the other side we can't feel pushing			
			when they were facing one way you felt the magnets attract
		and stick together	
			when you turn one of the magnets around you felt it repelling
		or pushing away	

The two middle columns in this table which 'span' the children's talk (column 1) and the more formal language of the curriculum (column 4) represent how the discourse operates as a linguistic bridge between students' current language abilities on the one hand and the demands of the school curriculum on the other. Exploring the mode shifts in this way also offers a linguistic perspective on one way comprehensible input may be achieved in tandem with the modelling of new language. The discourse is characterized by what can be described as a kind of code-switching as the everyday and formal codes mesh together in a hybrid register. I suggest that the kind of register-meshing that results in this hybrid discourse is an important factor in the successful learning of new academic registers with young second language learners, and one which is consistent with the notion of the ZPD, with its focus on both what the learner brings and what the task demands of them.

It could be speculated that the closeness of 'fit' between the teacher's and student's contributions offers an insight into how far the students' zone of proximal development is informing the teacher's response. As discussed earlier, the notion of the ZPD and the importance of contingent responses would suggest that teacher-talk should take student-talk as its starting point but extend it beyond what students are capable of producing themselves. This occurs in many of the texts. The degree of difference between student- and teacher-talk can perhaps more generally illuminate the appropriateness of teacher responses in classroom discourse. Too close a match would suggest that students are not being provided with a context in which learning will occur, too great a difference may lead to students failing to understand the teacher's discourse (see Lemke's thematic analysis of science discourse in the classroom, in which he demonstrates the outcomes of too great a gap between the thematics of teacher and student (Lemke 1990, pp. 28–48)).

Also from the point of view of second language learning, it is important to note that in the examples above the more unfamiliar lexis introduced by the teacher occurred at a time when students had *already* developed some understanding of the topic of the interactions (that is, they had begun to develop their own thematic patterns). Thus learners are given access to the more unfamiliar register in the light of the schematic knowledge they have built up by taking part in the activities. It follows that a teacher in this context is potentially able to use aspects of the lexico-grammar beyond what might be understood if learners had not first taken part in the small-group experiences, and were without these as a basis for interaction and interpretation. The teaching of new language at this point in a sequence of episodes suggests some parallel to the principle within bilingual programmes, which suggests that learning should occur first in L1 as a basis to learning in L2; here, though, the relationship is between different registers (from familiar to new register) rather than between different languages (from first to second language). As Lemke points out, the learning of science language represents the learning of a 'foreign register', and so students, in effect, 'learn "bilingually" in both colloquial and scientific English' (Lemke 1990, p. 172).

Talking about the talk: making the new register explicit

The classroom discourse produced many instances of the explicit teaching of scientific language, and of the use by the teacher of metalanguage. The following three examples show how in the context of actual language use, the teachers talked about the language to which children were being introduced, and developed metalinguistic understandings with them.

Example 6.3 Our proper scientific language

(1:8)

In this example the teacher is introducing the lexical item *attract.* This term is introduced after the students have used the term *stick to* to describe the magnets' behaviour, a fact that the teacher acknowledges by saying that the students had *told me and explained it well.* She is standing at the blackboard and writing as she speaks.

> Teacher:
> I'm going to help you with a word today . that we didn't . . . no one has said/ because remember we're scientists . and we need to use the proper words . all of you <u>told</u> me . and explained it very well/ now we're going to learn the proper scientific words for this . what happens is . that magnets <u>attract</u> (*great emphasis*) . certain things and so rather than say that it grabs it or it sticks to it . what we say is magnets <u>attract</u> and that means . this kind of thing (*demonstrating*) so if I . am a magnet and I attract . Carol Ann/ I . . <u>bring</u> <u>her</u> <u>to</u> <u>me</u> (*demonstrating*) . <u>attract</u> . so I'd like for us to think of the other things . that the magnet <u>attracted</u> (*writes 'attracted' on board*) and then think of the things that the magnet . <u>didn't</u> attract . . that didn't attract (*writes 'didn't attract' on board*) and I'd like for you to say it in a sentence so we get used . to our proper scientific language

This text, typical of many in this classroom, provides an illustration of what it means to work within learners' ZPD, as the teacher accepts the children's wording but then provides the means by which the knowledge can be recontextualized in scientific ways. As the new lexical item is introduced to students, the teacher makes clear that her recasting is not a 'correction' of what the children have said – indeed she acknowledges that the children have already explained it very well – but rather it is the *scientific* way. The purpose of the learning is made clear: *remember we're scientists*; *we're going to learn the proper scientific words*; *so we get used to our proper scientific language*. This emphasis on appropriateness rather than on formal correctness is intrinsic to a model of language which has as a fundamental principle the notion that language varies according to context and purpose, and here this is made explicit to learners. By validating the students' original contributions, the teacher is presenting science, in Lemke's terms, 'as one way of talking about the world among others' (Lemke 1990, p. 125).

It is also significant that the new lexical item is introduced after the experiential work the students have been involved in, and after students have come to understand a new item of knowledge through their everyday register, not, as in many traditional ESOL classrooms, presented and practised ahead of actual use. Instead, the new item is linked to current understandings: previous conceptual understandings developed through the experiments provide a cognitive peg on which to hang new linguistic knowledge. This new knowledge is constructed multimodally: the new item is written on the board, and meaning is partly constructed through the teacher's physical gestures. As in the previous example, the learners are presented with more than one source of meaning.

Example 6.4 I'm talking about all magnets

(1.12)
Up to this point in the lesson the students had been referring to the results of their individual experiments using recount-like texts, for example, *the thumbtack is magnetic*. In this example, the teacher initiates a further shift in the discourse, and models to the students how their findings can be recontextualized as generalizations. The discourse here begins to shift from meanings representing personal understandings to the arena of public knowledge.

	STUDENTS	TEACHER
1		right now we're going to talk about all thumbtacks/ so we're going to talk about magnets . .
	[attract thumbtacks	try it this way, magnets [attract thumbtacks let's try it
2	magnets attract thumbtacks	
3		remember I'm not talking about just one I'm talking about all magnets/ I'm talking about all thumbtacks so let's try it again
4	magnets attract thumbtacks	

5		the nail is magnetic . . . so you tell me
6	[the nail	[magnets
7	magnets attract the nail	
8	the nails	
9		again
10	magnets attract nails	
11		that's hard . . this paper clip/ remember the steel paper clips are magnetic
12	magnets attract steel paper clips	

Typical of many of the discourse shifts in the talk, the teacher accompanies the modelling of the language with explicit metalinguistic comments. She begins by pointing out that a different kind of response is required: *try it this way*, giving an explanation of the shift in meaning: *I'm talking about all thumbtacks* and providing a model: *magnets attract thumbtacks* (1) repeating the metalinguistic explanation in (3).

The wording through which this new meaning is realized is built up with the students bit by bit, with the scaffolding from the teacher gradually reducing as the students produce the target language alone. The students produce this language twice (2, 4), and then are required to transfer their knowledge with a new example: *the nail.* They rightly recognize that a generalization will require a different morphological form (*nails*), but initially begin with this, rather than *magnets*, as the theme of the clause (6). The teacher scaffolds the appropriate clause theme by speaking over the students, so that they 'shadow' her, which enables them to respond in the way she wants in turn (7). However, this time they fail to include the plural morpheme and a few students self-correct (8). The teacher asks them to repeat the response again which this time they do using the model structure (10), transferring the model structure with the new example (12).

This highly structured text exemplifies the importance of contingency in effective scaffolding. It highlights the need for a teacher to respond moment to moment to student needs, as she does in this text by 'overriding' inappropriate responses and providing models of the new structure.

Example 6.5 We would write it in the present tense

(2:19)

As this text occurs the teacher is writing up on the board suggestions given to her by the students about the words that they expect to use when they write their science journals.

	STUDENTS	TEACHER
1		what could be some words that we/ that I could put up here/ let's have a brainstorm of some words that we've learned about magnets so that we can <u>write</u> like scientists too . . so . . Josephine
2	J: repel	
3		good . . Amanda
4	A: magnetic?	
5		magnetic good girl . . em Francois?
6	F: unmagnetic?	
7		not quite but you've got the right idea Francois/ very good/ who can help him with that word . . Belinda?
8	B: non magnetic	
9		all right . . tell me Francois?
10	F: non magnetic	
11		non magnetic . . your idea was absolutely right and sometimes we do say 'un' meaning 'no' so you were . . that was clever . . . Joseph?
12	J: attract	
13		attract
14	M: Mrs C. when you're writing that . . . mustn't you use the past tense?	

15
no because I want you to tell me
what you <u>know</u> about magnets
from this . . . what do magnets
<u>do</u>/ that's a good question but it's
something that you've learned
about magnets/ so then it would
be something that happens
<u>always</u>/ so we would write it in
the <u>present</u> tense . . . good
question . . that was good

This example is of particular interest in demonstrating how the teacher
responds to the linguistic understandings of two students (6, 14) about the
use of aspects of the new register. In both cases the suggestions, though
not correct, are responded to in terms of a 'right idea' or a 'good question'.

Francois's suggestion of *unmagnetic* is acknowledged by the
teacher in terms of his 'idea' which is *absolutely right* (7, 11), although
she requires him to repeat the correct form before moving on. Michael's
question *mustn't you use the past tense* appears to refer to the work the
students had done the previous day, when the teacher had written
attracted on the board and elicited from the children the past tense form
in relation to their recounts about their experiments. His question is
indicative of the degree to which metalinguistic understandings and
terms had been integrated into this curriculum area, and been appropriated by the students. The teacher responds to the question by recapping
what she had said earlier about the meaning of generalizations, empha-
sizing through her own speech the correct tense for the generalization
she is seeking: *what you know about magnets from this/ what do
magnets <u>do</u>/ something that happens <u>always</u>.* She concludes with a
metalinguistic explanation: *so we would write it in the <u>present</u> tense.*
This text illustrates how knowledge about language can be built up in
the context of actual language use. In addition, it suggests how Michael's
knowledge about language appears to have enhanced his understanding
of the meaning and form of the language he is being asked to use.

One further short text illustrates the degree to which students had
appropriated metalinguistic understandings along with their actual use
of new meanings. Juan was an ESL child on a special education programme, and in general struggled with most school work and with
English. Asked to reflect in his science journal on what he had learned
from the lesson, he wrote:

I learned that the south pole and the north pole attract. And I learn how to
talk like a sciencetist (*sic*)

Reminding and handing over

The notion of 'handover' is an important one in sociocultural theory. The term 'handover' is used here in the neo-Vygotskian sense (see Bruner 1986), referring to the notion that once learners are able to carry out a task alone, the expert's scaffolding diminishes and learners are expected to take increasing responsibility for the aspect of the task they have now mastered. To put it another way, they begin the movement from more peripheral to more central participation in the production of the discourse. In both classrooms, and after teacher modelling and explicit talk about language, students were expected to begin to use aspects of the new register alone. As might be expected, however, since learning is not a linear process, students often reverted to more familiar ways of expressing meanings. In this situation the teachers usually did not recast the students' wordings as they had done earlier, but instead simply drew attention to the students' wordings, causing the students to 'notice' (Swain 2000) the inadequacy (in this context) of what they had said. Students were usually able to self-correct alone, leading to a mode shift within their own wording. It is worth noting, however, that the point at which teachers chose to hand over was individually and situationally determined and varied from student to student, with some students being given very much longer periods of scaffolding before handover than others, a process which is quite consistent with the nature of the ZPD.

In the following three examples (examples 6.6–6.8), the teacher is talking with students in the context of teacher-guided reporting. In each case she reminds them that they have learned an alternative coding, but hands over to them the responsibility for producing it. As Lantolf points out, novices do not simply copy experts' capabilities, but appropriate it as they transform it (Lantolf 2000a, b). Here the students are encouraged to use the new language in the context of making their own meanings and are treated 'not as a repeater but as a communicative being' (Newman and Holzman 1993 in Lantolf 2000a, p. 18).

Example 6.6 I want you to use that new word

(1:15)

STUDENT	TEACHER
1 S: one north pole standing up . . next to another north pole which you put on top . . will push it away/ like it will make it move	

2		I want you to use that new word that we talked about . . push away?
3	S: it can repel the other magnet	

Example 6.7 Remember we're scientists now

(1:17)

	STUDENT	TEACHER
1	G: the magnet doesn't stick on the . . cork	
2		tell me
3	G: the magnet doesn't stick onto the cork	
4		remember we're scientists now Gina .
5	G: em . ah! the magnet attracts	
6		the magnet . ?
7	G: the magnet <u>didn't</u> attract the cork	

Example 6.8 Let's start using our scientific language

(1:17)

	STUDENTS	TEACHER
1	M: we found out that the south and the south don't like to stick together	
2		now let's/ let's start using our scientific language Michelle
3	M: the north and the north repelled each other and the south and the south also . . repelled each other but when we put the/ when we put the	

two magnets in a different way
they/ they attracted each other

The teacher reminder is given either through a metalinguistic reference to the lexical item: *that new word* (6.6:2), or through a reference to the nature of the register that she expects students to be using: *remember we're scientists* (6.7:4); *let's start using our scientific language* (6.8:2). In each case this prompt is all that is needed for the students to reformulate their wording. The result is a mode and field shift by the student which incorporates the specific lexis the teacher is focusing on. It could be argued that these prompts by the teacher cause students to notice their own wording because, as Swain argues, it engages them in metalinguistic thinking, their language is consequently 'stretched' and as a result what they say is syntactically more complete and contextually more appropriate.

Unpacking written language

Mode shifting also occurred in contexts where the teacher unpacked register-specific language. Often this was associated with the use of written texts. In example 6.9 the teacher is explaining written instructions for an experiment that children would later carry out in groups. The experiment was designed to develop an understanding of magnetic attraction and repulsion in relation to the placement of magnet poles. It required students to place a magnet into a 'cage' of paddle pop sticks that had been inserted into a block of polystyrene, and then to place a second magnet on top. The second magnet then had to be reversed and the results recorded. The instructions were:

Place a bar magnet into the cradle made by the paddle pop sticks. Place a second bar magnet on top. Observe and record what happens. Repeat, alternating the poles. Observe and record what happens.

Some of the discourse has been omitted so that the transcription includes only those elements of the discourse that are relevant to the current discussion, and so that the layout illustrates more graphically the mode shifting of the teacher (following the conventions used in Figure 6.1). The text has been transcribed using three columns. The left-hand column contains the written wording: the instructions from which the teacher is reading. The middle column contains a more 'unpacked' recoding of these instructions: it is more spoken-like 'everyday' language with which the students will be familiar. The right-hand column contains language which is situation-embedded:

here the teacher is referring to the materials that she is holding or pointing to.

Example 6.9 Alternating, changing, like this

(2.8)

	Most written-like (written instructions, read aloud by teacher)	'Everyday'	Situation-embedded (use of material and visual context)
1	(*teacher reading aloud*) Place a magnet into the cradle, and place another magnet on top of the cradled magnet		
2			so you've got one magnet in here (*T. demonstrating*) then you have to put another magnet on top
	(*four turns later*)		
3	(*teacher reading aloud*) alternating the poles		
4		changing the poles	
5			if you put it facing/ you've got one magnet in there and you put it in facing one way/ change the poles around like this (*T. demonstrating*)
6		change it to the other side	
7	alternate the poles		

8   so you're trying it
                              each way/ you're
                              changing the poles

The teacher begins the unpacking of these instructions (2) without an interim step of recoding through familiar language, probably because the material object itself can be seen by all the students. In (3) the focus lexis *alternating* is initially explained through a more familiar lexical substitution: *changing* (4). In her next move the teacher once more embeds the text within the visual context, this time demonstrating what the students should do as she is speaking (5). She continues by shifting the text away from an exophoric orientation, repeating the substitution *change* (6) before returning to the written wording, *alternate the poles* (7). The meaning is then further recoded by the teacher once more in everyday language: *you're changing the poles* (8).

While the teacher focuses predominantly on lexical items, the written text is also unpacked through the grammar. Procedural instructions commonly foreground the material process in the clause through its choice as theme: here, for example, the written instructions have *place, observe, record, repeat, alternating*. A further feature of written procedures is, commonly, the absence of human participants. In the teacher's recoding however, the students themselves are put into the texts as participants (*you*) and are thematized in the clause. Circumstances are also recoded in the context of the visual demonstration, so that they become exophoric: *in here, in there*.

These mode shifts, where the same propositional content is being coded in several ways, produce an overall text characterized by what I referred to in the previous chapter as 'message abundancy': students are given opportunities to hear the message in several modes. But it is clear that language itself is not the only component which is important. The immediate and visual context and the concrete materials being handled by the teacher also play a significant part in comprehension and in the whole communicative event. Lemke (1998) argues that meaning cannot be adequately understood in terms of a single semiotic system such as language: we do not make meaning with language alone. We use a range of resources in the construction of meaning, including actional and visual semiotic resources. Even when text is referred to as 'situation-embedded', it does not 'mean' alone, but can only be understood because of its coordination with the visual, gestural and actional components by which it is mediated. (At an intuitive level most teachers recognize this, and seek to make language comprehensible for their ESL learners by the use of a range of semiotic resources such as pictures, objects, mime and gesture and a range of hands-on curriculum activities.)

The example highlights the inadequacy of any approach which equates comprehension with the avoidance of more complex language. In this example, linguistic simplification would probably also have served the purpose of making language comprehensible for students, or the written instructions could have been avoided altogether, but this approach would have restricted students in gaining access to models of alternative registers. Like example 6.2, example 6.9 suggests a much richer interpretation of how input can be made comprehensible: students have, within the same situational context, access both to written text and to more familiar ways of coding similar meaning, as well as to the semiotic resources provided by the visual and actional context. Thus aspects of the situational context, including other semiotic resources such as the teacher's or children's gestures, are not simply a background to the discourse, but are interrelated with the language to construct additional sources of meaning. In the classroom, texts carry residues of other texts and meaning is constructed out of this intertextual classroom history. But it is also constructed intersemiotically through the integration of texts into a larger non-linguistic context.

Mode shifting across episodes

The first part of this chapter has given examples of four ways in which teachers' contributions led to mode shifts in the discourse, usually moving from more spoken-like to more written-like discourse but also incorporating shifts in the opposite direction.

This section takes each classroom in turn and illustrates how mode shifting occurred across a sequence of episodes, so that the discourse becomes progressively more written-like and explicit. This linguistic movement can be characterized as one whereby newcomers to a discourse community (of science, specifically school science) are in their early stages of socialization into the activities, identities, artefacts, knowledge and practices represented by the science curriculum. The mode shifts illustrate how science knowledge is gradually and progressively recoded or recontextualized through the discourse jointly constructed between teacher and students, and through the artefacts the students are handling. Edwards and Mercer see the process of learning in the classroom as one whereby teacher and students 'relate discourse to context, and build through time a joint frame of reference' (Edwards and Mercer 1987, p. 65). The illustrative examples show how these frames of reference are jointly built up through the shared experiences of teacher and students and how, through their interactions, students and teacher develop shared meanings and a shared language. Through sequences of activities, teacher and students create a shared communicative space, or what Mercer refers to as an 'intermental development zone' which is 'constantly reconstituted as the dialogue continues' (Mercer 2000, p. 41). In the sequences of discourse that follow, this process hinges on the linguistic variation which results from changes in the situational context of each new episode, with each episode representing both a reconstitution of the previous episode and a shared starting point for the next.

As would be expected, the most situationally-embedded discourse occurs when students are carrying out science activities in small groups. In this context they are talking while doing, and their learning at this point is typically mediated through 'everyday' language which is familiar and shared by students and teacher. Language in these instances is used not simply to comment on what is happening, but also to direct action or discuss procedural matters. The outcome of this small-group talk is the development of some shared understandings and personal experiences.

In the teacher-guided reporting sessions, the discourse becomes less reliant on the immediate situational context. You will remember from Chapter 4 that each group of students was engaged in different experiments, involving different procedures, and so when information from the groups was reported, students were hearing new – although related – information from each group. This information gap was critical in providing a social purpose for the teacher-guided reporting session and so was integral to the overall organization of the teaching activities. In the reporting session, students report on what they did and what they found out, so that the understandings developed within the small groups are now shared with a wider audience. In this process, students are supported in their reporting by the teacher who, through responses contingent on what they offer, reshapes their talk, clarifying with them what they are saying, and frequently recasting their talk in contextually more appropriate wordings. These recasts typically incorporate field and mode shifts, and the scientific register begins to be jointly constructed via the kind of hybrid register discussed earlier.

The least situationally dependent texts occur during writing activities, often when students write in their science journals. This context is one where the appropriation of the new register is most clearly evident. During the writing task itself there is little explicit teacher support of the type evident in the teacher-guided reporting, and the journal writing represents one of a number of points where 'handover' is evident; that is, those points when teacher support is reduced as students begin to appropriate the new learning for their own purposes.

Examples from classroom 1

To illustrate more clearly the linguistic shifts between episodes, examples 6.10–6.15 are presented together, with discussion at the end of the sequence. The remaining examples are presented and discussed singly.

Examples 6.10 and 6.11 occurred as four students were engaged in carrying out an experiment. After the students had completed the small-group experiments, they were asked to report back to the rest of the class about the results of their own work. Prior to this reporting session the teacher talked with the students about the 'scientific words' they would use, and introduced the lexical item *repel* (example 6.12). The students then reported back to the class about what they had discovered, with Hannah as reporter (examples 6.13 and 6.14). Example 6.15 is taken from Hannah's science journal and is the result of an entry describing what she had learned that day. Example 6.16 is a journal entry from a student who had listened to the interaction between the teacher and Hannah. Following this reporting session, and after all the groups of students had reported on their various experiments, the teacher talked with the students about any generalizations they could now make on the basis of what they had done and heard (example 6.17).

Taken together, this sequence of texts tells a little of the 'long conversation' of this classroom, and illustrates how each episode provides a basis of shared understanding for the next, within which it is itself recontextualized.

Example 6.10 (Students carrying out activity)

The experiment involved students making a 'cage' with a block of polystyrene and paddle pop sticks, placing a bar magnet within this cage and then placing a second magnet on top. When like poles are in contact, the top magnet is repelled by the bottom magnet and appears to 'float' above the base magnet.

Hannah	try . . . the other way
Patrick	like that
Hannah	north pole facing down
Joanna	we tried that
Peter	oh!
Hannah	it stays up!
Patrick	magic!
Peter	let's show the others
Joanna	mad!

Peter	I'll put north pole facing north pole . . . see what happen
Patrick	that's what we just did
Peter	yeah . . . like this . . . look

(The dialogue continues for several minutes longer as the students try different positions for the magnet, and then they begin to formulate an explanation (6.11). There has been no teacher input during the course of the conversation.)

Example 6.11 (Students carrying out activity)

Hannah	can I try that? . . . I know why . . . I know why . . . that's like . . because the north pole is on this side and that north pole's there . . . so they don't stick together
Peter	what like this? yeah
Hannah	yeah see because the north pole on this side . but turn it on the other . . this side like that . . . turn it that way . . yeah
Peter	and it will stick
Hannah	and it will stick because . look . . the north pole's on that side because . .
Peter	the north pole's on that side yeah

Example 6.12 (Introduction of new lexical item)

Teacher: (*referring to reporting session about to begin*)
what are some of the words we are going to use?

(*children offer: magnet, attract, metal, north pole, south pole*)
Teacher: now I'm going to give you another word for what Joseph was trying to say . . . one more scientific word and that is when something doesn't attract . . . some of you were saying it pushes away . . . or slips off . . . so instead of saying the magnet pushes away/ I'm going to give you a new word . . repel . . it actually means to push away from you (*demonstrating with her arm*) so we're going to use words like . . .
(*children again offer associated lexis, and include 'repel'*)

Example 6.13 (Teacher-guided reporting, teacher interacting with Hannah)

STUDENTS	TEACHER
1	try to tell them what you learned . . . OK . . . (*to Hannah*) yes?

	STUDENTS	TEACHER
2	em er I learned that em when you put a magnet . . .	
3		yes
4	(*laughter from Hannah and children as Hannah is attempting to explain without demonstrating with her hands*) when I put/ when you put . . . when you put a magnet . . . on top of a magnet and the north pole poles are . . . . (*7-second pause. Hannah is clearly having difficulty in expressing what she wants to say*)	
5		yes yes you're doing fine . . you put one magnet on top of another . .
6	and and the north poles are together er em the magnet . . . repels the magnet er . . . the magnet and the other magnet . . . sort of floats in the air?	
7		I think that was very well told . . . very well told . . do you have anything to add to that Charlene?

The teacher invites other contributions, and then returns to Hannah. She invites Hannah to describe the experiment again.

Example 6.14 (Teacher-guided reporting, Hannah's second attempt)

	STUDENTS	TEACHER
1		now listen . . now Hannah explain once more . . . all right Hannah . . . excuse me everybody (*regaining class's attention*) . . listen again to her explanation

2   the two north poles are leaning
together and the magnet on the
bottom is repelling the magnet
on top so that the magnet on
the top is sort of . . . floating in
the air

3   so that these two magnets are
<u>repelling</u> each other and . . .
look at the force of it

Example 6.15 (Hannah's written text, which was accompanied by a diagram)

I found it very interesting that when you stuck at least 8 paddle pop sticks in a piece of polystyrene, and then put a magnet with the North and South pole in the oval and put another magnet with the north and south pole on top, the magnet on the bottom will repel the magnet on the top and the magnet on the top would look like it is floating in the air.

The initial small-group activities in the course of which examples 6.10 and 6.11 were produced led, as would be expected, to the use of highly situationally-embedded language. The interrelationship between the immediate visual context, the material action and the language being produced is likely to make this a supportive context for students in the early stages of learning through the medium of their second language. As a starting point then, this context provided a source of comprehensible input for learners and allowed children to develop certain scientific understandings about the topic using familiar everyday language, here the discovery that the position of the poles is significant to the movement of the magnets. A significant point is that students are being given an opportunity to develop this shared understanding *before* they are expected to understand and use more scientific discourse. The small-group work here is the first step in building up the shared understandings out of which later discourse arises.

Both examples 6.10 and 6.11 have many of the characteristics of spontaneous spoken language as it occurs in contexts where there is visual support for meaning. These include several exophoric references (*like that, like this, this side, that way*), which in this context are clear to the listeners. These references, of course, carry meanings which, in the absence of a visual context, must be realized in a different way, and it is precisely this aspect of discourse which later causes Hannah and many of the other students difficulty in the reporting session.

Discourse from this stage also indicates the foregrounding of inter-personal aspects of language: example 6.10 foregrounds social interac-tion rather than information about magnets. As discussed in Chapter 3, language enables speakers to exchange one of two items: goods and ser-vices (including action) or information (Halliday 1985b). Many of the texts produced in the small-group work were composed largely of action rather than information exchanges, and typically contained a large number of imperatives as students directed each other (in this text: *put, let*). In this text too language is used to control action rather than to share information: *see, turn, show, look.* There are also interpersonal adjuncts, indicating affect, such as the expression of attitude and feel-ings (*magic! mad!*). Participants are generally human and frequently thematized; and they relate to the interactants themselves (We *tried that*; *I'll put north pole facing north pole*).

As the discourse progresses, however (example 6.11), individual utterances become longer and more explicit, and this occurs as the stu-dents begin to formulate explanations for what they see (note the logical connectives *so, because*). Interpersonal elements are reduced; there is now a non-human participant (*the north pole*) which is thematized and this, rather than the interactants themselves, becomes the topic of con-versation. Perhaps this is partly the result of the instructions for the task: the teacher's instruction to *try to explain what you see* extended the task from simply 'doing' to 'doing and thinking' (note the use of *explain* rather than, for example, *describe*). An explicit focus on think-ing is an important one in the light of this particular teaching context, where a teacher must balance the need for suitably high levels of cog-nitive learning with learners' relatively low levels of English, and where learning activities aimed at development of the second language must also be linked to cognitive growth. Clearly within these examples there is evidence of children's learning of science: the beginnings of an under-standing of why the magnets are behaving as they are, and attempts to hypothesize about the causal relations involved. Through the kind of exploratory talk which begins to be evident here in the small-group work, 'knowledge is made more publicly accountable and reasoning is more visible' (Wegerif and Mercer 1996, p. 51).

In example 6.12, the teacher introduces a new lexical item to the students, which students are expected to use in the more public context of reporting to others in the following episode. In the next examples (6.13 and 6.14), the teacher and children jointly reconstruct their experiences, producing texts where information is being exchanged and developing common understandings. As Driver suggests in relation to the teaching of science, 'activity by itself is not enough. It is the sense that is made of it that matters' (Driver 1983, p. 49). Lemke writes in a similar vein: 'what the eye "sees" has little enough to do with science or learning. It is the sense we make of what we see, the meaning for us of what we see that matters' (Lemke 1990, p. 146). In these examples the teacher is working with the children to 'make sense' of the activities in which they have been engaged. Wegerif and Mercer suggest that it is through being encouraged and enabled 'to clearly describe events, to account for outcomes and consolidate what they have learned in words' that children are helped to 'understand and gain access to educated discourse' (Wegerif and Mercer 1996, p. 51). Examples 6.13 and 6.14 illustrate one type of situation in which this process can occur.

As already suggested in Chapter 5, the micro-interactions between teacher and students in these teacher-guided reporting sessions show several small but important variations from a traditional IRF pattern. These differences appear to have significant effects on the interaction as a whole. As Cazden points out, 'even small changes [to the more marked patterns of teacher-student interaction] can have considerable cognitive or social significance' (Cazden 1988, p. 53). In examples 6.13 and 6.14, the interactions approximate more closely what occurs in typical mother-tongue adult-child interactions outside of the formal teaching context, suggesting a different orientation by the teacher to talk in the classroom. Often, for example, teachers' questions are framed in ways which do not allow for students to make extended responses (Dillon 1990). Here, by contrast, the teacher begins the exchange by inviting students to relate what they have learned, rather than with a 'known answer' or display question. Thus a context is set up where it is a student, rather than the teacher, who initiates the specific topic of the exchange, and who takes on the role of 'primary knower' (Berry 1981). Although of course the teacher remains in control of the knowledge associated with the overall thematic development of the unit of work, individual exchanges like these locate control temporarily in the student. The effect is to modify relations of power by shifting the location of knowledge onto the student, thereby modifying knowledge asymmetries and typical teacher-student roles. In both classrooms, teacher-guided reporting episodes typically incorporated dialogic patterns of exchange like those in examples 6.13 and 6.14.

As discussed earlier, adult-child mother-tongue interactions in non-pedagogic discourse are characterized by the reciprocity and mutuality of the speaker roles, which lead to longer stretches of discourse in which meaning is jointly constructed. Here the teacher-student interactions are similar in quality. As the first part of this chapter illustrated, the teacher tends to guide students contingently, and while accepting as a valid contribution the information given by the student, simultaneously provides alternative linguistic forms to encode the learner's meaning in more context-appropriate ways. What is also evident here is the reciprocal nature of these dialogic interactions. In the final exchange in example 6.14, the teacher takes up the role of a conversational partner by expanding on what Hannah has said and adding a new element of meaning (*and look at the force of it*). While classroom interactions between teacher and students are very rarely truly symmetrical, this more dialogic teaching achieves a greater degree of symmetry than is the case in traditional teacher-student exchanges. Van Lier makes a useful distinction between symmetry and equality, arguing that even when one participant is more powerful or more knowledgeable, the talk need not necessarily be asymmetrical, if the rights and duties of speaking are more evenly distributed (van Lier 1996). The kind of interactional pattern evident here illustrates how even exchanges which overall retain an IRF flavour can produce more conversational discourse when the teacher scaffolds the interaction rather than instructs directly.

The dialogic pattern that occurs in the context of teaching-guided reporting is significant in relation to Vygotsky's claim that learning occurs with support from those more expert, at the learner's zone of proximal development (Vygotsky 1978), that is, at the outer edges of a learner's current abilities. In example 6.13 it can be assumed that the student has reached her own zone of proximal development, since she hesitates for approximately seven seconds, and can presumably go no further alone. The recasting and support she receives from the teacher (5) then appears to be precisely timed for learning to occur. It is largely in the ability of the teacher to make such contingent responses that the skill of dialogic teaching lies.

The context of teacher-guided reporting here, and the dialogic pattern by which it is realized in these classrooms, also gave students opportunities to produce longer stretches of discourse: their contributions are whole units of meaning which are more written-like than those that occurred in the small-group work. Throughout the reporting sessions, as can be seen by the illustrative examples in this and the following chapter, students regularly produced utterances of four or more clauses in length, which represents a considerable increase over the responses normally associated with the known-answer or display-type teacher questions which often typify the IRF structure. In many cases this required the teacher to increase wait time, and on occasions this was as long as eight seconds. Research suggests that when teachers ask questions of students, they typically wait one second or less for the students to begin a reply, but that when teachers wait for three or more seconds, there are significant changes in student use of language and in the attitudes and expectations of both students and teachers (Rowe 1986). The importance of wait time is likely to be increased for students who are formulating responses in a language they do not fully control. Krashen and Pon (1975 in John-Steiner 1985), describe the self-correcting behaviour of an adult second language learner, who, given sufficient 'processing time' was able to correct almost 95 per cent of her errors. It is also worth pointing out that in the classrooms observed, students did not appear to become uncomfortable or embarrassed by the length of the wait time; on the contrary there were many explicit and enthusiastic bids for turns to offer contributions. What is probably important from the perspective of the learner is that students speaking in this context were able to complete what they wanted to say, whether alone or through interaction with the teacher, and as a result were positioned as successful interactants and learners.

A major difference between examples 6.13; 6.14 and examples 6.10; 6.11 lies in the relative importance of the two major speech functions. Where the earlier examples were largely concerned with the controlling of action, here the business of the text is the exchange of information. While there are still human participants (*I* and *you*), there are many more references to non-human participants and their thematization than in the examples associated with doing the task.

The written text from Hannah's journal (example 6.15) suggests that the interaction between student and teacher provided a significant source of linguistic input for the student which she has taken up and appropriated in her writing. In Hannah's example, which was written without further assistance other than teacher provision of the spelling of *polystyrene*, her interaction with the teacher, and her own second attempt at wording, have influenced both syntax and lexis.

In addition there is also evidence that the reporting sessions influenced not only the interactants themselves but also those who listened to the interactions as part of the larger group. The following example (6.16), also a journal entry, was produced by a student who had not taken part in this particular experiment herself, but who had listened to the interaction between Hannah and the teacher. It echoes this collaboratively constructed discourse.

Example 6.16

> The thing made out of polystyrene with paddle pop sticks, one group put one magnet facing north and another magnet on top facing north as well and they repelled each other. It looked like the top magnet was floating up in the air.

The final example from classroom 1 (example 6.17) occurred after this reporting session and shows the teacher helping students make generalizations on the basis of their earlier experiments. The teacher is standing in front of the blackboard and pointing to a matrix to which the students are responding (Figure 6.3). As the students respond the teacher ticks the appropriate *attract* or *repel* box.

Figure 6.3 Matrix on board

		Attract	Repel
N	S		
S	N		
N	N		
S	S		

Example 6.17

	STUDENTS	TEACHER
1		good . . . what if I try the south pole of this magnet and the north pole of that magnet . . yes Francois come on a sentence
2	Fr: the south pole and the north pole will attract	
3		good boy/ good Francois/ all right and let's try the south pole of this magnet and the south pole of the other magnet . . Stephanie
4	S: the south pole and the south pole will re . . repel	
5		so I would like two ideas that we get from this . . two <u>general</u> ideas what we call <u>generalizations</u> . . . who can give me something that will happen <u>all</u> the time not what just happened to us today but what will happen do you think . . . Gina do you want to try?
6	G: if you put the north pole and the north pole together em that will not . . . . that will repel and if you put the south	

	pole and the south pole together that will repel too	
7		good all right that will <u>always</u> happen so we'll say south pole and south pole . . . ? (*pointing to* *matrix*)
8	Ss (*several*): repel	
9		north pole and north pole . . . ?
10	Ss: repel	
11		all right . . who can give me something else . . Jennifer
12	J: em . . the north pole and the south pole attract	

The students as actors have now disappeared from the discourse, and what is foregrounded is the field of science itself. Students now express what they have learned as a series of generalizations, realized through explicit written-like clauses. The personal recounts of the earlier texts are no longer in evidence, and this final example from classroom 1 represents a further shift from personal recounts to statements of generalized principles.

This set of examples from classroom 1 illustrates how the discourse shifted over the course of five episodes from an initial focus on personal activity, realized through context-embedded everyday talk within the small groups, to more written-like discourse which begins to incorporate some of the register features of more formal scientific writing. The talk with the teacher in the teacher-guided reporting sessions was significant in this process in providing a linguistic bridge from the situationally-embedded talk of the experiential activity to the more explicit discourse of the journal writing. Subsequent talk about generalizations provided a further step towards the public and shared discourse of the scientific topic.

The following set of examples, which come from classroom 2, illustrate a similar process of mode shifting within the discourse of a sequence of episodes.

Examples from classroom 2

The examples from classroom 2 involved a similar set of tasks. The discourse is tracked across a series of eight episodes. In the first example of the sequence (example 6.18) the students are engaged in doing an experiment in small groups (the same experiment as described earlier). The teacher joins the group briefly to check that the students are on task and to find out what they have done (example 6.19). In the next lesson, the students will be asked to report back their findings to the rest of the class, and in preparation for this the teacher asks them, at the beginning of this lesson, to first recall in their groups what had happened. Example 6.20 is an example of this small-group discourse in which students recall for themselves what happened. The teacher joins them briefly (6.21) after which the reporting session begins, and Julianne reports on behalf of the group (6.22). As each group reports, the teacher draws their attention to the similarities in each set of results, and after all the groups have reported on their individual experiments, the teacher asks the children what they can see in common with the results. The set of four examples from 6.23–6.26 illustrate how the teacher begins to build this common framework. At this point, which coincides with the end of a lesson, the students are asked to write down one thing that happened in their own experiment, and a more general statement about the commonalities of the results. This discussion around commonalities, now based on what the students have written, continues in the next lesson (6.27). The students return to work on the written generalizations they had begun at the end of the previous lesson. The writing samples are examples of this revised writing (6.30) and reflect the teacher-student talk of the previous episodes.

Example 6.18

Here a group of four students is experimenting with magnets.

STUDENTS

1   OK (*reads*) 'then place another . . magnet on top of the cradled . magnet/ observe what happens'
2   don't/ put it like that
3   oh! wow! (*loud exclamations as second magnet appears to float above the first*)
4   <u>look</u> at <u>that</u>
5   how'd that happen?
6   oh . . <u>look</u> at <u>that</u>
7   mad
   (*laughter*)
8   look I'm not touching that
9   [** no leave it it's making
10 [hey look at this Andre

11   yeah look
12   look what
13   watch this . . .
14   oh mad
15   turn it over the other side and it won't stick . .

This example shows similar language features as example 6.10 in classroom 1. Interpersonal aspects of language are foregrounded: imperatives are thematized (turns 2, 4, 6, 8, 9, 10, 11, 12, 13) and affect expressed (turns 3, 7, 14). There is little within the text that would identify its field, and, like example 6.17, the exchanges centre around the controlling of action rather than the giving of information. Participants are human – *I, you, Andre* – and there is little evidence of explicit reasoning or the use of 'exploratory talk' (Wegerif and Mercer 1996) at this point.

Example 6.19

The group is then joined by the teacher.

	STUDENTS	TEACHER
1		so when you had the poles that way . . what's happened there . . . .
2	em we turned the magnet over and . . we . the magnet didn't stick but it stuck to the	
3		so have you done it both ways?
4	yes Miss	
5	yes Miss	
6		all right you've done it both ways
7	yeah [we'll write	[so you're recording that one . . . . and what happened the other way?
8	the other way make it kept up	
9		can you turn it round for me and show me what it looks like/ I missed that I didn't see that
10	got it/ the one the one at the bottom/ turn it over	

11	it's not touching it	
12		let me have a look . . . . . . what's happening there/ can you describe that
13	em cos they're not touching each other	
14		the magnets aren't touching . right so there's some sort of space in between . . .
15	the the magnets there's one magnet here and when the the em power . comes down and gets powerful it it . . stays on the/ on the	
16		so what's this magnet trying to do? to that one?
17	it's trying to lift it up	
18		OK it's attracting isn't it/ it's not repelling like it did the other way . sorry to interrupt you . just wanted to hear what you've done

The addition of the teacher to the group changes the nature of the discourse. The function of the exchanges is now not to control action, but for the teacher to ask for and the students to give information. The nature of the teacher's questions – *what's happening there? can you explain that? can you describe that?* – requires students to produce longer stretches of talk than in the previous text, and now their responses incorporate complete clauses. The teacher's requests for information result in talk which begins to reconstruct the events for the benefit of a listener who had not shared them. This interaction provides a rehearsal for what follows in a later episode, when students will be asked to explain to the class as a whole the results of their own experiments.

Example 6.20

In the following lesson, and prior to reporting back to the class, the groups were given time to recall what happened in their experiments, in preparation for sharing this with the whole class. The teacher first explained to the class that the groups needed to remember that other students had not done the same things as they had, and so each group needed to be very precise in the language they used:

Teacher:
We all did different experiments so we don't know the results/ we only know the results of one experiment/ so the language you choose is going to be very clear and precise because people won't know what was going on.

Following on from this, the students 'rehearsed' in their groups how they would report on their experiment:

1	Emily	we have to talk about what we did last time and what were the results . . . .
2	Milad	we got em . . we got a . thing like . . this . . pu- we got paddle pop sticks and we got
3	Maroun	we [put them in a pot
4	Milad	and [have to try and put
5	Julianne	wasn't in a pot/ it's like a foam . . .
6	Milad	[a foam
7	Emily	[a block of foam
8	Julianne	and we put it
9	Emily	we put paddle pops around it . the foam and then we put the magnet in it =
10	Julianne	[and then we got
11	Emily	= [and then we got another magnet and put it on top . and it wasn't touching the other magnet . Maroun your go
12	Maroun	and when we turned it the other way . . it didn't stick . . . because . . . because .
13	Julianne	because?

This text is discussed in Chapter 8 within a larger section of discourse, thus only brief comments are included here. What characterizes this text, and those produced by other groups in this activity, is the jointly constructed nature of the discourse, evident in the overlapping speech and the completion of others' contributions. Through this process of joint construction wording was gradually refined towards more explicit and written-like language, the beginnings of which can be seen here. This example suggests the pedagogical value of this kind of discourse, in which both language and science learning are embodied, and where there is a focus not only on the message to be communicated, but on the form by which it is constructed. Telling others what they know allows learners to recognize the gaps in their own understanding, and pushes them to clarify thinking and to engage in what Chang and Wells refer to as 'literate talk' (Chang and Wells 1988).

In ESL classrooms there needs to be some conscious thought given to the ways that such group reflection activities can happen, not through functionally empty drills where language is simply rehearsed, but in the context of a curriculum activity that engages students in cognitively challenging ways. In this reflection activity the discourse was the result of a real and shared purpose for the students, who knew that one or more of them would be expected to share their learning with other members of the class, in the role of experts in relation to their peers, and with the expectation that what they chose to say would be heard as new information by their audience. The comment by one of the students in 6.21 below – *can we have another practice* – suggests that the students also valued the opportunity to talk in this way.

It is therefore not in a discussion activity per se in which the pedagogical usefulness of such discourse can be said to lie. Both in terms of a linguistic analysis, and in terms of classroom planning, the pedagogical significance of a learning activity needs to be located in its place within the broader context of the sequence of learning activities and ongoing classroom discourse, and viewed in the light of its communicative purpose.

Example 6.21

This example follows on from 6.20, when the teacher joined the group.

	STUDENTS	TEACHER
1		how did we go?
2	we finish	
3		OK so you've said/ described
	yep	what you <u>did</u> and you've
		described what your results were
4	yes Miss	

5		OK/ you've remembered that our language has to be really precise because the other children have got to try and get a picture in their mind of what you did
6	Miss can we have another practice?	
7		you certainly can . . .

Here the teacher's initial contribution to the discourse is not to do with the construction of science knowledge but with the group work procedures the students have followed, and in particular, with the language they are using. Turn 5 represents a field switch (illustrating the notion of different fields discussed in Chapter 5). The primary field at this point is language; the metalinguistic talk here refers back to discussion earlier in the lesson about how speakers need to be precise enough in their talk to make sense to an audience who has not shared in the experience being described. In her earlier talk with the group (example 6.19), the teacher's probing questions helped students produce a more explicit text. Here, in turn 5, her purpose is similar, but she uses metalinguistic talk to fulfil it. Whereas in the earlier example her focus is language *use*, knowing how to use language, here her focus is language *usage*, knowing about language. It is a further example of how tasks embodying both a content and form focus provide a context for talking *about* language.

Example 6.22

Here Julianne (whose group was featured in the two previous examples) is reporting back to the rest of the class.

	STUDENT	TEACHER
1		OK/ what did you do . .
2	J: what's that called (*pointing to polystyrene*)	
3		what's that/ that's polystyrene/ foam is another word
4	J: we put paddle pops around the foam and then we got a	

159

magnet and we put it in . and
we got another magnet and we
put it on top but it wasn't
touching the other magnet . and
then when we turned it around .
it attach together/ the two
magnets . and when we put on
the side they em attach together

5   OK so when you say the first
time/ you said that you put the
magnet and it wasn't attached
or it didn't attract to the other
magnet/ what was happening/
at that time/ the first time . . you
put the magnet in the cradle

6   J: it was em on the top of the
other magnet/ it wasn't
touching it . . .

7   so was it just sitting on top of it
     J: <u>no</u>   <u>directly on</u> top?

8   J: it was just like on top of it
like that
(*demonstrating with her hands*)

9   so it was like floating above it?/
OK that's interesting all right/
that's what happened the first/
tell us what you did then

10   J: we turned it around and they
got stuck together

11   so you turned/ which magnet
did you turn around?

12   J: em the one that was on the
top

13   OK and then what happened

14   J: it touched it

15   OK it attracted . . . interesting/
thanks Julianne

Julianne presents her recount almost without hesitation (perhaps the result of the joint construction of the recount illustrated in examples 6.20), but as in example 6.2, the teacher chooses to unpack the account into several stages: *so when you say . . .* (5); *so was it just . . .* (7); *so it was like floating . . .* (9); *so which magnet . . .* (11); *and then what happened* (13). The teacher's responses stay close to Julianne's meaning: for example, *so* provides a cohesive link within each exchange, and reflects the semantic link between student and teacher wording. But from the point of view of communicative need, this probing seems redundant, since the teacher clearly understands the student. Here for example the student's initial wording – *it wasn't touching the other magnet* – seems to be unnecessarily problematized by the teacher: *so what was happening*. The student repeats what she said earlier: *it was on top of the other magnet, it wasn't touching it*. Again the teacher clarifies apparently unnecessarily: *so was it just sitting on top of it*, to which the student responds by demonstrating the movement with her hands: *it was like on top*. This is perhaps the cue that the teacher is waiting for which allows her to draw out from the discourse what she sees as significant: she recasts (*it was like floating above it*) with a final comment pointing to the significance of this in the experimental procedure as a whole: *that's what happened first*. Only at this point does she allow the discourse to move on: *tell us what you did then*. There is, then, considerable communicative redundancy in this piece of discourse. But while much of this teacher-talk seems redundant, most classroom talk has a pedagogical as well as a communicative purpose. The breaking down of the retelling by the teacher gives the student a space to reformulate the wording, which mediates the later and more difficult task of writing about it. While ostensibly a conversation between teacher and student, it is also of course, like many teacher-student conversations, public speech which is meant to be heard by the whole class: it is conversation as performance. The teacher's role here is to control the pedagogical direction of the discourse. While her responses follow on from the meanings the student has initiated, the teacher inserts into the discourse her own contribution about what is significant.

In the following four examples (6.23–6.26), the teacher and students together begin to build a common framework from the children's individual experiences, into which individual contributions are drawn.

Example 6.23

T: have you started to think about that . for the first experiment . when we had the two lying down . . . one in front of the other . . . they/ they attached to one side but when . the magnet was turned around . it didn't attract or it didn't attach . . Fabiola said the same thing in her experiment . . . one pole was attracted . to the one pole . on the floor but when it turned around it didn't/ OK interesting . the same group who did that was Duncan's group was it/ Duncan would you like to tell us your results? were they . similar . or did you find out anything different?

S: the same

Example 6.24

T: thank you Andre . . so same results again as the other group . . . . when it was facing one way you couldn't get it to . attract to the other magnet/ but as soon as the magnet was turned around . it attracted straight away . .

Example 6.25

T: that's the same/ would you say that they were the same results as the other group?

S: yes

Example 6.26

	STUDENTS	TEACHER
1		OK thank you . . . three experiments and you all did very well/ three experiments/ three experiments . . . . . and if you'd listened carefully . . . you could find that there was
	ohh (*several Ss bidding for turns*)	something [in common . . . with the results
2	ohh	[of all three experiments
3	oh Miss Miss	
4	Miss	
5		there's something in common if you listened to the results and the descriptions . . that were used . and that was similar in all . three . experiments . Janet would you like to tell us what you think

6   em Miss when they first put
the magnet em on one side . .
em it attracted . em repelled . .
and the next time they did it
they put the magnet on the
other side and some of the
repel/ the * that did it the first
time it repelled em it attracted
next

In this group of examples the teacher begins to guide students to understand the significance of what they have been doing, ensuring that key understandings are jointly shared. Throughout this episode the teacher continues to acknowledge the expertize of the groups and name them as the source of the information: *Fabiola said the same thing in her group*. At the same time she inserts into the discourse what she wishes the students to see as significant:

> when we had the two (magnets) lying down . . . they attached to one side but when the magnet was turned around it didn't attract (6.23)

> when it was facing one way you couldn't get it to attract but as soon as the magnet was turned around it attracted straight away (6.24)

Human participants are beginning to be absent from the text, and the actor – the doer of the experiment – is left implicit in the passive form of the verb. The following pairs of examples from the same episode provide further examples of the mode shift that is evident in the discourse as a whole. Compare, for example, the change of clause theme, and consequent recoding of the processes, as a result of the mode shift from the first to the second text in each pair.

Individual student reporting on the group's findings
then when we turned it around it attach together
Later, teacher summarizing results
(as soon as) the magnet was turned around it attracted

Individual student reporting on the group's findings
then we moved one to the other side and then the other one was sort of
    pushing it away and we turned it around . . . and when you turned
    around the other it stuck to the other one
Later, teacher summarizing results
they attached to one side but when the magnet was turned around it didn't
    attract

There are clear implications here for the importance not only of making sense of *individual* activity, but also of placing individual recodings of personal experience into a larger framework of meaning. In the absence of this framework, individual discovery may, in cognitive terms, lead nowhere. As Edwards and Mercer suggest:

> when teachers go out of their way to avoid offering to pupils help in making sense . . . of experiences, the consequences may be that the usefulness of those experiences is lost.

(Edwards and Mercer 1987, p. 169)

The following example (6.27), which occurred in the following lesson, continues the discussion around commonalities, and shows the students beginning to make generalizations about the properties of magnets.

Example 6.27 (Constructing generalizations)

	STUDENTS	TEACHER
1	B: when you press two magnets together it attach	
2		so if I place that (*demonstrating*) to that (*demonstrating*) it attracts/ what about if I put that one (*reversing the poles of one magnet*)
3	B: when you turn one magnet around it doesn't attach together but/ cos it turns around by itself	
4	A: if you turn the circle around it won't attach (*referring to mark on magnet indicating north*)	
5		it won't attach . . if I turn that circle because . why
6	A: because Miss they're both/ like/ the north	

Later in the same discussion

14	An: if you put the south and north together then em they will	

	. . attach but if you put north and north or south and south together . . they will not attract	
15		so if the poles are the same . . they will repel however if the poles are different . they will attract/ well done/ thank you/ exactly what happened/ Robert?
16	R: the north pole and the south pole . . attract . whereas the north pole and north pole repels	
17		well done/ that's exactly what happened/ you joined those two together didn't you/ *whereas*/ some people used different sentences/ let's try again/ let's listen to it again
18	R: the north pole and the south pole attract whereas the north pole and the north pole repels	
19		like poles repel (*nods to Charbel from another group*)
20	C: Miss it's something like Robert's	
21		that's OK if it's similar that's because we got the same results
22	C: em the north pole and the south pole attract each other whereas the north pole and the other north pole repels	
23		well done/ that's exactly what happens/ you used *whereas*/ the same connective there/ well done

In the earlier part of this discussion the teacher continues to use the science materials to visually represent the meanings to the students, as she did when helping them to understand written instructions. Here the action of reversing one of the magnets, which she repeats, makes salient to the students the process she wishes them to think about (2). The demonstration elicits from Andre an explanation (4, 6), which later forms the basis of the scientific principle involved, which Andrew begins to formulate (14) and which is developed by other students (16, 22). Turns 14 and 15 provide a further illustration of the teacher providing the students with alternative ways of expressing the same semantic relations (Lemke 1990). Andrew states the scientific principle in one way, the teacher in another. She signals to the students the equivalence between the two versions by connecting them with *so*, and by the closing comment *exactly what happened*.

Again we see how metalinguistic knowledge can be developed in tandem with knowledge about science. When Robert uses the conjunction *whereas* (16), the teacher draws the students' attention to the fact that he *has joined those two [sentences] together whereas some people used two different sentences*. She asks him to repeat what he has said, thus focusing explicitly on language form. The teacher then returns to a focus on science and recasts what Robert has said as *like poles repel* (19). Charbel is nominated to speak but appears reticent because *it's something like Robert's* to which the teacher responds by reminding him that *we got the same results*, thereby also reminding the students of the point of the discussion they are involved in, namely to identify the common principle in the experiments. The teacher comments again on the use of *whereas*, this time referring to it metalinguistically as *the same connective*. Note that this connective is taken up by one of the students in the writing that followed this discussion (see below, 6.28).

Following the discussion the children wrote in their journals. Four examples are included here. For the purpose of comparison, and in order to illustrate how the discourse has shifted from personal recount to generalized principles, examples which the children had written earlier (immediately after they had completed their experiments) are also included.

Example 6.28

	Earlier text	Text after discussion
Julianne	The magnet which we put next didn't touch the other magnet. When we turned it over it stucked on the other.	All magnets have a side which repels and a side which attracts. Magnets don't stick if you put north with a north or south and a south

but if you put a south with a
north they stick.

| Emily | The magnet which we put over the cradled magnet was hanging in the cradle. When we turned the magnet over it stuck to the other magnet. | Magnets have two poles. A north pole and a south pole. If we put the south pole with the north pole they stick together. When you put N with N or S with S they repel. |
| Andre | The bar that was on the string was trying to find the pole that atract the one that was on the ground (*sic*) | The north pole and the south pole atch together wher as the north pole with the outher north pole repels (*sic*) |

Each pair of examples mirrors the movement which has occurred in the ongoing spoken discourse, from personal recount to a generalized principle. Julianne's two examples show this development clearly: the first is a personal recount and the second begins to approximate a report. Human participants are included in the first text, and appear as themes. Participants, both human and non-human, are specific, and the text is sequenced temporally as would be expected in a recount: *next, when*. Everyday rather than scientific terms are used: *didn't touch, stucked*. The second text has no temporal sequence; the participants are generic (if *you* is read in the generic sense of *one*) and the non-human participants are the major themes of the clause complex: *all magnets, magnets*. The processes are coded appropriately as *attract* and *repel* (although this is not consistent).

Emily's first text is also a sequenced recount. There is little specific field lexis, with the magnets being described as *hanging* and *stuck*. Her second text begins with a generalization about magnets, and there is a clear attempt to sequence the information as an explanation. Most of the text participants are non-human and generic (note that *we* and *you* can be read as generic), and some appropriate field lexis is evident: *north pole, south pole, repel*.

Andre's two examples also reflect a mode shift. Though the first text does not contain himself as an actor, *the bar on the ground* is represented as actor, and the process is essentially a human one: *trying to find*. The second text is a generalization. It is of interest too because the use of *wher as* (*whereas*) shows evidence of uptake from the previous discussion. Andre was seen by his teacher as a fairly low level student in terms of English language development, and his teacher commented that she would not have expected him to have used this comparatively sophisticated language. Although no generalization can be made from this single example, it seems likely that Andre's text was influenced by other students' interactions with the teacher that he had listened to.

While all the final written examples indicate some development of the subject register, it cannot of course be argued that this is solely the effect of the interactions in which the students had been engaged: causality cannot be assigned to a single pedagogic component. However, the written texts should be seen as reflecting the mode shift towards a more scientific register that is characteristic of this series of episodes as a whole. They are congruent with the pedagogical direction that the discourse is taking, and exemplify how the particular choice by the teacher of each of the writing tasks was in itself part of the context of the discourse. The written texts also reflect the nature of the writing task itself: as Halliday (1978, 1984) argues, language is the way it is because of what it does. The first of each of the students' texts was written as a recording of the experiment they had just completed, and the teacher had pointed out that the purpose of this was to help students remember what they had done the following week. The recordings were to be 'as accurate as possible'. With this purpose, it would be likely that students would produce a text with the characteristics of a recount. The second text of the pair, however, came after the teacher-guided reporting, and the task for the students was to write a statement or generalization from the experiments.

Thus while direct causality between teacher-student interactions and the written texts cannot be claimed, it appears likely that the students' written texts were influenced by their interactions with the teacher. The written texts are embedded in the discourse in which they had taken part, and it would appear unlikely that such writing would have been produced *without* the discourse which led up to and surrounded it. Talk with the teacher provided a bridge into new forms of language. Writing of the development of children's understanding of writing, Wells writes:

> this is most likely to occur when activities are carried out in collaboration with the teacher or other children, in which the new, synoptic mode of construing experience is related to the more familiar, dynamic mode through talk that *moves back and forth between the two modes, building bridges between them.*
>
> (Wells 1994, p. 82, italics added)

Implications for pedagogy: mode shifting and learning

The sequences of texts discussed have shown how the discourse in the two classrooms moved from situationally-embedded talk towards the more formal and public discourse of school science. With the help of the teacher, particularly in those episodes which incorporated teacher-guided reporting, the discourse is continuously refashioned to incorporate more of the features of written language. The talk in the teacher-guided reporting episodes has many of the characteristics of written discourse, attributes such as explicitness, connectivity and coherence and justification, the kind of talk described by Wells as 'literate talk' (Chang and Wells 1988). The process of recasting by the teacher supported the students in using literate talk to give clear descriptions, develop arguments and give explanations, and ultimately to produce successful written texts. In this process we have seen how students' individual ideas and ways of knowing are linked to a larger framework of meaning, and the voice of the individual begins to shift towards the public discourse of the discipline. Talk with the teacher functions as a bridge into this more written-like mode.

The discourse of both classrooms was characterized by two features, both of which were the result of the pedagogical practices of the teacher: the presence of what I have termed 'message abundancy' and the production of hybrid discourses. We have seen how message abundancy was achieved through mode shifts, involving shifts between spoken and written language and shifts between familiar and technical language, and through the integration of other semiotic systems. We have also seen how many of the teacher-student interactions involved register-meshing, where the familiar and everyday language of the students was blended with the more academic and technical language of the curriculum. This blending, I have suggested, can also be seen as a blending at a micro-level, of Bernstein's horizontal and vertical discourses. The presence of message abundancy and the construction of blended discourses appear significant in creating discourse contexts which are enabling of both second language learning and curriculum learning, and help to define an 'effective' ESL classroom.

The analysis has foregrounded the intertextuality of classroom events. In Lemke's words, 'everything makes sense only against the background of other things like it' (Lemke 1990, p. 204). In these classrooms, the discourse of each new episode was constructed by teacher and students out of the context of previous and familiar thematic patterns of semantic relationships, and 'heard' within this context. The context at any point in time both produced and then was subsequently changed by each new episode. Thus the discourse of each new episode contains traces of earlier voices; as Bakhtin and others have suggested, words always carry with them some of the meanings of their earlier users (Bakhtin 1981; Maybin 1994). As Mercer comments, 'the talk itself creates its own context; what we say at one time in a conversation creates the foundation for meanings in the talk which follows' (Mercer 1995, p. 68). Edwards and Furlong similarly suggest:

> Talk is not one distinct item after another. It involves what has been
> called 'conditional relevance': the meaning of an utterance arises
> partly from something else that has been (or will be) said, perhaps
> some distance away in the interaction.
>
> (Edwards and Furlong 1978, p. 41)

In this sense, content and meaning are not givens but 'are negotiated and renegotiated in the face-to-face interactions among members of a group at particular points in time' (Floriani 1993, p. 255). We have seen how these individual interactional 'histories' are first realized in external and scaffolded dialogue, and then later appropriated by individual learners for their own thinking and learning. The long conversation thus becomes a personal resource for learners, and new learning and language is pegged to what is known and familiar.

The dynamic perspective on context which this notion of intertextuality suggests puts learners at the heart of the learning process, by acknowledging what is for them a changing reality: participants within a sequence of events have a different sense of what and how things mean at different points in time. As we have seen in this chapter, the creation of a shared communicative space, based upon the participants' common knowledge and shared aims, allows teacher and students together to negotiate their way through a particular activity, and through this process to create further shared understandings. You will recall from Chapter 2 that Mercer refers to this shared space as an intermental development zone. The creation of this IDZ requires the teacher to be able to recognize how things mean to students at a particular point in time, to be able to stand outside her own adult thematic framework and history, to 'read' the context through the eyes of her students. This more dynamic view of context shows more clearly its significance for language learning: the 'long conversation' facilitates students' understanding and use of new forms of language and thematic structures. As suggested earlier, an understanding of the dynamic nature of context also suggests a much richer notion of what constitutes 'comprehensible input'.

Such a view of context clearly extends far beyond the notion of a static, synoptic view of context as 'setting'. As Mercer points out:

> 'context' is not simply those things that exist around the talk, the
> physical objects and so on; it is those things beyond the words being
> spoken which contribute to the meaning of the talk.
>
> (Mercer 1995, p. 68)

Classroom discourse cannot therefore be fully understood except as a single long conversation, or more precisely, a long conversation which is at the same time interrelated with other semiotic systems and with learners' personal understandings of the story to date. In this sense, every piece of language only 'means' in terms of the ongoing story known and shared by the classroom community. An understanding and analysis of the local moments of learning thus requires a recognition of how they have been influenced by prior events, contexts and texts.

A number of pedagogical implications arise from the discussions in this chapter. First, there are implications for the structuring and sequencing of learning activities in content-based programmes: teaching programmes need to be considered in terms of how far they have provided sufficient contextualization (in its broadest sense) for students to understand, and make use of, new curriculum content, and the language forms by which it is realized.

A further implication relates to the value of content-based teaching. The existence of the long conversation and the use of language for authentic purposes, such as reporting to others, was largely due to the fact that English was the medium for learning other things, namely science. In contrast, in classes where the primary aim is the learning of language itself, contexts often have to be 'invented', and the purposes for using language, and its field or content, exist only through this invented context (for example, a communicative language game where students must imagine they are marooned on an island, and must come to a consensus about what things they need to survive). These invented contexts may provide opportunities for the practising of specific language structures, but, if taken as isolated activities, they do not have the potential to create the dynamic contexts in which language is part of an ongoing conversation around the learning of other things. Without this ongoing conversation, learners are effectively robbed of a potential resource which could support them in understanding unfamiliar language and producing new texts. By contrast, the examples in this chapter show how the language the learners produced had embedded within it traces of previous events and processes that helped shape its existence; such traces indicate how these prior events serve as a resource for language development. Perhaps the language learning potential of the long conversation is one of the strongest arguments for content-based language learning for ESL children, especially when that content is the mainstream curriculum itself (the proviso here being that the teacher is sufficiently knowledgeable about language to understand and make use of the potential of the curriculum for language learning).

Also from a pedagogical perspective, the examples illustrate how different episodes create very different contexts for language use and how these contexts result in very different language outcomes. Mention was made in Chapter 3 of Saville-Troike's study, which showed that communicative activities and social interaction between students may not alone be sufficient to develop English language and academic skills.

Texts produced in the experiential group work suggest that this is not a surprising finding – subject specific language is simply not necessary for communication between the interactants; what was most important to the participants was social communication. In programme-planning consideration must therefore be given to the *probability* of the target language actually being used in particular activities. The mere use of scientific materials does not guarantee that scientific lexis will be used; on the contrary, the use of such materials in a face-to-face context is likely to obviate the need for it. Thus task design must take account of the relationship between text and context. For children learning curriculum content through the medium of their second language, it is important to consider whether action or information exchanges are most likely to be foregrounded in a particular task; how explicit and field-specific the discourse needs to be for the purpose of the task; and what opportunities there are for students to use more explicit spoken discourse – literate talk – prior to related writing tasks.

Finally, we can contrast what occurred in these classrooms to more traditional ESL and EFL programmes. Frequently in such programmes, a learning sequence begins with some formal study of grammar or vocabulary, which is then followed by opportunities to practise the target language, in increasingly less teacher-controlled contexts. By comparison with this approach, students here moved *towards* the target text, and little explicit attempt was made to present the more formal register ahead of the students' personal understandings of the science being taught: most attention to language was given at later rather than earlier stages of learning. And as suggested earlier, in many ESL/EFL programmes context is equated with setting. In contrast, as we have seen, context in a content-based classroom is a dynamic one in which meanings are made in the light of ongoing and jointly constructed and reconstructed understandings.

7 The teachers: teaching as mediation

Introduction

As we saw in Chapter 2, the teacher's role has been characterized in a variety of ways, depending on particular pedagogical orientations which differ largely in the extent to which the teacher is seen as retaining primary control over the discourse of the classroom. Pedagogical practice has been described, and frequently polarized, as either 'teacher-centred' or 'student-centred'. Such terms, however, are potentially problematic in that they present classroom practice, and teachers' roles, as uniformly constant and unvarying. Moreover, as Thorne (2004, p. 52) suggests in his discussion of activity theory, analyses based on a 'centred' conception of the classroom 'may put into shadow the important roles that "non-centred" actors play in educational settings' and set up 'blind spots' which work against an understanding of the teaching and learning process. The reality of the classroom is very much more complex than a 'centred' approach would suggest: the orientation of the teacher to the students, conversations between students, the other semiotic systems and artefacts at play in the classroom (such as mathematical symbols, board work, charts, graphs and pictures) and the curriculum itself, all mediate student learning. In addition, as the previous chapter demonstrated, if a sequence of episodes is examined they vary considerably from each other in the degree to which they could be characterized as student-centred or teacher-controlled.

Avoiding such one-dimensional and centred descriptions of pedagogy requires an alternative paradigm for considering the role of the teacher. As Maybin puts it, what is needed is:

> a model of the learning process which can accommodate the teacher as active participant (as opposed, for example, to a custodian of stimulating environments) and which, moreover, offers teachers a possible conceptual escape from the tired debate about 'traditional versus progressive' pedagogies.
>
> (Maybin *et al* 1992, p. 187)

This chapter conceptualizes the role of the teacher in student learning as one of mediation. Mediation is a familiar concept in social contexts: a lawyer, for example, mediates between a client's account of an event and the language principles and categories of the legal world of the court (Maley *et al* 1995). Mediation of this kind can broadly be described as occurring in situations characterized by difference, difficulty or social distance (Baynham 1993, 2000). Such characteristics are inherent in most teacher-student relationships, since in the great majority of school classrooms there is considerable linguistic and conceptual distance between teacher and students, and this is especially so when teacher and students do not share the same language, assumptions and life experiences. As in other forms of social mediation, mediation by the teacher, realized through classroom discourse, links an individual learner with the broader social world, and builds bridges between two discourses.

Mediation is central to sociocultural theory. Vygotskian theory asserts that humans do not directly act upon the world but that actions are mediated through social and cultural semiotic tools and artefacts. In the school context, semiotic tools include technological systems, numeracy and visual arts and, the most important tool of all, language. In the classroom context the process of mediation involves the cognitive and linguistic socialization of students, as they are initiated by their teachers into the common knowledge which comprises educational discourse (Edwards and Mercer 1987). Webster *et al* define mediation quite specifically as 'helping students to construct events in terms they understand' (Webster *et al* 1996, p. 28), by means of using students' personal experiences to make sense of broader phenomena. As Chapter 2 discussed, a significant aspect of mediated learning is the collaboration between expert and novice, whereby adults can help students accomplish tasks, (and we can include here ways of using language), which they would be unable to achieve alone. In Wells' words:

> Spoken discourse has an essential role to play in mediating the pupil's *apprenticeship* into the discipline, both as a medium in which to respond to and prepare for work on written texts and . . . as an opportunity to 'talking their way in' (Halliday 1975) to ways of making sense of new information . . . in forms that, *with the assistance provided by the teacher*, gradually incorporate the essential features of the discourse of the particular discipline.
>
> (Wells 1992, p. 291, italics added)

Central to a view of teaching as mediation, then, is the recognition that both language and content learning depend on the nature of the dialogue between teacher and students, the role that teachers play in the construction of discourse, and the specific assistance that the teacher gives to students in their role as apprentices in the subject learning.

In construing teaching as mediation, the nature of that assistance must be considered. In this book I have referred to this assistance in learning as 'scaffolding'. Interactional scaffolding is an outward manifestation of mediation in action, and its realization in practice. In short, it is a significant means by which mediation occurs, while its effect is intended to extend the learner's ZPD.

The metaphor of 'scaffolding' has been used by educators in the field of both mother tongue and second language to describe the nature of assisted performance, largely instantiated through dialogue (Cazden 1988; Hammond and Gibbons 2005; Lee and Smagorinsky 2000; Maybin *et al* 1992; Mercer 1995; Ohta 2000; Tabak 2004; Webster *et al* 1996; Wells 1999a). The term was originally used by Wood, Bruner and Ross (1976) in their examination of parent tutoring in the early years. In the classroom it can be defined as the temporary, but essential, assistance which helps apprentice learners into new skills, concepts or levels of understanding (Maybin *et al* 1992, p. 186). Webster *et al* (1996) suggest that rather than pedagogical tasks per se, it is the nature of the scaffolding within them that mediates understanding, and like Wells, Mercer and others see this as largely instantiated through the dialogue between teacher and students. Ohta has commented, however, that 'the interactional mechanisms involved in the obtaining or providing of assistance during language learning tasks have been little examined' (Ohta 2000). This chapter examines some of these mechanisms.

Maybin *et al* suggest two criteria for determining whether a particular example of help can be portrayed as scaffolding: there must be evidence of a learner successfully completing the task with the teacher's help, and evidence of the learner having achieved a greater level of independent competence as a result of the scaffolding experience. From the teacher's perspective the aim in the scaffolding process is ultimately to 'hand over' knowledge and control to the students. Central to the notion of scaffolding, then, is that it is increased or withdrawn according to the developing competence of the learner (Mercer 1995).

Webster *et al* suggest that scaffolding provides a metaphor for the *quality* of teacher intervention in learning, again meaning more than just help to accomplish a task. It is aimed at a new level of student competence achieved through teacher support of student activities and problem-solving, but without the teacher taking over, and actively assists learners to construct their own understandings (Webster *et al* 1996). Scaffolding, which they also term 'dialogic teaching', is only effective when the teacher has a thorough knowledge of both the starting point of the learner, and of the field of enquiry, so that the teacher is able to explore the best ways of achieving the aims of the teaching programme in relation to students' starting points. Thus what kind of help

175

is given, and how, is dependent on the situational context of the task, not on a hypothesized psychological 'level' of the students.

While every instance of scaffolding is by its nature a highly contextualized and situated phenomenon, the examples that follow illustrate two defining and underpinning principles of scaffolding which distinguish it from the more general notion of 'help'. First, they show how scaffolding is essentially a process of connection put in place by the teacher: it is a connection between the student (in terms of their contribution to the discourse), the task in which they are involved (including the task of participating in the conversation) and the discourse and knowledge of the broader curriculum. This bridge-building between student, task and curriculum is a common factor across all the illustrative examples in this chapter. Second, the examples illustrate how the process of scaffolding is focused on helping learners develop the cognitive and linguistic resources which they can later use for their own purposes in new contexts. In other words, scaffolding is oriented towards showing students *how* to do (or think or say), rather than *what* to do, think or say.

The illustrative texts have been selected not only because their interactional patterns and pedagogical purpose occur frequently in the data, but also because each instance offers a particular insight into the complex and situated nature of scaffolding. They appear to meet the criteria for effective scaffolding outlined earlier, in that they are aimed at enabling learners to achieve an aspect of language use, or grasp a particular conceptual understanding, which they are not yet able to do independently. In most cases, there is also evidence of this successful achievement as a result of the scaffolding. Of significance also is that the texts show how teachers can actively support learning without recourse to heavily directed instruction, and also without recourse to the deliberately non-directive strategies that have at times been associated with 'discovery' learning and extreme progressive approaches.

The analysis of a particular teaching event needs to take into account its situatedness and its pedagogical purpose, and needs to be 'read' within the particular stage of a teaching-learning sequence. For this reason, the organization of the illustrative examples follows the structure of the macrogenre identified in Chapter 5. You will recall that the sequence of learning and teaching activities which recurred within the programme was made up of four to five stages: *review/recap and orientation; setting up of new task; carrying out task; reflection on task; written work*, with stages 2–5 being broadly mapped onto the construct of the mode continuum[1]. The illustrative examples that follow are taken from each of these stages in turn. Reflecting the notion of the ZPD, they illustrate the 'Janus'-like quality (see below) of the discourse that results when teachers take account of both the current levels of an individual learner and the public discourse of the curriculum subject. They demonstrate how a teacher may

> engage in the co-construction of meanings with individual learners in ways that are responsive both to the particular meanings that the learners are *currently* making and also to the larger vision of the meanings that they *will need to be able to make* in order to become productive and creative members of the wider culture.
>
> (Wells 1995, p. 239, my italics)

Illustrative examples: mediating through scaffolding

Stage 1: Review and orientation

The ZPD suggests that if scaffolding is to be effective, then any new learning needs to be located in students' prior experiences. Chapter 6 demonstrated how each new episode was a recontextualization of the one before, which in turn became the prior experience for interpreting the next. The two examples included here take a close-up view on this, illustrating how the foregrounding of prior experiences become the building blocks of new learning. As Wong-Fillmore (1985) points out:

> If students remember what they did or learned on the earlier occasion, the prior experience becomes a context for interpreting the new experience . . . prior experiences serve as the contexts within which the language being used is to be understood.
>
> (Wong-Fillmore 1985, p. 31)

The mediating role of the teacher at this orientation stage is largely concerned with providing what Wong-Fillmore refers to as an anchor for new learning. At the beginning of a new topic teachers frequently elicited from students what they already knew in order to develop a shared basis for beginning the unit. In the examples that follow, the teacher's mediation provides through the discourse a bridge between the students' classroom experiences of the topic to date and the learning objectives of the next task, eliciting from them what they have learned so far, or what they did in the last lesson. These texts often have what van Lier refers to as a 'Janus' quality, both reflecting on what is past and pointing the way to what is to come: you will recall they are signalled in the episode summaries by the phrase *recap/review and set up* (for example see 2:10, 15, 21, 27, 29, 32, 36, where in every case they occur at the beginning of a new lesson). In this way, new learning and new language are constantly located within current understandings. Example 7.1 illustrates this review function.

Example 7.1 A picture in your mind of what we did on Monday

(2:21)

In the previous lesson three days earlier, the students had worked in groups to carry out experiments demonstrating magnetic attraction and repulsion. Here the teacher is reviewing what happened.

	STUDENTS	TEACHER
1		today/ well first of all let's . . connect ourselves back to last lesson/ was everybody here on
	<u>yes</u>	Monday . . . I think we were all here on Monday . . what did we do . on Monday? Marcel's thinking so's Andre/ just think/ try and get a picture in your mind . of what we did last Monday . Maroun? Maroun
2	M: Miss we had to go in our groups and everyone had . some people had . em things to do and we had to read each . instr . . . =	
3	S1: instruction	
4	M: = instruction	
5		OK so we were in groups/ what things did we have to do/ who can help Maroun explain that? Bernadette?
6	B: like we get . like people doing the groups like using magnets? . . in each group like using strings and the em . . cr . . . em the magnets . like in the cradle?	
7		mmm . so you're giving me some examples of the activities . . . what sorts of activities were they Diana?

8   D: em like there were three
     activities/ we were in our
     groups . . and like we had
     to follow the instructions

9   excellent/ that's exactly right .
                                                there were three different
                                                experiments or three different
                                                activities . each group had one
                                                of the activities we had two
                                                groups working on each
                                                activity and there were
                                                instructions that you had to
                                                do . . to use the magnets . .
                                                what I'm going to ask you to
                                                do now instead of . telling
                                                me what happened straight
                                                away/ I'm going to ask you
                                                to go back . into those
                                                groups . . OK for a minute or
                                                two . . and I want you in your
                                                group . to . retell or recount
                                                what you <u>did</u>

The scaffolding here serves to create a shared understanding of what the
last lesson consisted of, which is then used as a basis for the next task.
The use of 'we' serves to locate the teacher as part of this shared understanding, and represents what Edwards and Mercer (1987) describe as
a joint knowledge marker, marking the knowledge as significant
throughout the discussion. Meanings are initiated by students and
appropriated by the teacher, with part of each student's response being
reinserted into the discourse within the following question, which in
turn pushes the dialogue towards what the teacher wishes to mark as
significant. Figure 7.1 represents how the appropriation by the teacher
is realized through the lexical links across successive turns, and how
from the students' initial answer (1) she leads students back 'on track'
to focus on what she wishes to talk about. The text represents an
example of what it might mean, in discourse terms, to 'lead from
behind'.

The teacher begins by inviting the students to *connect [them-
selves] back* to the previous lesson, encouraging them not to answer
immediately but to first *get a picture in your mind* of what happened.
She appropriates part of Maroun's answer (*we had to go in our <u>group</u>*)
in her next question (*what things did we do <u>in our groups</u>?*). Bernadette

Figure 7.1 Leading from behind: appropriating responses

	Students	Teacher	
1	we had to go in our groups		
2		we were in groups	*T. appropriates student's response*
3		what things did we do	*T. elicits process from students*
4	using magnets, using strings, like in a cradle		*Ss name processes*
5		examples of activities	*T. provides generic description of processes as 'activities'*
6		what sorts of activities	*T. requests information about activities*
7	three activities		*Ss produce response teacher is seeking*
8		three different activities	*T. now focuses on the three activities which are the theme of the following discourse.*

begins to describe some specific experiments (using magnets), which the teacher summarizes as *giving . . . examples of the activities* (7). She locates this recontextualization within her next question: *what sorts of activities were they?* (7). Diana summarizes the work of the class as a whole (there were three activities) and the teacher responds by summarizing the work the students were involved in, *three different experiments or three different activities*. Having focused the students, briefly but very explicitly, on the events of the last lesson, she links the now shared understanding of what they did to the instruction for the new task, which is to return to the groups and *retell or recount what you did*.

The discourse thus serves to build up common understandings about what has already occurred. This shared agenda becomes the anchor for what is to come next. As van Lier comments:

> In order to learn, a person must be active, and the activity must be
> partly familiar and partly new, so that attention can be focused on
> useful changes and knowledge can be increased.
>
> (van Lier 1996, p. 171)

Edwards and Mercer (1987) describe such texts, where the teacher highlights events or learning as of significance, as 'reconstructive recaps',
and suggest somewhat cynically that in these contexts teachers often
rewrite history by highlighting events and understandings that they see
as educationally significant, while playing down events which they see
as less relevant or confusing, an issue which is taken up at the end of
this chapter. Nevertheless, such highlighting of key learning and concepts would seem to be of considerable benefit to students learning in
their second language.

Stage 2: Setting up the new task

The four illustrative texts from this stage indicate what it is that the
teacher considers to be important to enable students to complete the
tasks. The mediation by the teacher is oriented towards helping children understand what the task is about, the process of doing the task,
and how it is to be completed.

In text 7.2 the teacher scaffolds the task for students through
unpacking for them a set of written instructions. In text 7.3, the teacher
demonstrates the task herself by modelling it for the children. However,
scaffolding is not restricted to talk about the experiential content of the
task. As Chapter 5 pointed out, talk about language and talk about how
to be a student are sometimes foregrounded in the discourse, particularly when students are about to begin a new task. Thus in text 7.4 the
teacher focuses on the language that will be integral to a prediction task,
and in text 7.5 she focuses on how the students are expected to work
together and leads a discussion on the characteristics of successful
collaborative group work.

What all the examples of teacher-scaffolding in this section have
in common, the pedagogical function they share, is a deliberate attempt
by the teacher to set up and scaffold tasks in such a way as to make clear
to learners the boundaries and requirements of the task, the processes
by which it will be carried out and the expectations of the teacher.

Example 7.2 Reverse the other magnet

(1:18)
Here the teacher mediates the students' understanding of a set of written
instructions by unpacking the written language into a more familiar and

spoken-like register. The experiment to which the teacher is referring involved placing two bar magnets end on, and then reversing one magnet. The written instructions were:

> Use a glass table or a smooth desk. Using two bar magnets, lay them down in the same line with the poles close together. Observe and record what happens. Then leaving one magnet the same way, reverse the other magnet. Observe and record what happens.

As in similar examples, the layout of this text is intended to illustrate the mode shifting more graphically. The discourse has been transcribed using three columns. The left-hand column contains the written instructions that the teacher is reading aloud. The middle column contains a more unpacked recoding of the instructions: it is more spoken-like language with which all students are likely to be familiar. The right-hand column contains context-embedded language: here the teacher's referents are the materials she is holding or pointing to. Some of the original discourse in this text has been omitted to highlight more clearly the nature of the teacher's mediation. Students' contributions are in italics.

	Context-reduced (written instructions, read aloud by teacher)	'Everyday' language	Context-embedded (use of material and visual context)
1	'use a glass table or a smooth desk'		
2		your desks/ desk surfaces are smooth	
3			that sort of surface over there
4	'lay them down in the same line'		
5		does it mean . next to each other?	(T. demonstrating 'next to' with magnets)
6	no, in the same line		(T. demonstrating 'in the same line' with magnets)
7			lay them like that (T. demonstrating)

8	and it says 'with the poles close together'		
9		what are the poles?	
10		*ends/ sides*	
11		*those things on the side*	
12			I would call this the side (T. demonstrating)
13		*the edges*	
14		*the thing that attracts the metal object*	
15		we're talking about each <u>end</u> of the magnet so that's what we have to say	
16	that the poles are close together		
17	so there's the same line and the poles are close together		(T. demonstrating)

The teacher does not directly explain the meaning of the instructions, rather she chooses to exemplify them. In (2), she gives an example of the kind of surface to which the instructions are referring, using a familiar object (*your desks*). In (3) she further concretizes the instructions by referring specifically to what is within the visual range of the students; the text is exophorically referenced (*that surface, over there*). The teacher then focuses on the somewhat unusual wording *in the same line* (4). She poses a question *does it mean next to each other?* (5). While *it* refers to the wording of the instruction, the teacher is at the same time demonstrating *next to each other* with two magnets. Her next move is to expand on this negation, and she does this not simply by negating the original structure (which would have resulted in 'it does not mean next to each other') but by repetition of the written instruction: *no, in the same line* (6). This is then unpacked by her next move *lay them like that*

(7) where again the referent for *them* is found in the immediate visual context of the students. The reference system neatly exemplifies the relationship the teacher creates between the written text and the here-and-now context: the reference to *them* in the written text (*lay them down*) is to be found within the text of the written instructions, the referent to *them* in the teacher's spoken text (*lay them like that*) lies in the familiar world of the classroom in which the interactants are sitting.

Example 7.3.1 I'll just do this one as an example

(2:27)
Here the teacher is demonstrating to the students how they should record the results of a number of related experiments onto a bar graph. The aim of all the experiments at this point was to find out whether there are differences in strength between the north and south poles of a magnet, and between different types of magnets. The experiment that the teacher is using in her demonstration requires the students to dip each pole of a bar magnet into a jar of paper clips and then count the number of clips attracted. There is also a set of written instructions for each group of students. The two axes of the graph are already drawn up on the board, but they are not yet labelled.

	STUDENTS	TEACHER
1		so this is the first one . when you do a graph you know . that you always have the two axes/ OK this one which is the . vertical . and this one is the . ?
2	horizontal (*several voices*)	
3		horizontal good and it will actually tell you on the card what you are to call each axis/ OK so it's fairly structured . this side . you'll write the number . . . what do you think you'll do the number of?
4	clips (*several*)	
5		clips that's right (*labels 'vertical axis' 'number of clip'*) . . . and you can decide . . how you would like . once you've done your experiment you'll probably know how to go up . you might want to go up in . .

6	fives	
7		maybe twos . .
8	four six	(*writes 2. 4. 6. on the vertical axis*)
9		OK but you will have a better idea once you've done the experiment/ I'll just do this one as an example . if you've got the number of clips . up here (*points to vertical axis*) . down here (*points to horizontal axis*) we need to know . the type of magnet (*labels horizontal axis 'type of magnet'*) . . because you all . . . and you know that there are three different sorts of magnets so the first one that I asked you to use was the . ?
10	bar magnet (*all*)	
11		OK (*writes 'bar magnet' on horizontal axis*) so . . . you can use . . this to do a bar graph . so that you'll know here (*pointing to horizontal axis*) . . it might be a fridge magnet . which magnet you were using . .
12	bar magnet	
13		and how many paper clips were attracted to it
14	Miss can we go by one two three four five? (*referring to what needs to be labelled on the graph*)	
15		yes you will know . how to go better when you/ when you know the number of clips/ so if you're using the bar magnet/ what was the first thing I asked you to do/ use . you had to choose . a . ? you've got the bar magnet and you had to choose a . ?
16	pole (*several students*)	
17		a pole . . that's going to make a difference to your graph as well . so . if I'm using the bar

		magnet . . and I decide to start with my north pole . . I need to say that on my graph . . OK so I'd say bar (*pointing to 'bar'*) and what could I put there to help me say . ?
18	a little 'n' (*several students*)	
19		a little 'n' good (*writing 'n' beside 'bar'*) . and I would say/ let's . pick a number out of the air . . . six? I got six clips attached . so I would go . I'd/ you'd use a ruler of course I'm not doing it because I'm trying to be quick . . when I use my bar magnet and I use north I get six (*counting up the vertical axis and marking on graph*) . . . .
20	aah (*several students indicate understanding*)	
21		OK then when I use =
22	M: see what the strongest is	
23		= a bar . . . oh you're quick Maroun

This series of exchanges is characterized by the very unequal amount of teacher and student contributions, with the teacher relying largely on 'cued elicitation'; that is, the provision of strong clues to students about the desired response in order to obtain specific responses from the students. Although the use of cued elicitation results in minimal responses, these responses are significant in that the students are being required to name the lexical items which will eventually appear on the graph, for example *clips* (4); *four six* (8); *bar magnet* (12); *a little 'n'* (18). One of the differences between cued elicitation and other interactional patterns is that students are often not called on to answer by name nor are their responses overtly evaluated. The evaluation is inherent in the fact that the teacher usually repeats the response item and continues the discourse, here incorporating the contribution into the board work. This produces discourse which tends to feel more 'fast moving' than other patterns of interaction because it is not punctuated by anything extrinsic to the thematic development of the text.

In the context in which this text occurs, meanings are built up via the discourse, the written instructions and the graph on the board. As

Chapter 6 discussed, multi-modal sources of meaning can help make written instructions comprehensible. However the graph on the board is not simply a device for demonstrating to students how they should read the instructions. It also constitutes an additional text, a way of mathematically representing the information the students are about to obtain, and as such, a text type which students must learn to 'read' as they would a linguistic text. Hence perhaps the teacher's explicit demonstration of how to label the diagram and then how to record the information. Later in this stretch of discourse (not included here), the teacher made explicit the fact that a graph is an information source, saying *it must tell you something. . . . there must be some information that you can get from the way that you recorded*, while later in the discourse she referred to the graph as 'an efficient way of organizing information'. She then demonstrates a second example (7.3.2), this time using pins rather than clips, but doing so much more briefly, again cueing the responses she wanted. This time, as the excerpt below shows, the instances of overlapping speech and increased participation by more students suggest that the task is now understood.

Example 7.3.2

STUDENTS	TEACHER
	then . once again I would like you to use a graph to record your findings . . . OK because it is . an efficient way of organizing your information OK so for this graph it's a similar sort of thing . . . . two axes . . Simon right? . . . . . your
[horizontal (*many*)	vertical . . and your [horizontal what might go . on the vertical axis of this one . . .
number	
	number of what?
paper clips	
	are we using clips this time?
pins	
pins (*many*)	
	well done . exactly right . the number .
of pins (*several*)	
	of pins . . . . . . will go on your vertical axis . . and on your horizontal axis?

em bar	
	thank you for using your hand . Catherine
type of magnet	
	good. once again. the type . . . and . you need to indicate once again if you
[what we're using (*several*)	
	are using . . . [which pole . .

These two texts illustrate the temporary nature of scaffolding; the support reduces as it becomes redundant. While instructions for the first example are given very explicitly, they are only briefly repeated for the second. Each group was given a set of written instructions and they subsequently carried out the task with minimal help from the teacher.

Example 7.4 How could we make the language of prediction?

(2:27)
In this text which is taken from the same stretch of discourse the focus is on language itself. On other occasions the teacher had related the notion of predicting to 'thinking like a scientist', pointing out that scientists make predictions and hypotheses, and then test them. Here the teacher asks the students to predict the result of the experiments before they carry them out, and reminds them of how they can talk about 'predicting'. What makes this and other similar texts unusual is that this metalinguistic talk is occurring in the context of a science class. Its occurrence at this point, immediately before the group activity where students will need to use it, affords an opportunity for the learners to engage more readily with the task and to make immediate use of the language here being discussed.

	STUDENTS	TEACHER
1		I want you to try and predict the results with your group . . . without touching any equipment/ have a think . . . about what <u>might</u> happen . what <u>may</u> happen and just take some time talking about that . . . Diana might say 'I think that . . . the north pole is going to attract the most number of clips' . . . how else could we make the language of prediction . what could you say we could use 'I think' . what else could you say . . .
2	M: maybe	
3		<u>maybe</u> . the south pole . . will be stronger than?

4 M: the north?

5   that's something else you could say/ Julianne's
                         going to give us another one/ she's been
                         concentrating so well

6 J: em it could be?

7   OK it <u>could be</u> that the horseshoe magnet . . . is
                         stronger than . . . ? Belinda?

8 B: em . . . . oh .
   my prediction . .

9   good . . can you extend that a bit . Janet? my
                         prediction . . . ?

10 J: em/ is?

11   good/ my prediction <u>is</u> . . Robert?

12 R: em . . . em . . .
    probably the . .

13   good that's a good start . . <u>probably</u> . . OK
                         Simon . lots of language coming out here . . .

14 S: I predict that . .

15   excellent . . .

16 E: em . . perhaps

17   very good/ that's a good one Emma

The teacher first models an example of what she calls the *language of prediction* (1) by using a projecting clause to project the model of what students might say: *Diana might say 'I think . . .'* . This strategy involves the teacher playing the role of a student and using projection to model the focus language and ground it in what is familiar to students.

The students go beyond the teacher's model and offer several types of realizations of modality: subjective and explicit, like that modelled by the teacher: *I predict that* (14); explicit and objective: *it could be* (6); implicit and objective: *maybe, probably, perhaps* (2; 12; 16); and expressed through a nominalization: *my prediction* (8)[2]. The teacher extends the first three of these responses (3; 6; 9) to model a complete clause, again providing a more coherent model. Perhaps because of the potential grammatical complexity of the nominalization *my prediction*, she also uses marked stress to help the students notice the structural form: *my prediction is*.

It could be argued that since scaffolding has been defined as help given for a task that students would be unable to do alone, the apparent familiarity by the students with what is required might suggest that this is not scaffolding at all in this sense. Several points can be made here. The teacher is reminding students of something they know so that they are better able to complete the task successfully. The aim is not to 'teach' the use of modality but to help students express modality *in the context of this task*. Thus it becomes part of the broader scaffolding around the setting up of the task. What is also significant here is that the students who respond are the more fluent English speakers, and their responses provide peer scaffolding for others.

In the group work that followed there was evidence of the use of the focus language around prediction by many of the students:

> I predict that the north will stick/ will get more needles (*sic*) than the
>   south (Duncan)
> I think that the north pole will pick up more pins (Andre)
> Probably a hundred will stick (Gabriella)

Example 7.5 You have to do a lot of negotiating

(2:42)
The example provides an instance of explicit teaching about culturally valued ways of learning. Students (including adult learners) are not automatically able to work well in groups (see, for example, Reid *et al* 1989) and, given that much pedagogy, including second language teaching, encourages the use of group work, then it would seem important that teachers take time to talk with students about the interpersonal and language skills integral to participation in group work. Edwards and Mercer (1987) point out that the educational value of any kind of activities, including collaborative problem-solving, will depend on the extent to which students are able to understand the ground rules and relate them to their own experience and ways of learning, and on how well the teacher has set up the environment for generating and supporting talk.

This text occurred towards the end of the unit on magnets. The final task for the students was to design and make a game for younger students which used the properties of magnets in some way. The teacher had explained the task, referring to the written instructions that each group has been given, and had asked students to retell what they were to do. (In this lesson the students had to design the game and list the materials they would need.) Before the students begin, the teacher talks with the students about the need to negotiate in groups. As with the

previous text, this interaction is intended to facilitate the students'
engagement in the group discussion in ways that are likely to lead to a
successful outcome, which is to come to a collaboratively-reached
agreement about the design of their game.

	STUDENTS	TEACHER
1		you're going to come up with <u>one</u> game OK . so you have to do a lot of negotiating/ because you're all going to have lots of good ideas . but if/ is it going to be/ get into the group/ 'I know what we're doing/ me me me/ I've decided'? is that how we work in groups?
2	no (*many*)	
3		what sorts of things can we remember Simon?
4	S: em share your ideas?	
5		good take turns/ share your ideas . because four people's ideas or three people's ideas . have to be . better than one person's ideas don't they/ we have to get a lot more . Fabiola?
6	F: communicate with your group	
7		how do you communicate with your group . . that's very true but how do you do it?
8	F: like instead of . em when you start with your group you don't em shout . and don't . 'I know what we should do and this is what we can do' and if someone want to talk it over say 'no this is what we're going to do'	
9		OK so it's a lot of . . first of all . turn taking . and quiet group work voices .

and maybe sharing your ideas
certainly/ 'oh an idea I have' or 'one
idea I have' . or 'a suggestion that I
have' . put it forward as a suggestion
or an idea/ people will be much
more . willing to listen to it . than if
you say 'this is what we're going to
do' so be careful . with the sort of
group work language that you use/
well done .

(*later in discussion*)

10   (*J. raises hand*)   yes?

11   J: Miss how about if . like .
     you have four people in
     your group . one wants
     to do something and another
     one want (*sic*) to do
     something else and they all
     want to do different
     things?

12   they've all got different ideas? good/
                                      good question/ does anyone have any
                                      suggestions for Julianne . if you got
                                      into your group and everyone says
                                      'well this is my idea'/ 'this is my
                                      idea'/ 'this is my idea'/ 'this is my
                                      idea' and no one wants to . . move
                                      from their idea

13   what could be some strategies? .

     [Miss (*many bids*)   [Duncan

14   D: like . you could put them
     all together . like . like make
     them one

15   F: make up into one game

16   OK so maybe try and combine the
                                      ideas to make up one game/ that
                                      could be one thing/ what if they
                                      don't go together though . what if

the ideas are very . very different .
how could you work with it then .
Anne?

17   A: em you could em find a
piece of paper and write it
and scrunch up and put it
into a hat

18   OK choose it/ maybe say 'all right
we can't decide . so that the most
fair way to do it or the fairest
way to do it' . that could be
one way . that's another suggestion /
Janet

19   J: Miss em we could come
up with a different one . em
everyone . when they all
want to do it

20   Charbel

21   C: do an arm wrestle?

22   *laughter*   oh probably not the most
appropriate way/ certainly an idea
(*laughing*)

23   yes scissors paper stone/ arm
wrestle/ that sort of thing/ we
might get ourselves into real
trouble

laughter   though . . thank you I don't think Mr
W and Miss M would be too
impressed if they walked in and saw
us arm wrestling over what we
decide to do . they probably wouldn't
think that was . appropriate group
work behaviour . . Robert?

24   R: Miss em if you can't
think of one you can em
em you can you can . .
play it? and see which
one's a good one

25		OK so you could come up with a few to choose from/ Andre?
26	A: oh Miss like . . you're going to vote for which one is the most fun	
27		that's a good idea . maybe you could say you can't vote for your own but you can vote for one of the others . sometimes though it's just . . not being stubborn . . you know thinking . <u>really</u> trying to step back and think 'well it doesn't matter whose idea it is . . but what would be the best idea for the task that we're trying to complete'

The mediation of the teacher here serves to socialize students into the school's culturally accepted ways of taking part in collaborative learning. The talk is largely about talk itself, represented through projected clauses. It illustrates how the teacher scaffolds the difficult concept of 'negotiation' by appropriating each of the students' suggestions and elaborating, enhancing and extending them to make explicit particular school-valued beliefs about some key characteristics of effective group work. The discourse constructs with the students a particular kind of student identity: collaborative, polite and a constructive group member. Suggestions about such characteristics are likely by their nature to be somewhat abstract and culturally implicit, but here they are grounded through the bridging devices of hypothetical quotations and situated examples.

Throughout the interaction the teacher elicits suggestions which she then appropriates and expands on. She begins the interaction by setting up a hypothetical situation in which appropriate and inappropriate language can be reflected on, 'becoming' a student and modelling an imagined verbal projection. The rhetorical strategy of quoting rather than reporting a projected clause creates an immediacy in the discourse. Here the teacher takes as a starting point for the discussion an example of inappropriate talk, a situation with which students have probably had some personal experience in previous group-work situations. Simon's suggestion (4) is expanded by causal enhancement (Halliday 1985b): the teacher provides the reason why it's useful to share ideas (5): *because four people's ideas . . . . have to be better than one person's ideas.* Her response to Fabiola's suggestion (6) is to invite her to elaborate and she asks for clarification (7). Fabiola exemplifies, as the teacher had done earlier, by giving examples of what not to do through hypothetical direct speech. The teacher responds (9) by taking each 'quote' and showing its antithesis in terms of appropriate behaviour. Figure 7.2 shows how she appropriates student contributions to make explicit the kind of group-work behaviour she is constructing.

Figure 7.2 How do you communicate with your group?

Student suggestion	Recontextualization by teacher
don't shout	quiet group voices
if someone want to talk it over say 'no this is what we're going to do'	turn taking
	sharing ideas . . . put it forward as a suggestion
'I know what we should do'/ 'this is what we're going to do'	'an idea I have'/ 'one idea I have'/ 'a suggestion I have'

Julianne's question (11) concerns what they should do if they are unable to agree on an idea. The teacher responds positively to this and exemplifies Julianne's question again through hypothetical projection (12). The question is appropriated by the teacher and leads to a discussion about possible solutions. Most contributions are marked by the acknowledgement that it is a possible solution: *that could be one thing* (16); *that could be one way* (18). This marking of contributions as relevant to the ongoing discussion is one way that a teacher maintains a common thread in a discussion and reminds students that contributions should be linked to it.

Charbel's contribution is presented and responded to as a joke, but this too is similarly clarified, with a half-serious comment that the principal and deputy principal would not think this was appropriate group behaviour either. Robert's suggestion is also elaborated briefly, and Andre's suggestion about voting (26) is extended by the teacher who suggests a process for the voting.

At this point the teacher presents her own view, drawing the students' attention to the need to think in terms of which idea is the best for the task. Implicitly she suggests that the focus should be on the idea (foregounding the experiential content) rather than the person (downplaying the interpersonal content). Again this rather abstract message is concretized by the act of quoting; quoting here evokes a potentially real event, an effect enhanced by the orientation of the deixis: *well it doesn't matter whose idea it is . . but what would be the best idea for the task that we're trying to complete?* (27).

Stage 3: Doing the task

Since at this stage students worked in groups, the overt role of the teacher diminished and there was comparatively little teacher scaffolding except when she joined a group. It should be noted that in general there appeared to be little overt need for her presence, and this was perhaps largely the result of the strong scaffolding provided through the *setting up* stage. When she joined the groups, she took on a mentoring role, checking on whether students were 'on task', and whether there were any procedural problems. Often she would elicit from students what they had discovered or done so far, thus helping them to articulate their learning, see what they had achieved and understand how it fitted with the requirements of the task (see example 7.6). Since written instructions often accompanied the task, the students were not without help even when the teacher was not with them, and they were frequently reminded to consult the instructions if problems arose.

In addition, help with the task was often provided by other students, even when there was no one student who was clearly more knowledgeable than the others. Student-student talk is important for different reasons from teacher-student talk; it provides a context for 'the skills of disputation, the notion that all knowledge is questionable' (Edwards 1990, p. 66), which is less possible within the asymmetrical interactions between teacher and student. Since this chapter is specifically about the role of the teacher, these issues will be discussed in the following chapter which focuses on the learners. The most important role the teacher played at this stage, apart from clarifying the task with individual students, lay in the planning and organization of the materials themselves. In the 'doing' stage, it is these materials that are the mediating tools for learning.

Example 7.6 Are you people on track?

(2:28)
Here a group of students is carrying out the experiment presented in example 7.3, designed to explore whether both poles of a magnet have the same strength. The text can be seen as an example of 'repair contingency', the way that a teacher adjusts to the unexpected, providing support to get learners back on track. In this case, the students were part way through the experiment but found that all the pins in the jar

(numbering about 70) were attracted to the poles. Having laboriously counted about half of them, they are now questioning the teacher about whether it is necessary to count all the pins, and pointing out that all the pins that had been attracted had become magnetized.

	STUDENTS	TEACHER
1	how do you get . . . (*to teacher nearby*)	
2		what can I do for you . . are you people on track?
3	Miss do we have to count [all the pins?	
4	Miss do we [have to count all of them?	
5		what does it say here? look at your task card
6	it says	
7	put them back	
8		so tell me what you've done so far . . what have you done so far
9	like . em we put em both em bars like at a time	
10	Miss they both stuck	
11	put the north pole in and then . . put the south pole in	
12		OK well that's exactly what you do . . you have to count how many were attracted to the north pole [can you just show me/ show how you did it
	[Miss all of them were	
13	they're all stuck to it . . they're all spiky	
14	put them in back into the jar . . .	
15	that's/ do the horseshoe magnet	
16		put them back in/ that's it . . and it says you have to dip/ so put . the jar down in the middle all right
17	jar in the middle	
18		now what you just did then . was you . dipped it right in it so that (*indicating the pole*) was touching . .

		what it means on the task card is just try/ if you put it about halfway in like that *(demonstrating)*/ OK until they start . to pick it up *(several pins are attracted upwards and attach to the magnet)*
19	oh cool	
20	could we do it again?	
21		and . what do you need to do now?
22	count it	
23	count them	
24		OK now what pole did we just use then?
25	er . north?	
26	north	
27		so next step will be?
28	the south	
29	south	

Scaffolding was defined earlier as help which actively assists learners to complete a task they are unable to complete alone, but it is help to understand rather than simply help to complete. Here the teacher withholds direct help until the students check the task card (5, 6), summarize what they have done so far (8–11) and demonstrate how they did it (13–17). Only at this point does the teacher demonstrate part of the experiment, although significantly she does not refer to what the students should do but to what the task card 'means'. Again the sources of meaning are multimodal: the task card; the teacher's interpretation of what it 'means' (*put it about halfway in*) and the demonstration. The teacher then sets the students on the path she wants them to take, scaffolding the steps they need to follow through her three questions (21, 24, 27).

Stage 4: Reflection on the task: making sense of what has been done

It is at this stage that the mediating role of the teacher is most clearly foregrounded. This is not surprising, since it is at this stage that the teacher is concerned with linking students' personal experiences of the experiments with a larger framework of meanings, and with jointly constructing with the students aspects of the new register which realizes these new meanings. This stage most clearly distinguishes a sociocultural approach to teaching from more 'progressive' and process-driven approaches, since considerable time is given to the explicit apprenticing of students into the culture and discourse of the subject. Through the scaffolding the teacher provides in the interactional process, she mediates between learners' personal ways of knowing, built up through their engagement with the tasks; and the more public and shared knowledge that represents the subject-specific ways of knowing. The collaborative discourse between student and teacher builds bridges between students' spontaneous knowledge, expressed in the dynamic mode of action and everyday speech in which that action is directed and reported, and the more formal, schooled knowledge which is expressed in the synoptic mode of written language (Lemke 1990). As already discussed, it is this more academic register that minority learners are least likely to develop without planned intervention. Given the nature of the two classes, it is not surprising, then, that this was the stage that was given the most class time. It included a wide range of interactional patterns, varying from student-initiated interactions where contingent responses by the teacher recast student meaning into more register appropriate language, to teacher-initiated and heavily teacher-controlled interactions where the teacher's questions incorporated strong cues about the response she expected. But this variation, it will later be argued, is not arbitrary.

The texts indicate that the discourse at this stage focuses on two major areas: the cognitive and conceptual aspects of the topic itself and the linguistic aspects of the scientific register the students are developing (again recalling the issue discussed in Chapter 5, where it was suggested that the discourse incorporates fields other than science itself). While these focuses cannot of course be clearly separated, since language is the means by which knowledge is coded and realized in the discourse, it appears that teachers 'zoom in' on one or other aspect at particular moments, according to what appears to be the major concern of the teacher at a particular pedagogical moment.

Texts 7.7–7.9 illustrate how the teacher makes her own and her students' reasoning and thinking explicit in the discourse, and how she establishes and develops, through the way that she manages the discourse, a particular line of enquiry which is consonant with her own educational objectives. Not surprisingly, perhaps, given that the lessons were sited within the curriculum area of science, texts like the ones included here, which are most overtly concerned with the building up of scientific understandings, are extensive at this stage. This set of texts is glossed as *Mediating thinking: making reasoning explicit*.

Texts 7.10–7.12 show the teacher focusing specifically on supporting learners to use aspects of the scientific register. They include not only models of appropriate language by the teacher, but metalinguistic discussion of the language itself, and are glossed as *Mediating language: technicalizing the discourse*.

The texts illustrate that at this stage there are many common elements in the instances of scaffolding. Teachers consistently put new learning in the context of old, they recast individual contributions from students in more registrally appropriate ways and as public knowledge, they 'manage' whole-class talk by appropriating and recontextualizing student responses for their own pedagogical purposes, they signal what is significant in the discourse and they recap and summarize the group's shared knowledge.

Mediating thinking: making reasoning explicit

Effective teaching has been described as not simply knowing what, but of knowing how (Webster *et al* 1996). Talk between teacher and students will thus incorporate not simply reference to 'facts' but also to the processes of reasoning underpinning them. Through interaction between teacher and students, such reasoning is made explicit. In the examples that follow the teacher constructs from the students' contributions a line of reasoning congruent with her own teaching objectives and uses this shared reasoning as a basis from which to co-construct with the students the theoretical knowledge of the curriculum. The discourse serves to link the students' observations with the reasoning and scientific principles encapsulated in the science curriculum.

Example 7.7 What do you think she was thinking?

(1:7)
In the text that follows, the action of one of the students (Belinda) during earlier small-group work prompted the teacher to draw the attention of the class to what the student might have been thinking. The student had been testing a range of objects to see which were magnetic and which were non-magnetic. A gold-coloured nail was eventually shown to be non-magnetic, but not before the student had ruled out the possibility that its non-attraction by the magnet was simply the result of the nail's weight and the lack of strength of a single magnet. To test this she had used two, then three magnets to find out if the combined strength of the magnets would be enough to attract the nail.

	STUDENTS	TEACHER
1	B: em we put three magnets together/ it still wouldn't hold the gold nail	
2		can you explain that again?

3	B: we/ we tried to put three magnets together . . to hold the gold nail . . even though we had three magnets . . it wouldn't stick	
4		so . . . she put three magnets together . . . because she was concerned about that gold nail . . . where?/ here it is/ and she said/ she thought well . . maybe one magnet wasn't strong enough/ is that what you were thinking?
5	B: yes	
6		so she put three magnets together and she said <u>even though</u> she put three magnets together it <u>still</u> wouldn't hold that nail/ why did she put three/ what was she <u>thinking</u>? what was she thinking? Gina/ what was she thinking?
7	G: to try each side like if one side is not good then something like that?	
8		is that what you were thinking Belinda?
9	*(B shakes head)*	
10		Colin what do you think she was thinking?
11	C: that she thinks the golden nail was stronger . .	
12		that . that this (*indicating nail*) was stronger/ is that what you mean?
13	C: couldn't em make the magnet go on . . . it was too heavy	
14		she was thinking the nail was a bit heavy so she thought maybe one

> magnet wasn't strong enough/ but
> then with <u>three</u> magnets it <u>still</u>
> wouldn't attract

15   B: <u>ten</u> magnets
      wouldn't still

16   M: if you did twenty it
      wouldn't work still

17   S: yeah hundred

This text is unusual in that it suggests an appropriation of 'thinking' rather than the more usual 'saying'. Here is perhaps an example of Lotman's reference to text as a 'thinking device' (Lotman 1988); the student's thinking is made explicit and therefore open to challenge. The text demonstrates the reciprocal nature of appropriation to which Newman *et al* refer (Newman *et al* 1989). Not only do students appropriate the thinking and discourse of the teacher through the ongoing classroom talk, but teachers also appropriate the thinking and language of their students, in order to draw attention to what students are to see as significant in relation to a broader frame of reference. The appropriation of students' ideas by teachers, when this results in the development of new meanings and ways of thinking, is a powerful form of scaffolding, since it is the learner's ideas and meanings which lie at the heart of the interaction. Here the teacher draws on what Belinda did in order to make explicit to the class the concept of non-magnetic material, and to distinguish it from concerns about the weight of the material.

Belinda initially describes what she did (1), implicitly suggesting what she was thinking through the judgement-loaded adjunct: *still*. Her comment that *it still wouldn't hold the gold nail* is somewhat elliptical and assumes a shared knowledge on the part of her audience which they do not yet have (since the other students were not part of this experiment). It is interesting to note again the effect on Belinda's language of the teacher's request to *say that again*, to which Belinda responds by explaining what happened much more explicitly, (note that the adjunct *still* is recoded as a conjunction *even though*). The teacher taps into this evidence of thinking, appropriates it and projects it explicitly: <u>she thought</u> *well maybe one magnet wasn't strong enough* (4). Linguistically this is an interesting text because the teacher is quoting a mental act and presenting an idea as a wording. In these data, and probably in classrooms generally, it is far more common for a teacher to report a verbal act and present a locution as meaning: *he said that*; than it is to project an idea: *he thought that*. Even less common is the representation of thinking as wording. Where projected elements are quoted rather than reported they are 'more immediate and lifelike' (Halliday 1985b, p. 233) since the orientation of the deixis is that of drama rather than narrative.

The text is characterized by the teacher's drawing together of the students' contributions to construct with them a coherent line of reasoning, made explicit in her own contributions (4, 6, 14). Her clarification checks (4, 8, 12) ensure the students' line of reasoning remains within this script. Colin's suggestion (13) is appropriated by the teacher and embedded into her final comment, which represents the point of this piece of discourse: *but then with three magnets it still wouldn't attract.* The final three comments from the students (15–17) demonstrate that this has been well understood, and the talk later continues with a discussion about other materials which are magnetic and non-magnetic.

The kind of reconstructive recapping which is evident in the teacher's contribution allows a re-representation of students' experiences and the events of the classroom in a way which fits the broader pedagogic objectives of the curriculum: here Belinda's experimentation with the three magnets is reconstructed by the teacher in line with a wider framework of knowledge about magnetic and non-magnetic materials. But throughout the discourse the teacher continues to acknowledge the student as the source of the idea, and continues to defer to her in evaluating the responses of the other students (see, for example, turn 8). The discourse as a result is interpersonally more symmetrical in terms of who is positioned as the primary knower, despite its IRF structure. Also of significance is the fact that the teacher demonstrates through the discourse what most teachers would claim as a general educational objective, but which is often left implicit: that one function of talk in the classroom discourse is the development of students' reasoning skills. If we are to take seriously Vygotsky's notion of inner and outer speech, then the explicit overt formulation of how a line of reasoning proceeds needs to be seen as central to the development of students' independent thought.

Example 7.8 Magnets stick to some kinds of metal

(1:11)
Like the previous text, this text also exemplifies how teacher-guided reporting creates a space for reasoning to be made explicit in the discourse, this time through considerable repetition, marked stress of key words and message abundancy. Prior to this piece of talk, students had taken part in an initial exploration of the properties of magnets, and had reported back their findings. The teacher had then asked them, in small

groups, to think of some *general ideas* about magnets, based on what they had found out. Example 7.8 is based on this small-group talk.

	STUDENTS	TEACHER
1	A: magnets stick to some kind of metal	
2		<u>some</u> kinds of metals/ are you saying/ what does that mean/ they <u>don't</u> attract . .
3	A: all metals	
4		they don't attract . . <u>all</u> metals . and I think in the other group . they figured that one out too . . so they don't attract and I think maybe that's what you mean (*to the other group*)/ they don't attract all metals/ did we have that down/ yesterday?
5	Ss (*several*): no	
6		so that is something new we've learned then?
7	Ss (*several*): yeah	
8		they . <u>don't</u> attract <u>all</u> metals . right Rana?
9	R: we thought how about if the golden screw is em . gold and the thumbtack . colour gold as well . how come the thumbtack [attracted and the gold screw didn't? and we thought that they might be different metals . and they . . .	[aah
10		that was good/ that was very good/ now who else was in that group/ Joseph and Jennifer/ that was very good the way they were talking about that
11	S1: I thought of that	
12		see here's Rana's argument look . . (*demonstrating*) same colour . . the magnet/ the magnet <u>didn't</u> attract <u>this</u> (*gold screw*) . . but it <u>did</u> attract <u>this</u> (*thumbtack*)

13	J: and we thought	
14		so Joseph what did you think then .
15	J: and we thought . that . . it was different . different metals . different kind of metals	
16	S1 [that's lighter	different kinds [of metals . . . <u>so</u> Amanda read yours again then . it's different kinds of metals . <u>therefore</u> .
17	A: magnets only stick to <u>some</u> kinds of metals	
18		only <u>some</u> metals
19	A: yes	
20		only <u>some</u>

This text exemplifies an important characteristic of scaffolding: the explicit marking out by the teacher of what is significant in the discourse and the new knowledge being constructed. What is to be learned is marked not only by the marked emphasis of key lexis and textual markers (*so, therefore*), but also by the degree of repetition (which is unlike anything that could be conceived of outside of the school context and marks this text clearly as 'school discourse'!): *they don't attract all metals . . . they don't attract all metals* (4); *they don't attract all metals* (8); *it's different kinds of metals, it's different kinds of metals* (16); *magnets only stick to some kinds of metals* (17); *only some* (18); *only some* (20). The fact that this is 'new' knowledge is further marked by the teacher: *so that is something new we've learned then.* This marking of the significance of new knowledge may also function to encourage students' meta-cognitive awareness, as they are helped to recognize and reflect on this step in their learning. In turn 16 the logical conjunction *therefore* marks the progress of the discussion to this point, and pushes the discourse forward by indicating to the children that this is the conclusion of the argument: what follows is to be considered as the 'point' of the discussion and of their earlier experiments[3].

As in the previous text, however, the argument hinges on what has been initiated by the students. The teacher first appropriates Amanda's response, but unpacks it through elaboration to underline the point Amanda is making: *does that mean/ they don't attract . .* (2). Rana's contribution, which poses both a question: *how come the thumbtack attracted and the gold screw didn't?* and an answer: *we thought they were different metals* (9), is clearly related to the understandings the teacher is helping the students construct[4]. The overlapping *aah* from the teacher suggests her positive evaluation of this contribution, and her next move (10) is a further evaluation: she comments positively on *the way they were talking about that*. The teacher appropriates Rana's contribution, not by recoding it into the more academic register of school science, but by doing the reverse; she unpacks the generalization (that magnets attract only some kinds of metals) by giving a specific example and demonstrating with the materials themselves. This demonstration is introduced and 'named' as *Rana's argument*. Again, and as we have seen in other texts, the teacher appropriates students' ideas, but continues to acknowledge their source throughout the discourse, thus modifying the knowledge asymmetry and suggesting a greater equality of status within the discourse. Joseph's comment (15) repeats the same piece of information, which the teacher again appropriates. At this point the teacher reminds the students of the line of reasoning they are jointly building up, by summarizing the understanding so far: *different kinds of metal*, and then adding an explicit logical conjunction, *therefore*, which both marks the progress of the discussion to this point and pushes the discourse forward by indicating the conclusion of the argument. Amanda's wording at this point (17) encapsulates a subtle but significant change. This time she refers to *metals* rather than *metal*, recognizing perhaps that this is more appropriate (since types of metal are at issue in this context). In addition, she adds the adjunct *only* and a marked stress on *some*: *only some metals*. Like the teacher, she now marks what is significant.

The two-way register shifting that characterizes this text and many others – from common-sense to technical language and back again – makes explicit the relationship between two kinds of knowledge and two kinds of meaning. The generalization that the teacher is foregrounding is a 'scientific' concept: only some materials are magnetic. From a Vygotskian perspective this is a 'systematic' concept: it can be used voluntarily. What is unpacked is an everyday concept: the magnet didn't attract the gold nail. As a piece of information it cannot be manipulated in a voluntary manner because it lacks systematicity. In this text, both specific and generalized learning is articulated, and the relationship between them is made explicit through the discourse. Discourse is thus constructed which bears many traces of students' meanings while it is in the process of becoming the authoritative discourse of the subject.

Example 7.9 Something in common with the results

(2:22)
This example is part of a much longer stretch of discourse where the teacher elicited from the students the commonalities between the

results of their different group experiments, all of which had demonstrated how like poles repel and unlike attract. As in the previous text, the teacher mediates between the students' personal experiences and broader scientific principles, indicating to students how they should be thinking about their own experiments in the light of this broader framework.

STUDENTS	TEACHER
1	OK thank you . . . three experiments and you all did very well/ three experiments/ three experiments . . . . . and if you'd listened carefully . . . you could find that there was something in
[ohh *(many bids)*	common . . . [with the results of all three experiments
2 oh Miss Miss	
3 Miss	
4	there's something in common if you listened to the results and the descriptions . . that were used . and/ that was similar in <u>all</u> . <u>three</u> . experiments . Janet would you like to tell us what you think
5 J: em Miss when they first put the magnet em on one side . . em it attracted . but/ em repelled . . and the next time they did it they put the magnet on the other side and some of/ the first time it repelled/ em it attracted next	
6	so there was like an <u>opposite</u> . OK why/ why do you think that might be happening/ she's exactly right . . where the groups put the two magnets together and they found out they either attracted . they turned it round and then they repelled . . or . they repelled first of all . they turned

207

		the magnet around and attracted/ the magnets attracted to each other/ Andre?
7	A: em because Miss . the . magnet which you put on the other magnet which you turned around . . it's not the . . like it wouldn't stick to it because . it's it's the wrong one . . and it can still feel . . the . . other side of the . thing so it turned around and it touches to it	mmm

(A few minutes later)

29	*(several Ss)* [negative	you see that N [marked on there?
30		OK it's an N that <u>does</u> stand for something/ you're right/ it doesn't stand for negative . . . does anyone know what it might stand for?
31	emmm no	
32		it actually stands for North
33	*(several)* ohhh *(loudly, indicating understanding)*	
34	S1: and south north north south	
35		exactly right . and that's . . . you've heard of the north pole
36	S2: [they stick it together	[and the south pole
37		therefore . . let's look at this . . . there's my . north there . . and my north there/ if I put the <u>two</u> . <u>norths</u> together . who can predict what they think <u>might</u> happen/ Marcel?

38	Ma: Miss em Miss first they the * will go like that (*demonstrating by putting hands apart*)	
39		you think they will repel?
40	Ma: yes	
41		shall we try? well I'll try first and tell you
42	S3: oh yes	
43		(*demonstrating*) exactly/ they are repelling
44	Ma: Miss it it's pull/ it's [pulling	
45	S4: [pulling	
46	S5: ohh can I?	
	S6: ohh (*bidding for a turn*)	
47		what's it doing (*gives magnets to Milad*)
48	M: pushing it away (*demonstrating*)	
49		it's repelling isn't it . . all right . . come out here Milad . . .
50	M: it's like a strong wind	
51		what about . . if I turned it around . . I've got this pole which is the opposite to north it's the . ?
52	south	
	south (*many voices*)	

The nature of the response that the teacher requires (i.e. not an individual recount of a specific experiment) is made explicit in the teacher's initial two turns: *three experiments, three experiments, in common with the results of all three experiments, something in common, that was similar in all three experiments*. This kind of redundancy, which we have seen in many of the examples, could be expected to give less competent language users greater opportunities to process and understand the point being made; even if they do not participate as speakers, they have greater opportunity to be participants in the talk.

Later in the discourse (not documented here) students apply the learning that has now been constructed by predicting what will happen in each of the situations the teacher sets up (*what will happen if I put north and north/ south and north/ south and south*, etc.). Having reached this degree of shared knowledge, the teacher refers back to the beginning of this text, suggesting that: *this is exactly what you were saying*. She thereby legitimizes the students' earlier findings as relevant within the new piece of knowledge that has now been constructed. At this point – and not until then, when it appears that the understandings she has sought to build up have been appropriated by the class – does the teacher ask the students to write a generalization about what they had found out, a task that is now within their capabilities (see text 6.28). Without the scaffolding provided through the discourse to help students see the generalizability of their findings, this subsequent writing is likely to have been beyond their capabilities.

Mediating language: technicalizing the talk

Lemke (1990) argues that part of the teacher's job in teaching students to 'talk science' is to focus on those aspects of language which are peculiar to science. He argues that teachers should:

> model scientific language by explaining to students how they themselves are combining terms together in sentences. They should stop to point out special idioms and phrases, forms of grammar . . . and especially . . . identify the semantic relations of terms and the various ways of expressing the same relationship in different words.
> (Lemke 1990, p. 170)

The mediation illustrated by the texts in this section is concerned with this aspect of science teaching: the scaffolding bridges the everyday language of the students and the subject-specific ways of meaning.

Example 7.10 The north pole and the south pole attract

(1:17)

This interaction was discussed in Chapter 6 in the discussion of mode shifting. Here the focus is on the way the metalinguistic dimension of the talk results in the co-construction of generalizations. You will recall that the interaction occurred immediately after a teacher-guided reporting

episode, and that on the board was a matrix to which the teacher is referring (see Figure 6.3).

	STUDENTS	TEACHER
1		let's just see if we can . . . Belinda . . . let's just see if we can . . figure out something here . . if I put the pole of the first magnet . . the <u>north</u> pole . . to the north pole of the second magnet what will happen the north pole of one magnet and I try to put it on the . . by the north pole of the second magnet what will happen . . . George?
2	G: they repel?	
3	S: repel	
4		all right so I'll just put a little tick like that . . so the north pole and the north pole/ repel
		let's try this what if I try the north pole and the south pole . . of the magnet . . who can tell . . I want a sentence a nice sentence Carol Ann?
5	C: the north pole and the south pole attract	
6		good . . . what if I try the south pole of this magnet and the north pole of that magnet . . yes Francois come on a sentence
7	F: the south pole and the north pole will attract	
8		good boy good Francois all right and let's try the south pole of this magnet and the south pole of the other magnet . . . Stephanie
9	S: the south pole and the south pole will re . . repel	

| 10 | | so I would like two ideas that we get from this . . two <u>general</u> ideas what we call <u>generalizations</u> . . . who can give me something that will happen <u>all</u> the time not what just happened to us today but what will happen do do you think . . . Gina do you want to try |

11 G: if you put the north pole and the north pole together em that will not . . . . that will repel and if you put the south pole and the south pole together that will repel too

| 12 | | good all right that will <u>always</u> happen so we'll say south pole and south pole . . . ? |

13 Ss (*several*): repel

| 14 | | north pole and north pole . . . ? |

15 Ss (*several*): repel

| 16 | | all right . . who can give me something else . . Jennifer |

17 J: em . . the north pole and the south pole attract

| 18 | | right they attract . . each other . . north pole and south pole attract each other . . right |

The teacher's mediating role here is one whereby students' personal experiences of scientific forces at work are incorporated into their attempt to make sense of the phenomena. The teacher does this mediating work through the provision of three kinds of scaffolding by which she embeds students' individual findings within a broader framework of meanings. First (1–9), she makes use of an additional and parallel semiotic resource (the matrix on the board). Second, there is the use of metalinguistic talk concerning the nature of generalizations (10–12). Third, there is a brief but significant example of cued elicitation. Each of these is now briefly discussed.

Lemke's argument for the importance of visual semiotic resources in the construction and mediation of meaning is of particular significance in relation to the notion of scaffolding. As we saw in text 7.4, scaffolding may work in tandem with an additional semiotic resource to create a multimodal resource for meaning-making. In this case the matrix on the board drawn up by the teacher serves as a parallel semiotic system and provides a visual frame of reference for the more decontextualized language the teacher is wanting the students to use. At the same time, as the teacher completes the matrix by ticking the appropriate boxes, the students are presented with an alternative semiotic system by which they can represent the information they have built up. As pointed out in Chapter 6, the provision of the matrix in this instance is especially relevant to a context where students are learning both a second language and curriculum content in the second language. The matrix presents part of the semantic or experiential content as 'given' and the student can therefore focus more specifically on the form: this presumably would help to fulfil the condition that Swain argues for, namely that the learner give attention to comprehensible (and here registrally appropriate) output. It is significant that through the scaffolding from the teacher and that provided by the model of the previous student, Francois, a child on a special education programme and an ESL learner, is successful in this task (7).

Talk about language is also a feature of the text, with the teacher-talking explicitly about the notion of a generalization. The teacher-talk here encapsulates two fields, that of science and that of language itself. The relationship between these within the progression of the discourse is a significant factor in the scaffolding the teacher is providing. To give a more visual representation of the role these two fields play, part of the teacher-talk has been separated into talk about magnets and talk about language (Figure 7.3).

Figure 7.3 Two fields within the discourse

TEACHER (Field – language)	TEACHER (Field – science)
1	let's try this what if I try the north pole and the south pole . . of the magnet . . who can tell .

2   I want a sentence a
                     nice sentence Carol Ann?

3   C: the north pole
and the south
pole attract

4   good . . . what if I try
the south pole of this
magnet and the north
pole of that magnet . .
yes Francois

5   come on a sentence

6   F: the south
pole and the
north pole
will attract

7   good boy good
Francois south all
right and let's try the
pole of this magnet
and the south pole of
the other magnet . . .
Stephanie

8   S: the south
pole and the
south pole will
re . . repel

9   good (*to obs*) my
goodness aren't they
speaking well

so I would like two ideas
that we get from this . .
two <u>general</u> ideas

what we call
<u>generalizations</u> . . .

who can give me
something that will happen
<u>all</u> the time not what just
happened to us today

10			Gina do you want to try
11	if you put the north pole and the north pole together em that will not . . . . that will repel and if you put the south pole and the south pole together that will repel too		
12		good all right that will <u>always</u> happen so we'll say	
13			south pole and south pole . . . ?
14	Ss: repel		
15			north pole and north pole . . . ?
16	Ss: repel		
17			all right . . who can give me something else . . Jennifer
18	em . . the north pole and the south pole attract		
19			right they attract . . each other . . north pole and south pole attract each other . . right

The metalinguistic focus of the discourse is intended to help students understand the concept of a generalization, and based on this to recontextualize their personal experiences in a more written-like form. The metalanguage includes reference to the fact that the teacher wishes the students to use a *sentence* (2, 5), and several formulations of what she means by 'generalization': *two general ideas/generalizations/ something that will happen all the time/ not what just happened to us today* (9). As the dialogue progresses, however, the language field progressively 'drops out' of the teacher talk as students begin to master the structure of the generalization without her help. The metalinguistic scaffolding is progressively discarded as students show they are able to produce the target language alone. In Wood's words, the scaffolding withers away as the learner becomes more competent at the particular task (Wood 1986).

Further scaffolding is provided through cued elicitation, signalled by a rising/questioning intonation pattern (13, 15), with the teacher's contributions completed by the students (14, 16). This scaffolding also reduces, and Jennifer's response (18) is a complete clause, which, while syntactically parallel with the previous responses, contains different information and indicates how the new learning has now been appropriated and transferred by the student. The remaining two minutes of talk (not included here) continues in the same vein.

Example 7.11 Remember we're scientists

(1:8)
In this example the teacher is playing a highly controlling role, with most of the exchanges being of the IRF type and incorporating many examples of cued elicitation. The final section (29–37) is reminiscent of the uncontextualized 'language drill' common in many behaviourist approaches to second language teaching in the 1960s. As has been argued, however, the pedagogical significance of texts, how they are 'read', cannot be uncovered without considering their place within the ongoing discourse which has been built up over time. The intertextual nature of classroom events, as discussed in Chapter 7, means that any interactional sequence is simply an 'excerpt' of a much larger piece of discourse, namely the total discourse around the subject or topic to date.[5]

The text occurred after the students, in groups, had tested a range of objects to find out whether they were magnetic or non-magnetic. They had then reported on their results. At this point the teacher had taught the lexical term 'attract'. Until this there had been no explicit focus on language, and the students had used everyday informal talk to report on what they had found, for example *grabs it*, *sticks to it* and *attaches* to describe the process of attraction.

In this example, the teacher appears to have two linguistic focuses: the use of the lexical term itself (*attract*) and the structure *the magnet attracted X*, (its past tense form). The text is an example of what I have referred to as a 'zooming in' technique, whereby a teacher departs briefly from the broader contextual landscape to foreground and bring to students' attention a significant detail, before refocusing again on the wider landscape (Gibbons 2002). In this case, the 'zooming in' relates to the particular linguistic support the teacher perceives the ESL learners to need.

An excerpt of an extended section of discourse is included here to indicate the overall scope and sequence of the scaffolding, and to illustrate how it is progressively discarded as students learn to use aspects of the new register. Immediately before this excerpt began, the teacher had told the students that, while they had explained what they had done in the group work very well, they were now going to use, in her words, *the proper scientific words*, because *we're scientists*.

	STUDENTS	TEACHER
1		now think back in your groups . think of the things that the magnet attracted . attract<u>ed</u>/ this is yesterday (*writes 'attracted' on board*) and then think of the things that the magnet
2	G: didn't	
3		didn't attract . . that <u>didn't</u> attract (*writes 'didn't attract' on board*) and I'd like for you to say it in a sentence so we get used . to our proper scientific language . OK Joseph . either one
4	J: em . the golden nail . . em the magnet . didn't attract the golden screw	
5		all right it didn't attract the . .
6	J: golden screw	
7		it didn't attract the golden screw (*T. then points to the nail*)
8	V: it didn't attract the . .	
9		careful

217

10	V: em the magnet attracted the nail *(Several minutes later)*	
11		anything else anybody? Rena
12	R: the magnet attracted the thumbtacks	
13		Charlene? . . think of all the things that we've got Charlene
14	C: the magnet didn't attract to the cork/ didn't attract to the cork	
15		the magnet . didn't attract the cork/ the magnet didn't attract the cork/ tell me again Charlene
16	C: the magnet didn't attract the cork	
17		good/ Joseph?
18	J: the magnet didn't attract the coin?	
19		which one Joseph? . I had a two cent coin and a five cent coin/ they're different colours
20	J: the five cents coin? (The discourse continues in a similar manner for several minutes.)	
21	Fr: the magnet attracted the	
22		good boy
23	Fr: paper clip	
24		good boy
25	S3: we had that	
26		no we had the plastic one
27	S4: the plastic covered one	

28		OK .. now . . . could I just have us <u>say</u> it . because I want to make certain that we can/ we can <u>talk</u> like <u>scientists</u> . so if I point to something I'm going to call on people and see if we can just say it in sentences properly/ I'll start/ the magnet attracted . the nail . the magnet <u>didn't</u> attract the plastic top/ Vivienne (*holding up the coin*)
29	V: the . the . mag magnet didn't attract the two cent coin	
30		Amanda (*holding up the lid*)
31	A: the magnets attracted the lid	
32		Belinda (*holding up the coin*)
33	B: the . . magnets didn't attract the five cent coin	
34		good Belinda (*holding up the magnet*)
35	S: the magnet attracted . the other magnets	
36		good Silvio (*holding up a plastic coated paper clip*)
37	M: the magnet attracted the plastic covered . clip	

Here the teacher is providing strong scaffolding for the students to begin to use a more written-like register for talking about their learning. The notion of scientific language is mentioned twice more (turns 3, 28), and it is made clear to the students why they are being asked to respond in this way. Mention was made above of the 'drill-like' pattern of the discourse, beloved by audiolingual approaches. Such pattern practice, however, took minimal account of context and was functionally empty. Here, by contrast, talk about language, and formal language practice, takes place in the context of actual language in use: despite the formality and focus on a particular grammatical structure, what the students say comes out of their understanding of the experiential work they have taken part in, and is thus a recontextualization of their understandings rather than a rehearsal of language form devoid of speaker meanings. Van Lier (1996) makes the point that the IRF is advantageous only in so far as it is designed as a way of scaffolding interaction, and must therefore promote handover so that students can learn to handle more dialogic forms of discourse. Here it appears to be used for this purpose.

One of Lemke's recommendations to secondary science teachers is that students should be shown how to combine science terms in complex sentences (1990). It is unclear exactly what the term 'complex' might imply for younger students; however, this text provides an instance of the kind of practice Lemke appears to be arguing for when he suggests that:

> [Students] should be practising the use of one particular thematic pattern of semantic relationships among scientific terms . . . Following this they should use the terms in writing sentences and paragraphs deriving directly from oral discussion . . . [The work of the teacher] is not simply to set up these situations and tasks, but to teach the students explicitly to use scientific language.
>
> (Lemke 1990, p. 169)

One of the characteristics of interactional scaffolding is its contingent nature: what the teacher says, and how she scaffolds, is contingent on what she perceives to be the ongoing support needed by individuals. While most students were able to answer appropriately, three students – Francis, Gina and Francois – had difficulty in responding in the way that the teacher had planned. Their contributions, and the teacher's response to them, are included here to indicate the differential and contingent nature of interactional scaffolding.

Francis

	FRANCIS	TEACHER
14	the magnet attracts to	
15		careful this is what we did yesterday
16	the magnet attract . ed attracted to the other magnets	

17	the magnet attract<u>ed</u> . other magnets/ we don't need to say the 'to' . so tell me again Francis

18   the magnet attracted the other magnets

The teacher reminds Francis of the need for the past tense but does not provide the word, instead simply reminding him that this happened yesterday (see the section *Reminding and handing over* in Chapter 6). SLA theory suggests the importance of 'noticing' a new linguistic item, and here the scaffold provided by the teacher assists Francis in noticing his own language use and reformulating what he has said. Recalling the appropriate form himself presumably requires a greater cognitive effort on his part than simply repeating the word as given by the teacher (see Chapter 3 and the discussion of self-repair). While Francis produces the past tense correctly, he also makes an error in the grammatical structure itself. This time the teacher uses both a metalinguistic explanation – *we don't need the 'to'* – and models the correct form. Francis then gives the response the teacher wants.

Gina

Here the teacher again uses a *Reminding and handing over* strategy to help the learner 'notice' and self-repair.

GINA	TEACHER
54 the magnet doesn't stick onto the cork	
55	remember we're scientists now Gina .
56 em . ah! the magnet attracts	

Francois

Francois is a student on a special education programme who is also an ESL learner.

FRANCOIS	TEACHER
20 the magnet attract . ed to the em that thing that has em ***	

21   these are the things that we had
                                                (*pointing to materials*) . . what
                                                are you thinking of?

        Fr. points

22   V: paper clip

Francois' interactions with the teacher were regularly quite extended; she frequently spent time probing what he said in order to help him express it more appropriately. Often he did not know words in English that were usually known by the other students. The teacher's response to his lexical difficulty in this instance is to allow him to point to the object and for another child to prompt him. At this point she spent several turns discussing the fact that there were two types of paper clips and both were magnetic (text not included here). Having established which kind of paper clip Francois is talking about, and providing a language model for talking about it, she returns to him.

	FRANCOIS	TEACHER
33		so Francois can you tell me/ the magnet attracted . . ?
34	the magnet attracted to the paper clip	
35		the magnet attracted the plastic coated . we don't need to say the 'to'/ the magnet <u>attracted</u> . the plastic coated paper clip/ you tell me
36	the magnet attracted . to the plastic . covered paper clip	
37		let's try it once more Francois . . Francois you don't need to say the 'to'/ listen to me/ the magnet <u>attracted</u> . . the plastic coated/ plastic covered paper clip
38	the magnet attracted . . / magnet . . the . magnet . . the plastic paper clip	
		(*Francois was clearly struggling to find the words he needed at this point and*

> *the teacher said quietly that we should have a video.)*

It is worth noting that the teacher scaffolds for Francois more strongly than she has for other students, for example, modelling for him the beginning of the clause (33). Francois makes the same mistake as did Francis in the grammatical structure (a difficulty shared by several students throughout the unit) and the teacher offers both a metalinguistic explanation and a model. The one second pause after *attracted* (35) might be expected to draw Francois' attention to this as the 'critical' point at which to listen, and gives him a longer time to process what he hears. Since he still does not produce a correct form on the second attempt (36) the teacher repeats both the explanation and the model again, this time with a longer pause after *attract*. This time Francois comes closer to producing the response alone.

There is a happy ending to this snippet of classroom life, and to one child's struggle with unfamiliar language. Later in the discourse Francois twice more bid to respond along with the other students, and in both cases produced the target form successfully. His final contribution is significant in that it contains considerable self-correction, and suggests he has appropriated both the past tense and the structure that were the teacher's focus in this interaction.

FRANCOIS	TEACHER
	(holding up a thumbtack)
the magnet attached/attract/attracted	
	attracted/ good boy
the thumb . thumbtack	

Text 7.11, along with the scaffolded interactions with three individual learners, is characterized by its quality of contingency. You will recall that this was defined earlier as the way that teachers pace the amount of help on the basis of moment-to-moment understanding. As the final example has illustrated, what is also significant is the differential nature of the scaffolding provided for different learners. Effective scaffolding is fluid and dynamic in its various enactments, becoming more necessary not only at certain *points* in the teaching/learning cycle, but also playing a differential role with different *learners*.

Teaching as mediation: some implications for the classroom

The analysis of classroom discourse as the mediation of learning suggests a number of issues relevant to the development of pedagogical theory and to classroom practice. Foregrounded by the data are three related issues: mediation as a theory of teaching-and-learning; mediation as a process of recontextualization and mediation as contingent interaction.

Mediation as a theory of teaching-and-learning

One of the realities of the classroom is that there exists a generally asymmetrical distribution of knowledge and power. As Edwards and Mercer suggest:

> If the educational process is not to be completely compromised by the asymmetry of teacher and learner, then we need to develop an understanding of the process which recognises and encourages that asymmetry in a manner that fosters rather than hinders learning.
> (Edwards and Mercer 1987, p. 201)

We have seen how the notion of teaching as mediation, and the closely related concept of scaffolding, acknowledges and builds on this asymmetry, since this constructs both teacher and student as active participants who play interrelated but differential roles in the learning process.

Central to a theory of teaching as mediation is the question of the means by which that mediation is achieved. I have suggested that the notion of interactional scaffolding is a productive way of examining how mediation is enacted. The analysis has attempted to uncover some of the pedagogical and situational parameters that impact on how scaffolding is constructed through teacher-student interactions. We have seen how productive scaffolding is a process of connection, creating links between the learner, the task and the broader curriculum, with interactions carrying traces of all three. In particular, attention has been drawn to the relationship between the various instantiations of scaffolding and their appearance at different points of the pedagogical sequence.

In viewing the texts as situated events, it has become clear that a particular interactional pattern cannot be evaluated for its learning potential away from the context in which it occurs and its pedagogical purpose. Excised from their contexts, the cued elicitation of example 7.4 or the drill-like pattern of 7.11 may appear overly teacher-directed and form-focused, but they take on a different hue when embedded within the ongoing discourse at a particular point in time. Particular patterns in interaction are not in themselves 'good' or 'bad', but need to be examined in terms of whether they are contextually appropriate. To critically examine classroom discourse we need to consider the degree to which particular kinds of interactions are justifiable in terms of their consequences for students and their learning, and their effect upon the teaching-learning environment. IRF and cued elicitation patterns may be appropriate when a task is being set up, so that teacher-expectations are made explicit and students are ultimately less dependent on the teacher while they are engaged in the task itself. Used in the early stages of developing understandings about a topic, however, it may constrain student thinking and the development of principled understandings, and lead to merely ritualistic responses in interactions with the teacher.

As suggested earlier, a theory of teaching as mediation offers a productive alternative to debates around the binary notions of teacher-centred and learner-centred education. As Mercer contends, the pedagogical principles around which diverse discourses of pedagogy often compete, are not to be found in a theory of teaching or a theory of learning but rather within an interrelated theory of 'teaching-and-learning' (Mercer 1994). Despite the large amount of experiential group work and talk between students in these classrooms, the learning that occurred was not simply a matter of individual discovery; the discourse is not that of the so-called progressive and 'learner-centred' classroom. Neither was it a matter of the simple transmission of educational 'facts'. As the examples have shown, the changing roles of both teacher and learners suggest a far more complex process than a centring analysis allows. The introduction to the conceptual and linguistic world of the teacher came only after initial opportunities for students to develop understandings and to communicate together in familiar language as they took part in the group experiments. Although each new piece of learning originated in student activity, their learning began but, importantly, did not end at this point. Students were not left to create their own understandings: the final interpretation of what occurred, what was said and what was done, was ultimately controlled by the teacher, and congruent with her frame of reference and broader curriculum-based scientific principles. This supports the conclusions of others; see for example Edwards and Mercer 1987; Stierer and Maybin 1994; and Mercer 1995. Stierer and Maybin write:

> The overriding impression from our studies is that classroom discourse functions to establish joint understandings between teacher and pupils, shared frames of reference and conception, in which the basic process . . . is one of introducing pupils into the conceptual world of the teacher and, through him or her, of the educational community. To the extent that the process of education can be observed taking place in the situated discourse of classrooms, it is

on our evidence essentially a process of cognitive socialisation
through language.

(Stierer and Maybin 1994, p. 200)

What can also be learned from the examples is that the degree to which
the teacher retains the primary control of the discourse is not static but
varies according to the pedagogical purpose of particular tasks. As we
have seen, the four types of interactions defined in Chapter 5 appear to
cluster around similar stages in the sequencing of activities, and serve
fairly distinct pedagogical purposes. Exchanges at the *Review and orientation* stage, when students were asked to reflect on what they had
learned, tended towards dialogic interaction. *Setting up the task* tended
to produce teacher monologues or IRF/cued elicitation patterns. *Doing
the task* involved participatory interaction and, where the teacher
joined the group, dialogic interactions. *Making sense of the task* used
predominantly dialogic patterns to share and construct knowledge, but
more teacher-controlled patterns, realized through IRF and cued elicitation, were used to remind students of what had been learned. With the
increase in focus on 'talking like scientists', when the language itself
began to be less familiar to students, teacher-talk incorporated stronger
scaffolding as students were helped explicitly to use the new register.
Unitary and centring descriptions of classrooms have historically
tended to fail to take this dynamic aspect of the role of the teacher into
account.

What is also evident from the examples is the significance of the
teacher as reciprocal listener. In the process of socialization into the
conceptual world of the teacher, students were listened to and their contributions taken seriously. As Lemke points out, this is critical if teachers are to avoid the inequity of regularly taking certain students'
contributions more seriously than others (Lemke 1990). Cummins (1988)
likewise argues that students' identities are constructed in the school
context through their interactions with teachers, and Philips (1972),
Heath (1983) and others have demonstrated the possible negative effects
of interactions between teachers and minority students when certain
students' contributions are regularly ignored or restructured. In these
classrooms, rarely were contributions passed over in favour of a specific
answer, and teachers in general took considerable time to clarify with all
students their intended meanings. Students were encouraged to articulate their thoughts and to listen to those of their peers. At times, particularly in the teacher-guided reporting, there was some temporary transfer
of perceived expertise from teacher to student, the initiating moves of the
teacher reflecting the fact that when students were reporting on findings,
she was not, at least in discourse terms, the primary knower. Questions
such as 'What have you found out?' locate the source of information with

the student, and frequently lead to responses from students far longer than the one-word or single-clause response associated with heavily teacher-controlled discourse. Ultimately, though, how far a teacher listens to the meanings students are trying to make, and how she or he responds to them, is not simply a matter of the interactional 'technology' the teacher is drawing on, or on an isolated list of strategies, but rests rather on his or her epistemological orientation towards what counts as valued knowledge. If knowledge is seen as something held by the teacher which must be transmitted to students, there is little motivation or justification for according much airspace to hear and probe a student's view of things.

Mediation through recontextualization: 'rewriting history'

Teacher mediation in the classroom, as we have seen, involves the recontextualization of knowledge. Typically, knowledge derived in one context (such as doing an experiment) is appropriated and recontextualized by the teacher in another context (such as teacher-guided reporting). These new meanings may in turn be recontextualized once more (as when the teacher uses these understandings to develop broader scientific principles).

As we have seen, recontextualization commonly occurs in an exchange between student and teacher in which the student's contribution is recast through a field and mode shift. At other times the teacher's mediation incorporates a more radical shift, when the overall theme of the ongoing discourse is shifted away from the individual experiences of the students towards a discussion of theoretical principles. Students as actors are then decentred, and theoretic knowledge is foregrounded in the discourse. Typically at these times the teacher marks the significance of these recodings through the use of *tell*, saying to the students for example: *what does that tell us?* that is, 'what does that signify?' As we have seen, however, recontextualization may not always move in a more written-like direction, but may also move the discourse towards the more immediate and concrete. It would be a misinterpretation, therefore, to see classroom discourse simply as reflecting a unidirectional movement towards more written-like discourse.

Though interactions between teacher and students are the most usual way for information to be recontextualized, we have also seen how information can be reconstructed through the use of parallel semiotic systems in interplay with the discourse, so that several meaning systems are built up simultaneously, for example, through the use of a bar graph (7.4) or a matrix (7.11). In these texts, the information sources provide a visual context for students to interpret the discourse of the teacher because of the opportunities for demonstration and modelling that they allow and because they 'mean' in their own right. Earlier I suggested the notion of 'message-abundancy' to describe such contexts[6]. These parallel semiotic systems play a dual role in the recontextualization of meanings. They may provide a referent for context-embedded discourse, and hence they are integral to the meanings being built up. At the same time they represent already-recoded information, which, in this case, had as its source the science activities carried out by the students. What is significant here is that these systems of meaning are an additional basis for more written-like language to be developed. Other semiotic systems in the classroom interrelate with language, they are not simply a backdrop to it.

Though I have suggested that marking what is significant is helpful to second language learners, a more critical lens on recontextualization can be taken. Commenting on the way that teachers recontextualize the contributions of their students, Edwards and Mercer (1987) suggest that teachers often 'rewrite history' by a kind of editing process: they highlight certain events and understandings (those they see as educationally significant) and downplay others (those they see as irrelevant or confusing). Such rewriting involves the removal of irrelevant content, the modelling of new and subject-specific language, and the appropriation of student-initiated wording, (all of which I have argued is important in the kind of explicit teaching supportive of second language learners). However typically, the teacher's use of *say* projects *reported* student wordings as meanings. In these very common situations the reported projection encapsulates the teacher's version of events, while the locutor remains the student, as in the following example: *Amanda was saying she was trying to show the power of magnets.*

Halliday points out that a projected clause stands for wording, whereas in reported speech it stands for meaning (Halliday 1985b). Unlike quotation, reported speech makes no claims about holding to the actual words of the speaker[7]. Thus when a verbal act is reported, it is reported as meaning, which may or may not concur with the speaker's view of what they said (see, for example, Hill and Irvine's work (1992) on evidence in oral discourse). As subsequent examples will suggest, teachers make particular use of the licence this offers, and on some occasions a contribution is attributed to a speaker which bares minimal resemblance to what had actually been said. Such are the shared understandings of students and teacher about how classroom discourse works, and the status of both the official discourse and the reporter, that the 'accuracy' of the reporting goes unchallenged. Much classroom discourse appears to rest on a benevolent conspiracy between teacher and students which maintains that while it is students who do the 'saying', it is the teacher who knows the intended meaning of their verbal acts. Here for example, the teacher is clarifying what an individual student has just said, but the reported meaning bears little relationship to what the student had actually said:

S: em the two poles they like to like er stick to some things * or
       otherwise they will pull away/ stick to something something that * * *

T: so you're saying that you've got a pole on each end . . and one pole
       will only stick to some things (6.14)

This 'meaning differential' is further illustrated by Figure 7.4 (Two version of events), and is based on a text (not included) where the teacher is recapping with the students the shared knowledge of the class about the properties of magnets. The jointly produced discourse between students and teacher has here been pulled apart so that each set of contributions can be read as a separate version of events. While this layout works against the representation of discourse as a joint production, it does serve to represent how teacher-talk selectively appropriates and expands on student-talk and thus how student contributions and the recontextualized teacher-version each produce a different set of meanings.

Figure 7.4 Two versions of events

Note: The original text has been edited to remove hesitations, false starts and unfinished clauses, and conventional punctuation has been used, since the focus here is on the experiential content of the discourse. Where the teacher used a cued elicitation in the original, the question has been replaced with a statement and placed under the teacher's version of events, on the grounds that the teacher is the initiator of the utterance and the proposition in this case comes from her. The word originally provided by the students is then italicized.

Students' versions of events	Teacher's version of events
The north pole and the south pole attract to each other.	There are two parts of the magnet, the north pole and the south pole.
	The north and the south attract each other.

Most north and north don't attract to each other	We learned opposite poles attract. The same poles, north and north and south and south, don't attract to each other, they *repel*.
and all magnets are strong. All metal twisties are magnetic.	
Magnets can attach to other magnets strongly.	Magnets can attract to other magnets.
Not all metal attracts to magnets.	Before we started we thought that metals attract to magnets; now we know it's not all metals, just some metals.

Examining the discourse in this way illustrates how the teacher's version, while related to that of the students, contains different experiential content, uses different wordings, leaves out seemingly irrelevant information and hence produces a different set of meanings. Here the teacher adds extra information about the parts of the magnet, introduces the item *opposite poles* as a lexical substitution for *north and south*, and summarizes the students' contributions as *opposite poles attract . . . the same poles . . . repel*. She recodes *attach* as *attract* and *don't attract* as *repel*. She also marks what has been learned: *we learned that; before we thought . . . now we know*. But she chooses to ignore what the students say about the strength of the magnets and metal twisties.

Lemke refers to such examples as 'retroactive contextualization':

> Retroactive recontextualization . . . is of considerable importance to the theory of meaning. In essence it means that after an answer has already been given, which had one meaning in the context of the dialogue that preceded it, the teacher says something to alter the context and make it seem that the answer had quite a different (or additional) meaning.
>
> (Lemke 1990, p. 103)

Examining the transcript with this perspective demonstrates the control that teachers exert over what counts as knowledge, and how it gets constructed. The experiments in which the students took part did not intrinsically 'have' meaning. Meanings had to be made for them, in this case by teacher and student, yet always, as we have seen, these meanings are ultimately controlled by the teacher. I have argued that the process of schooling is in part the socialization of students into subject-specific discourse, and that for minority students in particular this process is essential if they are to develop the skills to participate in the broader society; in Delpit's view, teachers must coach the voices of their students 'to produce notes that will be heard clearly in the larger society' (Delpit 1988, p. 285). And as has been shown through the examination of the discourse in this chapter, the kind of scaffolding provided by teachers as they socialize students into school learning offers great potential to the English language development of ESL students. Nevertheless examples like the one above should also signal the problematic nature of dialogue that 'socializes'. In the construction of classroom discourse, even when it appears benign and responsive, there will always remain the potential for some students' voices to become pale reflections of their original ideas and thoughts, or to be silenced altogether. The production of discourse situated within more complex science, indeed in any curriculum subject, may result in more subtle but potentially more significant differences between the dominant versions of events and the world views of minority students. As Lemke argues, 'it is the sense we make of what we see that matters . . . meaning is always an interpretation of what we perceive' (Lemke 1990, p. 147). As we have seen, it is the teacher's view, reflecting the 'official' and mainstream curriculum, that represents this interpretation. Lemke's comments about science teaching are applicable to school learning in general and represent a major challenge to all teachers:

> Teachers should show respect for common-sense views and alternative religious or cultural views, while presenting the view of science and the reasons for that view . . . science education only needs to ensure that [students] learn the view of science, not that they prefer it to all others, or give up any other view.
>
> (Lemke 1990, p. 171)

Making connections: mediatation through contingent interactions

As I have suggested throughout the book, the process of social mediation is essentially one of connection between differing ways of thinking and different discourses. It involves talk between individuals which results, at least in successful mediation, in both participants reaching a level of intersubjectivity on which new understandings can be built. Central to effective mediation in the context of the classroom is the notion of contingency. As we have seen in this chapter, contingent interactions are responsive to a learner's current understandings and finely tuned to the intended meaning of the learner, while at the same time they are located within the learner's 'challenge-zone', ahead of their current powers of meaning, so that they point the way to new learning. Making a similar point, Halliday refers to the principle of 'filtering' whereby learners decide what is and what is not on their agenda:

> Students will attend to text that is ahead of their current semiotic potential, provided it is not too far ahead. They will tackle something that is far enough beyond their reach to be recognised as a challenge, if they have a reasonable chance of succeeding (cf. Vygotsky's 'zone of proximal development'). Whatever is too far beyond their powers of meaning they will simply filter out.
>
> (Halliday 1993, p. 105)

Classroom interactions, if they are contingent, are anchored within the shared agendas of the participants, and oriented towards symmetry, that is, the discourse is based on shared understandings of the topic and proceeds on the assumption that each interactant is seen by the other to be a worthy conversational partner. For this to occur, as the examples have shown, classroom conditions must be set up where what is familiar to the learner is both validated and explicitly connected to the new. Through contingent interactions the individual learner is connected to the broader social world: the effect of contingent interactions is to create the threefold connection discussed earlier – between the individual learner, the task or topic in which they are engaged, and the broader school curriculum. Van Lier suggests:

> The conditions for a contingent language act are set up by alluding to the familiar, the given, the shared, then a surprise is sprung in the form of the new, the unexpected, and then joint interpretive work is undertaken which simultaneously connects the new to what is known . . . The contingent utterance manifests itself in discourse first of all by its new-ness or known-ness, then by its various connections both to the world around the speakers and listeners, and to the thoughts, beliefs and intentions of the participants.
>
> (van Lier 1996, p. 172)

But contingent interactions in the classroom do not simply 'happen': interactional contingency is rarely a random occurrence. It occurs in planned contexts where teachers have a long-term vision of where they want to take students, so that the contexts in which interactional contingency arises have their own purpose and direction. It is both this long-range vision and the ability to respond contingently in the ongoing sequences of discourse that I would argue characterizes the most effective teaching. It is in the planned curriculum that the *contexts* for interactional contingency are set up, but in the enacted curriculum that it occurs.

To conclude this chapter on teaching as mediation I refer back to Chapter 2, and the discussion of 'deficit' views of minority learners in the context of psychological or biologically oriented views of the learner as a lone individual. In the discourse around such views, the cause for educational failure, implicitly or explicitly, may be directed towards the students themselves, with blame for educational failure placed on their home background, their personal motivation or their bilingualism. But a view of teaching as mediation requires a major shift of focus away from this view of the learner as an isolated individual. Within a socio-cultural framework, learners' achievements are viewed as largely determined by the strength of the cultural and linguistic frameworks (or scaffolding) which support their learning (Mercer 1994). The notion of teaching as mediation represents a shift 'away from the notion of learners who succeed or fail on their own resources, towards a view of learning as a situated, culturally contextualized activity' (Mercer 1994, p. 101). Through contingent interactions and scaffolded learning, learners are more likely to develop the conscious sense of achievement and autonomy that ensures the kinds of engagements in school that work against constructions of failure. In a view of teaching and learning as mediation, a learner's individual successes or failures depend critically on the quality of the contributions of others. It is the nature of those contributions from others that has been the focus of this chapter.

Notes

1 Webster *et al* (1996) suggest a similar mapping for theorizing scaffolding through what they term the components of scaffolding. They name these components as *recruitment and management* (orienting the students to the task); *representation and clarification* (representing the task in terms the students can understand); *elaboration* (helping students to develop or adapt their concepts); *mediation* (using literacy to work through a learning process); and *finishing* (drawing together students' classroom activity and reflecting on its process and worth).

2 See Halliday 1985b for discussion of these terms.

3 The teacher's focus on conjunctions could be seen as significant for two reasons. First, conjunctions are often a late development in students' second language (Lock 1983; McKay 1992), perhaps because they are often a feature of more academic and written-like registers, and second, following Vygostsky, their use in the explicit formulation of argument throughout the discourse is likely to aid the development of students' inner speech.

4 This is also an unusual interaction in that a student initiates a question, a relatively rare event (Webster *et al* 1996) and also reports on the *thinking* of the group rather than giving procedural information.

5 From a methodological perspective, this text is an argument for looking beyond the formal structural characteristics of classroom interactions.

6 Of course, non-linguistic semiotic systems may, in themselves, be no more transparent to learners than language itself, since they must first learn to 'read' them, and to recognize the recontextualized information they display. The teacher implicitly acknowledges this when she suggests to students that the graph *must tell you something . . . there must be some information that you can get from the way you recorded.*

7 Note, however, that wordings do not necessarily concur with what a speaker has said either; they only claim to do so.

8 The learners: affordances for learning

Introduction

The focus of the previous two chapters has been on the discourse teachers and learners produce together, and the mediating role of the teacher in this. The point has been made many times that this discourse is both a function and an outcome of the specific activities in which the interactants have been involved. We have also seen how discourse is interrelated with other semiotic systems and material artefacts in the situational context, and with the previous conversations of the classroom. Discourse then has been viewed in both its situational and historical context. This chapter considers the affordances for language learning offered by this situational and historical context, and considers what factors favour learners becoming participants in the practices and discourses of school. The chapter concludes by suggesting some broad implications for pedagogical practices and second language research of this discussion, and of the previous two chapters.

In the course of the book it has at times proved useful to pull apart the dialogue in order to examine the nature of the contribution of one or other of the interactants: what can be broadly referred to as the 'input' or the 'output'. But a distinction needs to be drawn between what may be useful as an analytical tool for specific purposes, and what is needed for an understanding of the language learning process in context. In discussing the impossibility of separating thought and language in understanding human mental capacities, Vygotsky has commented that, in much the same way, an independent analysis of hydrogen and oxygen does not generate an explanation of water's capacity to extinguish fire (Lantolf 2000a, b). Much the same can be said about the metaphors of 'input' and 'output' if discourse is considered from the perspective of the learner: in situated dialogue the interactant is concerned with the meanings being negotiated with their partner, meanings which cannot be excised from their social and historical context. Swain (2000), van Lier (2000) and Kramsch (1995) have commented on the constraining effect for our understanding of second language learning of the conduit metaphor of communication. As we have seen in the two previous chapters, to look at learning is to look at an active learner in his or her environment. Or as van Lier, drawing on Reber (1993) puts it, we should 'ask not what's inside your head, ask what your head's inside of' (van Lier 2000, p. 247). The context is not there simply to provide input, rather the environment itself (in this case the classroom), provides what van Lier refers to as a 'semiotic budget' (p. 252). This refers not simply to the 'input' available, but to learners' opportunities for engagement in meaning-making activities.

But as van Lier points out, no ready-made research procedures exist for what he calls an 'ecological' approach, which requires a researcher 'to show the emergence of learning, the location of learning opportunities, the pedagogical value of various interactional contexts and processes, and the effectiveness of pedagogical strategies' (van Lier 2000, p. 250). Throughout this book I have addressed these aspects of learning, by drawing on situated discourse examples of the classroom through the course of a topic, and through drawing on the range of theoretical perspectives presented in Part 1.

In this final chapter I examine the kinds of affordances for learning that are available within the meaning-making activities described in the previous two chapters. Taking the perspective of the learner begs the question of how the semiotic budget to which van Lier refers is actually to be accessed, for affordances do not of course in themselves cause participation by learners or ensure learning, they simply make it possible, or 'afford' it. In this chapter I suggest some of the affordances for learning in discourse contexts where there is not simply the opportunity to participate but also factors that make it more likely that affordances will be taken up by learners. I identify these from the learner's perspective as: taking part in proleptic discourse; collaborating with peers; talking as an expert; participating in extended dialogue with the teacher; having the right to speak; opportunities to reconsider how things are said; and talking about talk. Each of these is discussed below.

Taking part in proleptic discourse

The first three examples (8.1, 8.2 and 8.3) are taken from the *review* and *setting up* stages of the cycle and are characterized by the explicitness of the information they carry. They are examples of what van Lier refers to as 'proleptic discourse'. Proleptic discourse 'is aware of gaps in understanding and invites the less-competent into sharing with the more-competent'; the hearer 'is given clues for the enlargement of common ground' (van Lier 1996, p. 182). A speaker or writer who uses ellipsis, on the other hand, leaves the listener to provide information which is considered redundant by the speaker and hence left out, and so 'does not explicitly check or facilitate the listener's interpretive processes, or invite the listener into a shared intersubjective space' (van Lier 1996, p. 182). In school discourse, ellipsis can shut off affordances for the enlargement of common ground, since the learner may not have the information necessary for continuing participation. Proleptic discourse, however, as we see below, offers affordances for *subsequent* participation and engagement in tasks. It is significant that the three texts are taken from the initial stages of the curriculum cycle when students are preparing for new learning.

Participating in reviews

As suggested in Chapter 7, the review stage of the macrogenre offers students an opportunity to hear again what counts as significant knowledge, and provides a context for interpreting new experience, a context within which the language being used is to be understood. For learners, it 'anchor[s] the new language in things that [teachers] have reason to believe the students already know' (Wong-Fillmore 1985, p. 31). In non-pedagogic discourse, the familiarity of interactants with the 'given' (the assumptions about what has been previously understood) is an inherent part of understanding the 'new' (the as yet unknown or new information)[1] and a prerequisite for participating in further dialogue. The given thus remains implicit, except when implicit assumptions begin to be questioned. Here, however, the review stage is a time when the given is explicitly articulated, rather than being taken for granted. It represents a curriculum space for the 'given' to be reinserted into the discourse, and to be made explicit. What is later going to be taken as assumed in the new episode is re-articulated: the given is held up for inspection. Example 8.1 illustrates how through dialogue between teacher and students, learners are engaged in this process of articulating the known.

Example 8.1

STUDENTS	TEACHER
1	can you tell me . . anything . . anything at all . . think about it in your mind first/ take some thinking time . . . anything that we have learned about magnets so far . . . just have some thinking

		time . . . anything that you have learned about . magnets so far . . . . . think . . . . OK Janet
2	J: Miss . the north pole and the south pole attract to each other	
3		OK . . there are two parts of the magnet the north pole and the south pole . . which parts attract to each other?
4	J: Miss the north and the south	
5		OK so we learned last week didn't we/ that opposite . poles attract/ good/ Andre
6	A: most north and * em (don't) attract to each other =	
7		well done =
8	A: = and	
9		sorry keep going
10	A: = and all magnets are strong . like .	
11		that the same poles/ north and north and south and south they don't attract to each other/ they . . . ?
12	S2: separate	
13	M: push	
14	S3: repel (*several voices*)	
15		<u>repel</u>/ well done

A dialogic review such as this creates a kind of 'safety net' for learners who need a second chance to access key information that may not previously have been fully comprehended, and makes certain linguistic forms more salient because of the likelihood of the repetition of key information and language by both teacher and students.

Engagement in teacher instructions

While explicitness and clarity of task instructions is of obvious importance for second language learners, most teachers are aware that their students' understanding of them is not a given. Understanding a sequence
of instructions is in fact a difficult task for a second language learner
(Lock 1983). I have also on occasions observed language classrooms
where the instructions given by the teacher were linguistically considerably more complex than the intended task. The transcripts of instruc-
tion-giving in earlier chapters suggests that engagement of students at
this stage is perhaps best achieved when the giving of instructions is not
seen simply as a prerequisite for a later task, or as information transmitted by the teacher, but rather viewed in itself as a potential teaching and
learning context. The teacher may, for example, deliberately unpack the
language into more immediate here-and-now talk, or she may seek to
involve students as participants in the discourse. Two examples are
given here.

In example 8.2, the teacher is explaining the procedure for an
experiment the students are about to carry out in small groups. Part of this
text was examined in Chapter 6 (example 6.9) in order to look at the way
in which mode shifts were realized in the discourse. Here a longer section
of the teacher-talk is presented, with a fuller commentary on the actions
of the teacher and her verbal behaviour. The teacher is referring simultaneously to the materials themselves and to the written instructions.

Example 8.2

TEACHER	COMMENTARY
place it like that sitting in there .	puts first magnet in cradle
OK/ it says *place another magnet on top of the cradled magnet*	reads slowly from card
so you've got one magnet in here .	points (*here*)
then you have to put another magnet . on top . . OK? of the cradled magnet	holds second magnet above first
once again . . *observe what happens . . and record using words and diagrams . .*	reads slowly from card, holding it up so that students can see the text
OK then it asks you . to repeat . . <u>alternating</u> the poles	*alternating* enunciated slowly and with stress, preceded by a pause

what does that word . <u>alternating</u> mean? anyone know what <u>alternate</u> means? . . . just simply . <u>changing</u> . .	defines unfamiliar (formal) lexical item using familiar (everyday) term (*alternate/change*) stress on *changing* preceded by a pause
OK so if you put it . facing you've got one magnet in there	pointing (*there*)
and you put it in . facing one way . change the poles around . . change it to the other side .	uses familiar term (*change*) holds second magnet above first and turns it around
<u>alternate</u> the poles . and what happens now . .	models new lexical item (*alternate*)
so you're trying it each way	summarizes process in familiar language: *trying it each way*
. . once again each card will tell you how you have to record . by writing or drawing . right that's just a quick explanation . . . but as I said the explanations are on each card so it might be a nice idea as a group . to read through this . the instructions . . together . make sure everyone understands what's going on . and then . . start your experiment .	gives strategy for solving possible later difficulties (*the card will tell you*)

Multiple opportunities are given to the students to understand and interpret the task: each step of the process is demonstrated while the written instructions are read aloud, and each step is interpreted using familiar terms to explain an unknown lexical item. As we saw in example 7.2, the teacher's talk moves back and forth between the written language of the instructions, the 'everyday' equivalents, and the context-embedded language of the demonstration. Learners are therefore afforded multiple opportunities to interpret what they hear. The teacher includes only essential information: what is critical for the students to know in order to carry out the task. She reads slowly and clearly, holding up the card so that students can read with her (and thus have access to another mode of information). Key words receive marked stress and there is also use of the 'pregnant pause', often less than a second but clearly perceptible, that teachers use immediately before a word or phrase of some significance (*it asks you . to repeat . . <u>alternating</u> the poles*). Such features make these key words salient and, we can assume, bring them to the notice of learners.

Once again, we can note that, from the perspective of the learners, meaning resides in the interrelationship between the verbal and actional behaviour of the teacher, the material context and the written instructions. This is, in van Lier's terms, part of the semiotic budget that is available to the students at this moment, or, in the terms I used earlier, it is a context that is rich in message abundancy. The significance of this, given the temporal context of the text (immediately before students carry out the activity) is that the explicitness of the instructions helps pave the way for learners' fuller participation and engagement in the subsequent activity.

In example 8.3 the teacher involves the students in retelling the instructions she has just given.

Example 8.3

STUDENTS	TEACHER
1	something else that's very important . what else <u>must</u> you do? Philip? what else <u>must</u> you do . . . you also <u>have</u> to do something/ Belinda?
2 B: you have to record what you did	
3	you have to <u>record</u> . . what you found . and what are we going to do tomorrow Philip?
4 P: em we're going to/ we're going to/ going to	
5	what are we going to do tomorrow?
6 P: we're going to tell . what we found out	
7	good boy/ you were listening/ that's good Philip . . you're going to tell what you found out . .

The teacher's questioning affords an opportunity to some students to recall and retell the key components of the subsequent task, and to others an opportunity to hear again an explanation of the task. The active involvement of the learners in the 'set-up' stage transforms the giving of instructions by the teacher into a language-using context.

Collaborating with peers

The value of peer learning to second language learners in collaborative situations has been well documented (for example, Brooks *et al* 1997; Donato 1994; McGroarty 1993; Swain 2000; van Lier and Matsuo 2000). The examples that follow suggest some of the affordances for language learning offered by working with peers, although two examples (8.6 and 8.7) also suggest that in some cases the perceptions of learner and teacher of the purpose of a task differ. While affordances may be real, they do not always concur with the pedagogical intentions of the teacher.

The first of the examples (example 8.4) was briefly examined in Chapter 6 (6.20). A longer section of the transcript is included here.

Example 8.4

Prior to this piece of discourse being produced, the teacher had reminded the students that they needed to be precise in their use of language when they shared their learning with others, since other children had not shared in the experience (see Chapter 6). In Example 8.4, students were 'rehearsing' as a group how they would report back.

1	Emily	we have to talk about what we did last time and what were the results . . . .
2	Milad	we got em . . we got a . thing like . . this . . pu- we got paddle pop sticks and we got
3	Maroun	we put them in a pot
4	Milad	and have to try and put
5	Julianne	wasn't in a pot/ it's like a foam . . . =
6	Milad	[a foam
7	Emily	= [a block of foam
8	Julianne	and we put it
9	Emily	we put paddle pops around it . the foam/ and then we put the magnet in it
10	Julianne	[and then we got

11	Emily	[and then we got another magnet and put it on top . and it wasn't touching the other magnet . . Maroun your go
12	Maroun	when we . . when we turned it the other way . . it didn't stick on because . . . because
13	Julianne	because?
14	Maroun	because em . . . . it was on a different . side
15	Milad	Emily your go
16	Emily	OK . last week we . . . we . . . . did an experiment . . . . . we had a . em a block of foam and we um . . stuck paddle pop sticks in it and we put . . . a . magnet . a bar of magnet . . into the em cradle that we made with the paddle pop sticks =
17	Milad	that's enough from you . .
18	Emily	= then we put another magnet on top and the result of this was . . . the magnet that we put on top of the cradled magnet did not . stick to the other magnet
19	Julianne	then when we turned it around . when we turned the other magnet around it it
20	Maroun	stuck
21	Milad	it stuck together because
22	Maroun	and it stuck together because . [it was
23	Emily	it [was on a different side
24	Julianne	[it was on a different side and the other one's and . . .
25	Emily	and the poles are different
26	Julianne	and the poles are different
27	Milad	and em when . . we put on the . . . side it stuck together . . .
28	Julianne	because em it was on different sides/ because we put it on the on the thin side and it didn't and we didn't/ it didn't stick . .
29	Maroun	because the flat side is stronger than the thin side?
30	Emily	no because the poles are different

| 31 | Milad | because the poles are different all right? |
| 32 | Julianne | we/we finish |

Swain argues that through collaborative dialogue and co-construction of knowledge, students who are 'novices' as individuals are simultaneously 'experts' collectively (Swain 1995b). Probably only one of the speakers here (Emily) would have been able to produce the recount alone, but collectively they were able to reconstruct what they had done. Thus the lexical choice *block of foam* is reached through a progressive clarification of an appropriate way to name it, and this is built up by three speakers: *a pot, not a pot, a foam* (repeated), *a block of foam*. No one student's contribution can be regarded as the source of the information, and no one contribution can be regarded as a solo text, even though Emily is clearly the most competent speaker. The other three students are scaffolded by the contributions of the group as a whole, and by taking part in the ongoing negotiation of meaning. Thus, for example, turn 11 continues the clause started by the speaker in turn 10. The prompt in turn 13, *because*, forces the speaker to continue and complete his statement. The main scientific understanding of the experiment is built up across eight turns (19–26) which together construct the statement: *when we turned the other magnet around it stuck together because it was on a different side and the poles are different.* Through the process of joint construction the discourse becomes more explicit, and scientific understandings are reworked and modified (note that *different sides* becomes *different poles*). Telling others what they know allows the children to recognize the gaps in their own understanding, and pushes them to clarify thinking and to engage in what Chang and Wells refer to as 'literate talk' (Chang and Wells 1988). While the notion of comprehensible output traditionally refers to the language produced by an individual, the nature of the talk here suggests that this is exactly what the group as a whole is striving for. As in most jointly constructed discourse, 'output' is not captured through a focus on contributions in isolation, but through attempting to understand the shifting and ambiguous patterns of meanings which Maybin (1994) has referred to as 'provisional meaning'.

Donato (1994) describes a similar process in a study of students learning French as a second language, as the students are negotiating the construction of *tu t'es souvenu* (you remembered). Although no student possessed the ability to construct this alone, they are able collectively to reach the correct form, leading Donato to argue that 'these three learners are able to construct collectively a scaffold for each other's performance . . . and minimize frustration and risk by relying on the collective resources of the group' (Donato 1994, p. 45). The situational context of example 8.4 provides similar affordances: a safe environment for trying out language and the collective contributions of the group. And because this was to lead to the students sharing with others, there was a simultaneous focus on both the message, or experiential content, and the form, or textual component. As we saw in Chapter 6, the value of this kind of reflective talk is suggested by Julianne's request to the teacher: *can we have another practice* (see 6.21). It is also evident in her solo attempt at the recount in the later teacher-guided reporting episode (see example 6.22).

Another interpretation of the affordances offered by this kind of clarifying talk relates to Vygotsky's notion of egocentric speech. In Chapter 2, this was referred to as signifying the transition from the interpersonal to the intrapersonal plane, the point at which outer dialogue begins to turn inwards to create the resources for thinking. Egocentric speech is the organizer of private mental functioning and helps an individual make sense of their experiences of the world. Though this text is not a true example of what Vygotsky would see as egocentric speech, it is nevertheless akin to it in that the discourse renders visible students' implicit reasoning in the process of helping them make sense of what they had seen. This explicit verbalization of thinking here mediates both the experience itself and the students' second language development, as demonstrated by their later production of more formal language in the reporting and writing sessions. There is some evidence for the appropriateness of applying Vygotsky's ideas regarding the mediational function of egocentric speech to the L2 learning context (McCafferty 1998; Alijaafreh and Lantolf 1994), although the ideas have not been taken up extensively. Yet it seems that an activity or task which requires students to reflect aloud on their thinking and their understanding can play an important cognitive function in terms of curriculum content, and also create affordances for participation in the later production of new forms of language. I suggest that in ESL classrooms there needs to be a 'curriculum space' for such group reflection activities, not through functionally empty drills where language is simply rehearsed, but in the context of a curriculum activity which engages students in cognitively challenging ways, and where the discourse is the result of a real and shared purpose for the students.

Examples 8.5 and 8.6 show very different kinds of affordances at work. Here children are asking each other for help in the course of written work. In the first of these examples, the children are sorting objects into two groups, those that are magnetic and those that are not, and individually recording the results. They have also been asked to draw the objects.

Example 8.5

Maroun	and the needle/ you didn't write needle (*checking his list has the same number of items as Emily's*)
Julianne	no I never wrote needle
Emily	no I didn't write needle/ I just put pin
Julianne	I wrote pin
Milad	what's that called . . .
Maroun	[a paper clip
Julianne	[paper clip
Emily	I never wrote that (*comparing lists*) . . . . a a paper clip we've got to write paper clip
Julianne	elastic . . (*holding rubber band*)
Milad	what's this called again em/ what's this called?
Julianne	crayons
Maroun	now this pasta/ I draw a pasta for this
Emily	pasta
Milad	what's this called? paddle pops
Maroun	rubber band/ rubber band (*speaking to Julianne*)
Julianne	what's this called?
Emily	coin/ just write a coin . . or a token
Milad	pasta . . is this pasta?
Julianne	yes

Later, as children are finishing their lists.

Maroun	Emily how much do you have? (*checking how many items on list*)
Emily	what/ for what
Maroun	for em this
Emily	1/ 2/ 3/ 4/ 5/ 6/ 7/ 8/ 9/ 10/ I got 10
Maroun	1/ 2/ 3/ 4/ 5/ 6/ 7/ 8/ 9 . . one more

Emily	do you have dice?
Maroun	yeah
Emily	and paddle pop stick?
Maroun	no
Emily	that's it
Julianne	have we finished?
Maroun	now we have to draw pictures
Julianne	pictures
Maroun	yeah
Julianne	I can't even draw a paper clip
Milad	copy it
Maroun	the Bambridge's scarecrow (*referring to his drawing, laughter from all children*)
Julianne	with lipstick! (*laughing*)
Milad	what is this?
Maroun	oh lid
Milad	lid
Julianne	thumbtacks (*drawing*)
Maroun	what does split pin mean? (*referring to Emily's list*)
Emily	it's actually a paper fastener/ you can write split pin <u>and</u> paper fastener
Milad	what's a needle . . what's a needle
Julianne	this (*showing*)

There were frequent requests for help in this and in similar peer activities, mainly restricted to questions of vocabulary, spelling and task procedure. Even the more fluent speakers had difficulty with less common vocabulary items, particularly those that related to the home domain. But what is significant here is that every request for the name of an item is responded to, sometimes with more than one group member contributing. It is doubtful whether such instant and ongoing help would have been as accessible in a whole-class context, or that the students would have asked for it so readily.

What is also significant is the foregrounding of the interpersonal function of language (such as humour), in the children's talk. As I have argued throughout the book, language in any instance of use simultaneously incorporates both an experiential and an interpersonal function. In Western contexts there has been a tendency to focus on the intellectual functions of language, rather than on the interdependence between feeling, thought and action, but as Vygotsky has commented, 'thought has its origins in the motivating sphere of consciousness, a sphere that includes our inclinations and needs, our interests and impulses, and our affect and emotion' (Vygotsky 1987, p. 282). Maroun's reference to the Bambridge's scarecrow, to which he likens his drawing of a paper clip, is a reference to an illustration in a shared class book recently read by the teacher, and Julianne's comment about lipstick appears to refer to the fact that Maroun was using a red crayon. The insertion of references to other experiences shared by the children (both in and out of the classroom), and the subsequent extension of the discourse could, we might speculate, 'extend' the semiotic budget of the classroom, and create a further source of language learning opportunities. It may be that what is sometimes described as 'off-task' talk has unplanned advantages in providing just such opportunities.

Example 8.6 provides further examples of peer help. The teacher had asked the students to write down one thing that had happened in their own experiment, and then a generalization about what they had learned 'overall'. The three short texts come from this same episode.

Example 8.6

(1)	Maroun	genulization (*sic*) how you spell it? *(Julianne and Emily spell)*
(2)	Milad	what you write?
	Julianne	'all magnets have a side pole'
(3)	Maroun	he (*referring to Milad*) have to do a over a overall [generalization]
	Milad	what's a overall?
	Emily	just write like . . 'if you put the north and the north together'
	Milad	yeah that's what I'm writing
	Emily	no that's/ write overall here
	Julianne	so Miss knows

The children here are primarily concerned with what they perceive to be the procedure of the task and the end product (the writing). As the last comment suggests, the work is really for 'Miss'! Emily's help to Milad is concerned with what to write and where to write it. As such it is not scaffolding in the sense identified in Chapter 7, since peer help in these contexts usually focused on *what* a learner should do (in some cases with other students doing it for them), rather than on *how* something could be done. Emily, for example, simply tells Milad what to write rather than answering his question. The interpersonal function of language is again foregrounded, with children directing each other and commenting on their own action; talk about the curriculum field itself, (the behaviour of magnets) is noticeably absent in this and in other group activities involving collaborative writing. Nevertheless, the help given by peers is at the point of need and is ongoing; such help doubtless made it possible for children like Milad to participate in and complete tasks that would be daunting for them to do alone. While their participation may at times be more 'peripheral' than other students, the support they obtain from their peers enables them to participate *as if* they are more competent language users.

Example 8.7 suggests how a teacher's and students' perceptions of the function of a task may differ. While there may still be affordances for learning, these may not necessarily coincide with the teacher's pedagogical purpose. Here the teacher's purpose was to have the students retell their findings and develop some generalizations. To this end she had constructed an information gap activity: after the groups had developed some generalizations, they were split into pairs, and then regrouped with a pair from another group. Each new group of children was then to share what they had brought from their original groups and come to a consensus about the generalizations, which were then to be recorded on a large sheet of paper for class display. However there was little talk indicating the kind of thinking the teacher had been hoping for, or even discussion about how the generalizations should be worded. Children simply read their existing lists to each other and copied each others' statements down. As the example shows, most of the talk is in fact about procedural matters such as the colours of the crayons they should use, whose contributions should be written down, turn taking and the neatness of the handwriting. (Note that it was not possible in this text to accurately identify which children were speaking.)

Example 8.7

I'll write it down/ which
no no write the heading first
magnets . .
I write heading/ let me write heading

she's neater
well I'm writing
neatly
neatly I know/ I do go neatly
you have to use the ruler so you
make it
no no straight lines
straight lines/ straight lines
straight lines
I'm doing it
swap/ want red?
what do I have to write?
you have to write the first one/ 'all mag -/all bar magnets' (*dictating*)
'all . . . . bar . . . . magnets . . .' (*writing*)
wait/ you've got finger prints in it
already
very sorry
that's not straight

Taken in isolation, then, some of the group work indicated that students and teacher appeared to have different ideas about its purpose. Although the end product was usually in fact very close to what the teacher had requested (for example, here the students successfully produced a list of generalizations), the students' concern was more often with the procedure of the task rather than the principles the teacher had been attempting to help them develop, and consequently there was sometimes little evidence of the kind of reasoned talk that the teacher had been planning for.

But rather than simply dismissing such examples as unsuccessful second language teaching tasks, the point should be made that, even when the students' and teacher's ideas of the purpose of the group work appeared not to coincide, the group work still fulfilled an important function: it created the intersubjectivity and common experiences necessary for the long conversation of the classroom discourse to be maintained. What followed from the episode above, for example, was a whole-class sharing of the writing of all the groups, with explicit discussion of the wordings of the generalizations and the accuracy of the science information. All children were involved in presenting the ideas on the posters, and this level of participation in both talk about science and talk about language would probably not have occurred if that particular activity had not taken place.

From the perspective of second language learning then, working with peers offered a number of contexts and affordances for language development. It provided a context for discourse to be jointly constructed so that individual novices collectively became experts as a group; it made available an ongoing and immediate source of help for individual learners and it provided the shared experiences on which later discourse was built. The affordances offered, though, may not be those expected by the teacher.

Talking as an expert

It has been suggested that the teacher-guided reporting episodes were particularly significant in the contexts and opportunities they offered for language learning. Teacher-guided reporting was discussed at length in Chapters 6 and 7, and those discussions will not be repeated here. In summary, these chapters illustrated that in the process of teacher-guided reporting, learners were supported in developing the academic registers of school, and that a feature of this process was the strong guidance provided by the teacher through interactional scaffolding. This guidance included the contingent recasting and recontextualization of student-initiated contributions, along with explicit metalinguistic talk. It included within its structure the gradual removal of scaffolding and handover to students.

From a learner perspective, however, one of the features of teacher-guided reporting is that built into its structure are opportunities for students to 'take the floor' as knowledgeable learners who had something to say that was not already known by others. Such exchanges have been analysed in earlier chapters in terms of clarification requests and opportunities for output and 'stretched' language, and the point has been made that a built in 'information gap' within class activities, whereby reporting-back has an authentic communicative purpose, is a context where clarification requests are more likely to occur. But from a learner's perspective, teacher-guided reporting represents a curriculum space whereby they can initiate the topic of exchanges; they enter the discourse as 'experts' with something to say to others, rather than displaying what is already known. It was worth noting that there were always enthusiastic bids to speak at these times by students, even from those less competent in English.

Participation in extended dialogue with the teacher

In their research in French immersion classrooms, Swain and Lapkin (1990) have pointed out that even after many years in input-rich classrooms learners may fail to control significant grammatical aspects of their second language. Swain suggests that this is due to the constraining effects on language development of classrooms dominated by the IRF structure, where there are minimal opportunities for extended learner-use of language. Likewise Shuy (in van Lier 1996) suggests that whereas recitation IRF structures basically elicit from students what they already know, talk with more of a participation orientation can lead students to higher levels of linguistic and cognitive development.

In recent years, studies of school reform in Australia and North America (for example Newmann and Associates 1996 and the Productive Pedagogies study in Queensland, Australia) have underlined the importance of students having opportunities to participate in 'substantive conversation'. In substantive conversations, learners will take part in extended interactions with each other and with the teacher about the ideas embedded in a topic. These interactions are reciprocal and promote coherent, negotiated and shared understandings of subject matter. The Queensland School Reform Longitudinal Study (1997–2001) includes a further two perspectives: the degree to which knowledge is presented as problematic rather than fixed, and the degree to which metalanguage and explicit discussion of how language works takes place in the classroom. Their study argues that these aspects of substantive conversation need to be promoted in any attempt to generate more equitable and productive student outcomes.

Many of the interactions in the teacher-guided reporting sessions could be described in similar ways to substantive conversation. While they are not truly symmetrical – teachers clearly impose an external agenda and participants do not take equal responsibility for the maintenance and progress of the discourse – they allow for more student ownership of the content of the discourse, and thus have a more participatory orientation. As a number of illustrative examples have shown, they also provide occasions for students' thinking to be made explicit through the discourse, and for talk about how language works.

But affordances for students to take part in extended and substantive dialogue with the teacher depend on classroom discourse moving away from the triadic IRF structure. To understand where these affordances lie, the structure of more extended dialogues is here examined drawing on Wells' notion of 'prospectiveness'. For illustrative purposes, three examples are included, which together represent a movement along a display–participation orientation. As the examples show, this orientation has important consequences for students' engagement and participation and for the possibility of 'opening up the IRF into more mutually contingent interaction' (van Lier 1996, p. 154). Example 8.8 occurred at the end of a teacher-guided reporting episode when the teacher was focusing on a particular language form. Texts 8.9 and 8.10 are also taken from teacher-guided reporting episodes.

Example 8.8

STUDENTS	TEACHER
1	what if I try the south pole of this magnet and the north pole of that magnet/ yes Francois/ come on/ a sentence
2 the south pole and the north pole will attract	
3	good boy/ good Francois/ all right and let's try the south pole of this magnet and the south pole of the other magnet/ Stephanie?
4 the south pole and the south pole will repel	
5	good

Example 8.9

STUDENTS	TEACHER
1	Maroun . something that you can tell me that you found out last lesson
2 Ma: Miss I thought that all metal can stick on magnets but when I tried it some of them they didn't stick	
3	OK so you thought that no matter what object/ if it was a metal object/ it would be attracted to the magnet/ OK interesting/ Milad?
4 Mi: I thought I thought that em the metal coins stick onto the magnet . . it wouldn't/ I put it near it and it didn't got stuck onto it	
5	OK/ it was attracted to the magnet?
6 Mi: no	it wasn't/ OK good/ Fabiola?

7   F: em em I thought that em the
. . . em . . Miss what was the
object that em could st . . em
like . . the coin could stick onto
the magnet but it wouldn't

8   OK you/ you predicted that it
did/ it would be attracted to the
magnet and it wasn't

Example 8.10

STUDENTS   TEACHER

1   tell us what you found

2   L: if you put a nail . onto the
piece of foil . . and then pick it
. pick it up . . the magnet will .
. . . . . . that if you put a . nail .
under a piece of foil . and then
pick . pick the foil up with the
magnet . . still . still with the
nail . . under it . . . it won't

3   it what?

4   L: it won't/ it won't come out

5   what won't come out

6   S: it'll go up (*prompt*)

7   L: it'll go up

8   wait just a minute . . can you
explain that a bit more Lindsay?

9   L: like if you put a nail and
then foil over it and then put
the nail on top . of the foil . .
the nail underneath the foil .
Miss I can't say it

10   no you're doing fine I/ I can see

11   L: Miss forget about the
magnet/ em the magnet holds
it with the foil up the top and
the nail's underneath and the

foil's on top/ and put the
magnet in it and you lift it up
.. and the nail will em . . . hold
it/ stick with the magnet and
the foil's in between

12   oh so even with the foil in
                                         between/ the magnet will still
                                         pick up the nail/ all right does
                                         the magnet pick up the foil

13 L: no (1:7)

Example 8.8 is an example of a traditional IRF sequence. The teacher
expects a particular kind of response (here, *a sentence*) and there is only
a narrow range of possible answers. In her feedback move, the teacher
evaluates the student (and by extension, his answer) positively, but her
feedback move brings closure to the interaction (although this is not
inappropriate in this case since there is no further 'thinking' to be done).
As we have seen, a major function of such a feedback move is that it
enables the teacher to supply the 'correct' information through presenting a point of view that is congruent with the curriculum objectives.
Newman *et al* (1989) describe it as a gatekeeping function where the
teacher is not only saying more, but doing most of the cognitive work too.

Text 8.9 is somewhat more dialogic in its orientation, in that the
topic of the exchange is determined by the student, and the feedback
move is contingent on the student's meaning. It remains IRF-like
however, in that each of the exchanges is closed at the third move, and
the teacher then moves on to another student.

In addressing the criticisms against the traditional IRF structure,
van Lier notes that 'it is important to emphasize that [these criticisms
are] neither a necessary or an exclusive consequence of the IRF structure, merely that this structure may favour this state of affairs' (1996,
p. 151). Even quite small changes may change the orientation of the discourse, as example 8.10 illustrates. This example is the most dialogic of
the three. Like the previous text, the topic of the exchange is determined
by the student, but unlike that example, the teacher, though still leading
the discourse through her questioning, elicits from the student a more
extended contribution through a sequence of exchanges. The teacher's
first initiating move is to invite Lindsay to contribute information about
the topic, then following Lindsay's response she elicits from the student
a clarification and extension of the response. The teacher's feedback
move is therefore not an evaluation but a further question designed to
elicit further information from the student. In this way the initial

255

exchange becomes extended as the teacher helps Lindsay to extend each response in her subsequent moves.

Wells (1996) suggests that in most analyses of classroom discourse, more extended texts between teacher and student (like 8.10) could be analysed as a succession of topically related exchanges or as a single instance of triadic dialogue, with the teacher's request for more information being analysed as a type of follow-up move. However, as he points out, this interpretation does not capture the essential difference in the feedback move between texts like 8.8 and 8.10. Sinclair and Coulthard (1975) propose three functional categories of act for this move: *accept/reject, evaluate* and *comment. Comment* is further broken down into *exemplify, expand,* and *justify.* Mehan's category of evaluate (Mehan 1979) is also broken down to include *reformulate* or *correct.* It would seem then that the feedback move is realized in a number of different ways each of which significantly affects the progress and quality of the discourse.

Wells proposes an alternative analysis for extended interactions like text 8.10. He argues that in conversation there is a tendency within an exchange for moves to decrease in 'prospectiveness'; that is, the degree to which a move expects a response, the most strongly prospective move being a demand. In the classroom, a teacher's initiating move realized as a question to a student is thus strongly prospective. Outside of the classroom, conversations made up of single nuclear exchanges in fact occur far less often than more extended sequences, since, as Wells points out, a second principle accompanies the principle of prospectiveness. At any point following the initiating move, a participant can increase the prospectiveness of their own move so that it in turn requires or expects a response. Thus, in example 8.10, the third move in the first exchange (the teacher asks: *it what?*) can be interpreted not as an evaluation or a feedback move that closes the exchange, but as a 'pivot' for two linked exchanges. As a question, it is a highly prospective move. (In Wells' proposal, Sinclair and Coulthard's categories of feedback such as *exemplify,* or *expand,* could also be analysed as pivotal response moves.) Through these pivot moves, sequences of exchanges can be built up, with each pivot initiating a further exchange which extends or qualifies the previous exchange in some way. Wells refers to such an extended set of exchanges as a 'sequence', defining this as a nuclear exchange plus a number of dependent exchanges which extend and are dependent on the initial nuclear exchange. He argues that in understanding how discourse is jointly constructed (and I would add, how some teacher-student interactions offer more affordances for learning than others) it is this unit, the sequence, that is the most functionally significant.

Wells suggests that when the third move is exploited to become a pivotal move, then the 'division of labour' shifts as the student takes on more of the responsibility in helping to jointly construct the information. The nature of this third move in the exchange is therefore critical: when it is realized as a pivot, rather than as a reformulation or an evaluation, it can lead to more extended sequences where the discourse is opened up and the student's (and teacher's) thinking is made explicit within the discourse. The choice of a pivot move both depends on and develops the intersubjective understanding by the participants about the goal of what they are engaged in.

The teacher's choices at the third move of the exchange can help define more precisely what is meant by a 'contingent' response. As Shuy (1991) suggests, responsive teaching uses contingency questioning rather than evaluation questioning. The use of a pivotal move by the teacher also means that what is about to be said cannot be predicted: the exact meaning of a sequence of discourse which is about to be constructed cannot be anticipated in advance, even though the 'point' of a sequence is typically to be found within the initiating move of the teacher. Wells concludes that it is in such moment to moment joint construction of meaning that the 'craft' of teaching is found (Wells 1996).

Wells' theoretical analysis is valuable in its potential to show alternative discourse patterns that are likely to offer more affordances for second language development. The three examples are analysed here in the light of Wells' framework (see Figure 8.1) and demonstrates how increasing the prospectiveness results in more dialogic patterns of interaction.

Figure 8.1 Increasing the prospectiveness

KEY to abbreviations

Type of exchange
Nuc   = nuclear exchange
Dep   = dependent exchange

Type of move
Init   = Initiation
Resp   = Response
F/back   = Feedback

Function of move
dem.   = demand for information
inf.   = giving information
ack.   = acknowledgement of response, and/or evaluation
reform.   = reformulation

(Adapted from Wells 1996)

Example 8.8

	STUDENTS	TEACHER	
1		what if I try the south pole of this magnet and the north pole of that magnet/ yes Francois/ come on/ a sentence	**Nuc** Init. *dem*
2	F: the south pole and the north pole will attract		Resp. *inf*
3		good boy/ good Francois/	F/back *ack*
4		all right and let's try the south pole of this magnet and the south pole of the other magnet/ Stephanie?	**Nuc** Init *dem*
5	S: the south pole and the south pole will repel		Resp. *inf*
6		good	F/back *ack*

Example 8.9

	STUDENTS	TEACHER	
1		Maroun . something that you can tell me that you found out last lesson	**Nuc** Init *Dem.*
2	Miss I thought that all metal can stick on magnets but . . when I tried it		Resp. *Inf*

	some of them they didn't stick		
3		OK so you thought that no matter what object if it was a metal object it would attracted to the magnet/ OK interesting Milad?	F/back *Reform.*
4	I thought I thought that em the metal coins stick onto the magnet . . it wouldn't/ I put it near it and it didn't got stuck onto it		**Nuc** Resp *Inf*
5		OK it was attracted to the magnet?	F/back *Reform.*
	<u>no</u>	<u>it wasn't</u> OK good	
6		Fabiola?	**Nuc** Init *Dem.*
7	em em I thought that em the . . . em . . Miss what was the object that em could st . . em like . . the coin could stick onto the magnet but it wouldn't		Resp *Inf*
8		OK you/ you predicted that it did it would be attracted to the magnet and it wasn't	F/back *Reform.*

Example 8.10

	STUDENTS	TEACHER	
1		tell us what you found	**Nuc.** Init. *dem*
2	if you put a nail . onto the piece of foil . . and then pick it . pick it up . the magnet will . . . . . . that if you put a . nail . under a piece of foil . and then pick . pick the foil up with the magnet . . still . still with the nail . . under it . . . it won't		Resp. *inf.*
3		it what?	**Dep.** F/back (realized as pivot) *dem*
4	it won't/ it won't come out		Resp. *inf*
5		what won't come out	**Dep** F/back (as pivot) *dem*
6	it'll go up (prompt)*		
7	it'll go up		Resp. *inf*
8		wait just a minute . . can you explain	**Dep** F/back

		that a bit more, Lindsay?	(as pivot) *dem*
9	like if you put a nail and then foil over it and then put the nail on top . of the foil . . the nail <u>underneath</u> the foil/ Miss I can't say it		Resp. *inf*
10		no you're doing fine I/ I can see	**Dep** F/back (as pivot) *dem*
11	Miss forget about the magnet em the magnet holds it with the foil up the top and the nail's underneath and the foil's on top and put the magnet in it and you lift it up . . and the nail will em . . . hold it/stick with the magnet and the foil's in between		Resp. *Inf*
12		oh so even with the foil in between . the . magnet will still pick up the nail . all right	F/back *reform.*

As Figure 8.1 illustrates, in examples 8.8 and 8.9, the feedback move allows no opportunity for a sequence to develop. Its replacement by a 'pivotal' move in example 8.10 produces a sequence in which the dependent exchanges allow for an exploration of the student's meaning. The reformulation eventually comes after five exchanges, unlike unextended sequences where the reformulation is given in the feedback move at the end of the first exchange. Because the teacher holds back the reformulation there is a redistribution of participation in the discourse. Significantly the teacher's move in turn 12 could have come much earlier (in 3) if she had used a feedback move in the nuclear exchange, but this would have greatly reduced the opportunities for negotiation and student learning. What this text suggests is that extended teacher-student talk is not necessarily the result of what has been learned, but the process of learning itself.

There is of course a range of ways in which teachers realize moves that occur in the third position but produce an increase in prospectiveness. In the two classrooms they included the following:

> wait just a minute . . can you explain that a bit more Lindsay?
> so what does that tell us?
> can you explain that again?
> what do you mean *could only stick to one side*?
> I don't understand / what do you mean Francois?
> can you come up here and tell us what you meant by that?
> can you just expand on that a little bit more about what you mean?
> what makes you say that?
> what do you mean/ 'the wrong one'?

The variation of interactional patterns that have been discussed in this section is also significant in providing contexts for subject learning. Lemke (1990) has pointed out that students need to be able to extract science meanings from the classroom dialogue available. Where triadic dialogue is the norm, questions are often only thematically complete with their answers, yet on the basis of a sequence of questions and answers students are required to construct coherent and thematic patterns of discourse. To do this they need to be able to recognize the relationship of one move in a dialogue structure to another, for example how a teacher's cued elicitation question can be pieced together with its response (Lemke 1990). In a broader range of interactional patterns students have increased opportunities to recognize and produce in their own talk the thematic relationships embedded in the field.

It has not of course been the intention in this section to argue that all teacher-student exchanges should be extended sequences, since, as Chapter 6 has argued, exchanges like texts 8.8 and 8.9 are more appropriate on some occasions and for some purposes. But such an analysis is a way of foregrounding discourse *options* for teacher-student talk, options which may offer more affordances for certain aspects of language and subject learning.

Having speaker rights

I have suggested that entering the discourse on one's own terms and engaging in sustained talk encourages participation. But simply being invited to take the floor is not necessarily enabling of language learning, and indeed it may have very much the opposite effect if students are made to feel inadequate or left without guidance at a point of need. Neither can it be described as an affordance for learning if a speaker's participation 'rights' are not upheld. In Chapter 3 I argued that successful classroom language learning is tied to a teacher providing learners with official participatory rights to engage in opportunities for learning (see Hall 1998). One tangible example of the protection of speaker rights was the refusal by both teachers to allow interruption by more competent or confident speakers during reporting episodes, especially the periods of often extended wait time. Despite the dialogic quality of the interactions in the teacher-guided reporting, where as we have seen in general teacher-talk is less strongly marked for status, both teachers regularly asserted explicit control when it became necessary to protect the participation rights of a speaker. Students were not therefore simply invited to engage in the dialogue but afforded the opportunity to do so. Example 8.11 illustrates this.

Example 8.11

Belinda is referring to the fact that two magnets only attract when opposite poles face each other. When faced with the teacher's clarification question, Belinda hesitates for some time, and George attempts to interrupt with the 'answer'.

	STUDENT	TEACHER
1	B: the magnet could only stick on one side	
2		what do you mean could only stick on one side?
3	*(B hesitates for 5 seconds, George interrupts and tries to explain)*	no no George . <u>let</u> <u>her</u> <u>try</u> . . *(said with emphasis)*
4	B: Miss . . . . like if you put the magnet together	

5		two magnets together?
6	two magnets together . then it sticks and then you try the other side it doesn't stick	
7	[yes	[ahh . . so you tried putting two magnets together and . one side . they would stick together and the other side they didn't/ all right we're getting some good information

An increase in wait time has been associated with significant changes in a student's use of language and in the attitudes and expectations of both students and teachers (Rowe 1986). The five-second wait in turn 3 is considerably longer than teachers typically allow, but that wait time is 'safeguarded' by the ground rules of the classroom. In both classrooms, the insistence by the teacher on a student's right to speak without interruption, and their consistency in maintaining this, appeared to create the kind of interactional environment where extended wait time was seen as usual, and was not a source of unease for the speakers nor impatience for the listeners.

If classrooms are to be constructed as communities of enquiry which offer affordances for learning to all students, then attention must be given not only to the planned curriculum – the learning activities in which learners participate – but to the processes by which the curriculum is enacted. In the classroom, destructive social processes are those that undermine social cohesion (Wells 2002), for example, by demonstrating a lack of consideration for others or preventing or constraining their participation. As we saw in Chapter 5, teachers made the social rules of the classroom community explicit, but this did not occur simply when the teacher had cause to admonish a student or to overtly control behaviour. Rather, the cultural and social rules of the classroom, such as the importance of working collaboratively, of respecting the contributions of others, and of recognizing the consequences of one's actions, were an integral part of the common knowledge that was being built up. Not only the participatory roles of speakers but also the responsibilities of listeners were taken into account. Viewing this explicitness of 'how to be a student' not as an aspect of teacher power and control but as an apprenticing of the students into the social rules governing the activity system of the classroom, suggests a different reading of texts like 8.11 and the examples in Chapter 5. Perhaps because most students understood and in general followed the rules of classroom behaviour, teachers were subsequently able to use the more dialogic, and less controlling, interactional patterns associated with discourse contexts more enabling of language learning. Making explicit the cultural values and behavioural boundaries of the classroom thus resulted in a teaching environment where little time was wasted on overt control of behaviour. For most of the time, teachers managed learning rather than learners, and as many examples have shown, students were positioned as worthy conversational partners and as persons in an educational relationship, rather than as instructional objects.

Opportunities to reconsider how things are said

One of the characteristics of many of the examples has been the time and opportunities allowed to students to reconsider their responses and reformulate their earlier attempts. The positive effect of this on students' language has been shown in a number of examples (see, for example, 6.6, 6.7, 6.8, 6.13, 7.7 and the discussion of Francis, Gina and Francois in 7.11). Other studies have suggested similar results when learners are given time to reformulate their own contribution to the discourse (see, for example, Forman and Cazden 1985). An additional example of student reformulation is included below (8.12). Gina is attempting to describe how a gold-coloured nail was not magnetic and therefore was not attracted to either of the magnets the group was using. Her second attempt is considerably more explicit and coherent than her first, yet as in similar examples this appears to come about simply through being given extra time to reformulate a response: it is not simply teacher 'wait time' that is important here, but the slowing down of the typically fast pace of classroom discourse.

Example 8.12

	STUDENTS	TEACHER
Gina	we had a . . gold nail . . and . the gold nail . . neither of them/ neither/ both of the magnets won't . touch to the gold nail	
Maroun	that's not real gold	
Janet	it's a screw	

265

	say that again very loudly so that . Veronica can hear you back there
Gina	we had a gold nail and the gold nail would not touch/ attach/ attract to any of the magnets

Entering the discourse as expert, having extended conversation with the teacher, being given time to reconsider the form of the message and having one's participation rights respected produce affordances for language development. But equally important is that through scaffolded interaction with the teacher, students were almost always able to successfully communicate their intended meanings and as a result they are positioned pedagogically as capable interactants and learners.

Talking about talk

The case has been made in this book and in other studies (for example, Moll 1994) that interactional scaffolding is central in the building of Vygotsky's zone of proximal development and that such scaffolding is of particular significance for at-risk second language learners. In the two classrooms we have seen that what was involved here was not only the deliberate scaffolding of subject-specific knowledge, and explicit talk about being a student, but also a focus on how language works. Many educational linguists and curriculum and syllabus documents in Australia now call for explicit attention to be given to all aspects of language across subject areas, including vocabulary, sentence-level grammar, connectives and conjunctions, the range of text types associated with learning across the curriculum and an awareness of the relationship and differences between spoken and written language (Christie 1990; Cope and Kalantzis 1995; Freebody, Ludwig and Gunn 1995; Hasan and Williams 1997). Many examples have already been given of how the two teachers integrated this language focus into talk about science. But what is of interest here is the learners' perspective on what they found useful in the kinds of talk in which they took part.

Example 8.13 comes from the end of a reporting session, prior to the students carrying out some writing. The teacher and students begin by talking about some of the differences between speech and writing, but continue with a short discussion about the usefulness of talk as a preparation for writing:

Example 8.13

STUDENTS	TEACHER
1	we've helped each other to find some words that we're going to write . . now before we write . . what are some differences/ what are some differences that you can think of between writing and speaking?/ I want you to think about when you talk and when you write . . what are some differences? Amanda?
2 when you talk it's hard because you have to put your hands in your pockets (*referring to a reporting session when the teacher encouraged students to explain without using gestures*)	
3	oh (*laughing*) when we did that exercise/ yes that was hard/ Jennifer
4 when you talk/ when you write/ em the/ you think . . when you talk you don't know what to say	
5	so Jen's saying that she has time to think when she writes and that/ that helps a lot . . you don't have the same <u>thinking</u> time/ good anybody else have . . the difference between writing and speaking, George?
6 Miss when you're writing you need more detail than what you . . . when you're speaking	
7	mm/ what does he mean by that Joseph?

8 when you're writing you have
to make the people . . you
have to let the people
understand what you're
writing and when you're doing
something they could <u>see</u> what
you're doing . . . what you mean

9 good/ he said that when you write
you have to let the people
understand what you're writing/
but when you're talking they can
see/ so George says you need more
detail when you write than when
you talk . just a question/ which do
you find easier/ writing or speaking

10 writing

11 writing

12 you find writing easier . . that's
interesting Francois

13 speaking Miss because the/
explaining like if like/ if
someone didn't understand
you got to ask them what does
it mean/ that's how it's easier

14 ah so you can/ you can talk to
somebody right away and get an
answer/ anybody else have any
other comment before we go away/
of what helps you to write better?

15 what we've been doing
here/ (*referring to the reporting
session*) what we've been doing
here/ does that help you at all to
write? Lindsay?

16 it helps when you share with
others

17 it helps when you share with others
what . . by writing or by talking?

18 both

19   both/ so you like the idea of talking
                                             before you write or no/ does that
                                             help at all? what we've been doing
                                             here/ I don't know/ that's what I
                                             need to know/ does it help to do
                                             this first? Belinda would it have
                                             been easier to just have you go off
                                             and write/ do you find this kind of
                                             thing is easier first/ before you
                                             write or do you like just to go and
                                             write?

20 when you speak you know
    what you're going to write in
    the book/ what you're going
    to write in the book and

21   (*teacher nods*) what do you find
                                             Carol Ann? do you like to talk
                                             about things first before you write
                                             or do you like to just go directly
                                             and write

22 I like to speak out so I can
    (*unclear*)

23   mm/ one last comment

24 Miss in writing you have to
    like draw a few pictures so
    they get a picture in your mind
    of something

25   you have to/ you have to/ Mario
                                             you haven't had a chance to say
                                             anything

26 Miss I think that em/ I/ I think
    you go and do/ talking/ before
    you write you have all . . the . .
    more information to know
    what you're going to write

27   so/ so you like to talk about things
                                             first?

28   yes Miss because if you talk
about things first you you/ the .
the . . person might helped you
get more information

A student in the same class wrote the following comments in her journal:

Not only did I learn from what I have experimented but from others who have shared their ideas with the class and I. They shared things about the two sides of the magnets and why they repel. In that time I learned how to respond to others what I think the answer was.

A year after this study was completed the teacher had grown increasingly interested in the role of spoken language in learning and literacy development, and in what students themselves could tell a teacher about what helped them to learn. In the science unit the children had then just completed (on how gears work), she had followed closely the same sequence of activities as those described in this study: children had first taken part in experiential work, reported on it and then written in their science journals. The context is similar enough for the following student comments to be of relevance. The discussion took place after students had completed journal writing, which was particularly well written by many of them, and was in response to the teacher asking them what had helped them to write.

Teacher question: Can you tell me what helped you to write clearly?
Individual student comments:
I discussed it with my group
talking helped me
we all had a turn at speaking
the others helped
it helped when we discussed
it was easier because we learned about it a lot/ like I knew about it
everyone in our group talked
talking helped me know what to do

These comments reveal that many children found helpful the opportunities for talking about what they were learning, and listening to what others said. They also reveal a surprising sophistication about language itself. In both sets of examples students appear to have quite clear ideas about the differences between speech and writing. They indicate some understanding at a metalinguistic level of the increased decontextualization of written language: *when you're writing you have to make the people . . you have to let the people understand what you're writing and when you're doing something they could see what you're doing . . . what you mean.* They are aware of how a lack of immediate feedback makes written language more complex: *when someone didn't understand you got to ask them what does it mean/ that's how it's [spoken language] easier.* And they are aware of the way that written language must therefore create a fuller context for the audience: *when you're writing you need more detail than . . . when you're speaking.* One student also comments that writing is easier *because we learned about it a lot, like I knew about it,* supporting the importance of field-building prior to beginning to write.

Implications for practice and research

A major implication of this study for second language research is the impossibility of analysing students' language learning in isolation from the cultural, historical and linguistic frameworks in which it occurs. Yet as mentioned at the beginning of this chapter, there exists no ready-made research procedure for an approach that shows the emergence and development of learning, the contextual location of specific learning opportunities and the value and effectiveness of differing interactional contexts and pedagogical strategies.

One way to develop such an approach is through the ontogenetic approach used in this study, which can show, even over a relatively short period of time, the relationship between particular interactions and language learning. Only by focusing on a sequence of activities (in this case, a unit of work), rather than a single lesson or exchange, is it possible to show how the changes in the nature of the discourse, and the differential interactional roles played by the teacher, impacted on students' language and curriculum learning.

Such situated research needs to be underpinned by both a socially oriented view of learning and a theory of language-in-context. This book has attempted to develop such an approach by drawing on sociocultural theory and systemic functional linguistics as a way of interpreting the interactions in two second-language classrooms. I suggest that both theories are necessary in this endeavour. What is often lacking in studies of second language development is a model of language which goes beyond a description of its phonology, morphology and syntax, one which allows for the study of discourse both as 'process' and 'product', as what is being said and what has been said. Such a model also makes it possible to recognize the development of a learner's range of functional varieties of language, including the academic registers of school. But a classroom also reflects both a social and a historical context, thus also needs to be interpreted in terms of how it means to the learners who are currently participants in the discourse and who have been participants in earlier classroom conversations. Learning involves the interpretation and production of meanings which for the learner are interrelated in a dynamic and changing context. The notion of context then must also include the existence of the 'long conversation' in which teacher and learner have been engaged over time in constructing shared meanings.

The integration of social theories of learning and language has allowed, for example, a richer interpretation of how discourse can be made 'comprehensible' to learners. Examples have shown that this occurs through the existence of multiple sources of meaning within a single situational context: the immediate visual situational context, alternate semiotic systems (such as graphs), the use of linguistic mode shifts by the teacher and the existence of shared information which had previously been built up over a sequence of episodes. It has also been possible to illustrate the problematic nature of classifying classrooms in terms such as 'open' or 'closed, or 'centring' descriptions such as teacher or learner centred. Rather, the classroom can be interpreted as one kind of activity system (see, for example, Engerstrom 1990; Wells 1999; Michell and Sharpe 2005), and as in all activity systems, when actions (or in terms of the classroom, teaching and learning activities) change, then so too must participant roles and cultural rules. Conversely, if there are to be changes in participant roles, so too will there be changes in the nature of activities and the talk that enacts them. A recognition that different pedagogical purposes require different teacher roles, at different times in the activity of learning, resolves the tension between approaches that focus on the 'transmission' of culturally valued knowledge and those that aim towards the 'development' of individual growth. Such an approach to teaching-and-learning as an interrelated activity brings together both the personal resources that learners bring to the learning situation, and the valued and systematized knowledge and language of the culture.

At the beginning of this book I argued that classroom-based research has the capacity to make explicit teachers' intuitive understandings of their practices. Chapters 6 and 7 concluded with some observations relevant to practice and these will not be repeated here. Several major implications for educational practices emerge, however.

First is the need for teachers (as well as researchers) to have as part of their own cognitive resources an explicit model of language-in-context that enables them to recognize the predictable relationship between a particular situational context and language use in that context. Central to this is an understanding of the relationship between spoken and written language in the educational context. Moving away from the notion that language is transparent and unproblematic and a 'given' for students and instead viewing the curriculum through the lens of language, is essential to the design of programmes that are concerned both with students' language development and with the development of subject knowledge. So too is teachers' critical awareness of their own language use. While teaching and learning activities are usually consciously planned by teachers, the interactional means by which they are played out is rarely at the level of explicit awareness. Becoming aware of the range of interactional options available to teachers means holding up to the light what is frequently below the level of conscious thought, but as this book has suggested, such scrutiny may lead to recognizing points of 'leverage' for interactional and educational change.

A second major implication is the significance for second language learners (and probably for others too) of an explicit curriculum, a curriculum where talk is not restricted to the primary instructional field but also includes a focus on how language is used and how collaborative learning is to be enacted in the classroom. As many examples have suggested, an explicit curriculum also demonstrates the three-way relationship between students' prior knowledge and experiences, the learning task they are engaged in and the broader concepts and generalized meanings of the curriculum. I have also argued that the intertextual links between classroom activities, as well as the nature of the activities themselves, are significant for second language learning (and for this reason I have suggested that content-based language teaching offers an advantage over language classrooms where language itself is the primary field). In an explicit curriculum, the 'long conversation' remains coherent and ongoing at the macro level (that is throughout a unit of work or sequence of units), and is characterized by discourse that is proleptic rather than implicit, and by talk in which reasoning and principled forms of knowledge are marked as significant. When significant linguistic and cognitive links are not made explicit in discourse, the long conversation is cut short, and language may then become truly 'decontextualized'[2] for learners. This may occur, for example, when teachers fail to make explicit the thematic links between their questions and the students' responses, or between texts which students are expected to read or write and the spoken discourse of the lesson. Scaffolding for second language learners thus includes the active encouragement of sustained long conversations through coherent sequences of activities, so that discourse is always 'contextualized' in this more dynamic sense.

I have argued throughout the book that the creation of classrooms where teachers encourage the dialogic function of discourse to emerge, is likely to lead to the kind of teacher-student talk that also offers affordances for language development. Ultimately of course, the development of a more dialogic classroom does not come about through a checklist for teachers of procedures to follow, but is the result of the epistemological orientation and dispositions of the teacher. Where knowledge is viewed as co-constructed between teachers and learners, or between learners, not as a commodity to be transmitted to learners, there is potential for more symmetrical and collaborative classroom interactions to occur.

One of Wittgenstein's dictums is that 'there are remarks that sow and remarks that reap' (in van Lier 2000). As van Lier has observed, in second language learning research we have traditionally tended to look for evidence and examples of the 'reaping' kind. This book has attempted to identify some of the 'sowing' events for young second language learners in classroom life.

Notes

1 For more detailed discussion of 'given' and 'new' see Halliday 1995, p. 277; van Lier 1996, p. 172.
2 That is, without a situational or a historical context. While written language is sometimes referred to as 'decontextualized', it may, as we have seen, be highly contextualized if it is intertextually related to the long conversation.

Glossary of systemic functional linguistic terms

actor:
the 'doer' with respect to a material process.

circumstance:
the circumstances associated with the process and typically realized by an adverbial group or prepositional phrase.

exophoric reference:
reference to something/someone outside the text, within the immediate concrete situation in which the language is being used.

field:
the field of discourse refers to what the language is being used to talk about, and is realized in terms of the ideational metafunction.

lexis:
the 'content' vocabulary of a text

metafunction:
there are three metafunctions of language which express three kinds of meaning, each expressing one kind of semantic organization, ideational (experiential and logical), interpersonal and textual. Experiential meaning is realized through the lexis and transitivity structures. Interpersonal meaning is realized primarily through mood choices, modality and modulation and also forms of address. Textual meaning is realized through the thematic structure of the clause.

modality:
modality refers in a general way to the linguistic resources which code meanings between positive and negative polarity. It also refers more specifically to the expression of possibility, usuality and probability. Included under the general term of modality is *modulation*, which codes degrees of obligation in relation to offers and commands.

participant:
the persons, things and abstract concepts associated with the process, typically realized by the nominal group(s).

process:
the core of the structure typically realized through the verbal group.

register:
the linguistic register of a text is made up of three situational variables, field, tenor and mode, each of which determines the appropriateness of the linguistic options and the choices made by the speaker.

tenor:

the tenor of the discourse refers to the relationship constructed between the speaker/listener or reader/writer, and is realized in terms of the interpersonal metafunction.

theme:

the 'point of departure' for the speaker, realized by first position in the clause.

transitivity:

the system for realizing the experiential aspect of meaning at clause level. It specifies the different types of process in the language, and the structures by which they are expressed.

Appendix: Episode summaries

Classroom 1

No.	Teaching/learning processes	HOW		WHAT		
		Dominant participant and interaction structures	Mode/degree of context-embeddedness	Knowledge constructed about science	Knowledge constructed about language	Knowledge constructed about how to be a student
	LESSON 1					
1	**Introduction to Unit** T sets problem (how to get a pin out of a glass of water)	T/Class: IRF	Spoken	Introduction to properties of magnets.		
2	**Discussion of problem**	Pairs: Participatory	Spoken			
3	**Sharing of solutions** Ss suggest solutions to class	T/Class: Dialogic	Spoken			
4	**Sharing of prior knowledge of magnets**	T/Class: Dialogic	Spoken: Construction based on previous experience. T writes up suggestions as concept map.	Prior knowledge: e.g. *Magnets can pick up things.* *Magnets don't stick to steel.*	Talk by T about *key words, how ideas go together, organizing information.*	*Good that you were watching.* (Spoken when T made a mistake on the board.)

| No. | Teaching/learning processes | HOW | | WHAT | | |
		Dominant participant and interaction structures	Mode/degree of context-embeddedness	Knowledge constructed about science	Knowledge constructed about language	Knowledge constructed about how to be a student
5	**Setting up new task** Task is to use magnets and a selection of magnetic and non-magnetic objects, find out something and record it. Told they will report to class tomorrow.	T/Class: Monologue and IRF	Spoken: T gives instructions. Ss retell.	Magnetic and non-magnetic materials.		
6	**Carrying out the task** Testing whether objects are magnetic or non-magnetic, and recording results	Group: Participatory	Spoken: context-embedded, language accompanying action.	Magnetic and non-magnetic materials, e.g. *Magnets don't stick to money.*		Reminder about group work, need to work together. T talks about listening behaviour and turn taking: *one person at a time.*
7	**Teacher-guided reporting**	T/Class: Dialogic	Spoken: reconstruction of personal experience.	Magnetic and non-magnetic materials. *Magnets are strong. They can attract through things.*		*We have a rule* (said when child interrupted the speaker). *Why didn't your hand go up to tell us?* (to child who

					had not heard previous speaker). If you talk I can't hear. One person at a time. I only talk to people with their hand up.
8	**Teaching new lexis** Teacher gives new lexis and focuses on form	T/Class: Monologue and IRF	Spoken: Construction based on reconstruction of experience. Ss using more 'written-like' discourse, responses given as full sentences.	Magnetic attraction. Written on board: *The magnets attracted/ didn't attract.*	Science lexis: *attract* Focus on tense *attracted/ this is yesterday.* T: *Say it in a sentence.* ⟨*Raise your hand when you have something to say.*⟩
9	**Setting up new task** Language-based task, making generalizations about magnets	T/Class: Monologue IRF	Spoken: T gives examples of generalizations.		
10	**Carrying out task** Making generalizations about magnets	Groups: Participatory	Spoken: Construction based on earlier reconstruction of experiences.	Magnets don't attract all metals. It doesn't depend on the colour of the metal.	*One at a time (spoken by students in group).*

No.	Teaching/learning processes	HOW		WHAT		
		Dominant participant and interaction structures	Mode/degree of context-embeddedness	Knowledge constructed about science	Knowledge constructed about language	Knowledge constructed about how to be a student
11	**Teacher-guided reporting** Reporting back of students' ideas re: generalizations	T/class: Dialogic	Spoken: Construction based on earlier reconstruction of personal experiences.	Magnets don't attract all metals. Magnets only attract some metals.		T to child calling out: *I love it when you have good things to say but not when you call out.*
12	**Teaching new lexis**	T/ class: IRF	Spoken	Meaning of *magnetic* and *non-magnetic*.	Science lexis: *magnetic, non-magnetic* *Magnets attract . . . Magnets don't attract . . .* Non-words (e.g. *non-magnetic, non-toxic, non-fiction*) T refers *to talking like scientists.*	
13	**Setting up new task to test repulsion** T gives new lexis. T gives instruction.	T/Class: Monologue and IRF	Spoken: T gives instructions. Ss retell.		Science lexis: *north pole, south pole*	

14	**Carrying out task: doing experiment** Testing repulsion	Groups: Participatory	Spoken: Context-embedded.	Like poles repel, unlike poles attract.	Science lexis: *repel*
15	**Teaching new lexis**	T/class: IRF	Spoken	Like poles repel, unlike poles attract.	Science lexis: *repel*
16	**Teacher-guided reporting**	T/Class: Dialogic	Spoken: Reconstruction of personal experience.		
17	**Making generalizations** Ss make generalizations based on matrix on board	T/Class: IRF	Spoken: Construction based on earlier reconstruction of personal experiences.	The north pole and the north pole repel. The south pole and the south pole repel. The north pole and the south pole attract.	T defines/explains meaning of *generalization: something that will happen all the time/ not just what happened today.*
18	**Teacher-guided reporting** (Continued from episode 16.) Discussion of George's experiments.	T/Class: Dialogic and Participatory	Spoken: Context-embedded, language accompanying action.		
19	**Setting up new task** (journal writing)	T/Class: IRF and Dialogic			Review of field lexis, and discussion of differences between speaking and writing. T refers to *writing like a scientist.*

No.	Teaching/learning processes	HOW		WHAT		
		Dominant participant and interaction structures	Mode/degree of context-embeddedness	Knowledge constructed about science	Knowledge constructed about language	Knowledge constructed about how to be a student
20	Journal writing	Individual	Written	Personal learning (what I have learned about magnets).		
21	Recap and set up for new task Testing strength of magnets	T/Class: Dialogic Monologue and IRF	Spoken: T gives instructions. Ss retell.			
22	Carrying out task: doing experiment Comparing strengths of different magnets	Groups: Participatory	Spoken: Context-embedded, language accompanying action.	The size of the magnet affects its strength.		
23	Teacher-guided reporting	T/Class: Dialogic	Spoken: Reconstruction of personal experience.			
24	Review of what has been learned	T/Class: Dialogic		Review of knowledge.		
25	Setting up new task To test effect of magnets on iron flings; filings on paper, magnet held underneath	T/Class: Monologue IRF	Spoken: T gives instructions. Ss retell.			

26	**Carrying task out: doing experiment** (effect of magnet on iron filings)	Group: Participatory	Spoken: Context-embedded, language accompanying action.	Iron filings are magnetic. The position of the magnet affects the movement of the iron filings.
27	**Teacher-guided reporting**	T/Class: Dialogic	Spoken: Reconstruction of personal experience.	Magnets have a force field.

Classroom 2

No.	Teaching/learning processes	HOW		WHAT		
		Dominant participant and interaction structures	Mode/degree of context-embeddedness	Knowledge constructed about science	Knowledge constructed about language	Knowledge constructed about how to be a student
1	**LESSON 1** **Introduction to Unit** T talks about what students are going to do. Elicits Ss' prior knowledge of field.	T/Class: IRF	Spoken. Written on board: *What do you know about magnets?*	Prior knowledge, e.g. fridge magnets for advertising.		
2	**Individual reflection** Ss write down what they already know	Individual	Written: Personal knowledge.	Prior knowledge. Ss suggest: *Magnets stick to metal. Magnets can stick on fridges. Magnets can stick to each other.*		
3	**Sharing of individual reflection** Ss exchange information with partner	Pairs: Participatory	Spoken: Talk based on written texts, i.e. written language spoken aloud.	Prior knowledge.		
4	**Setting up concept map** T models how to organize concept map, using Ss' ideas. T gives instructions to students about how to	T/Class: IRF and Dialogic	Spoken: Ss give ideas and T scribes (writes as students say, unedited) T gives	Prior knowledge: e.g. *Magnets have a forcefield. Magnets are used on fridges to stick notices.You can stick magnets on the fridge. Magnets stick to metal.*	Talk by T about key words, how ideas go together, organizing information.	*Good that you were watching.* (Spoken when S pointed out mistake T had made on the board.

#	Stage / Activity	Interaction	Mode	Examples	Student language
	construct their own concept map		instructions. Ss retell.	*Magnets are good for putting messages.*	
5	**Constructing individual concept maps** Ss organize personal knowledge using concept map	Individual	Written: Personal knowledge.	Prior knowledge: e.g. *Magnets can stick on fridges. I know that magnets can move things. I know about magnets that they stick to metal.*	
6	**Setting up for new task** (to share concept maps). T gives instructions and models sharing of individual concept maps.	T/Class: IRF	Spoken: T takes on role of students: *Let's pretend I'm working with M, I might say '........'*		
7	**Explaining personal ideas to others** Ss share and justify their concept maps	Pairs: Participatory	Spoken: Based on what Ss have written.	*I attach 'stick' to 'powerful'.* *I put 'attach' and 'messages' because you can attach the magnet.*	Ss asking each other for lexis: *What's that called?* — Ss refer to: *Your turn, Your go.*
	T interrupts pair-work briefly: reminds Ss to ask each other questions, and gives instructions to make some generalizations about magnets based on what they already know	T/Class: Monologue			S to group: *What we should do if we're going to make a generalization on magnets we should start with the main idea.*

No.	Teaching/learning processes	HOW		WHAT		
		Dominant participant and interaction structures	Mode/degree of context-embeddedness	Knowledge constructed about science	Knowledge constructed about language	Knowledge constructed about how to be a student
8	**Teacher-guided reporting** Making generalizations. Ss share information gained in previous episode with whole class.	T/Class: Dialogic	Spoken: Ss reconstructing shared knowledge of group. T expanding, rewording.	Prior knowledge of the groups.		Listening behaviour. Listening to each other and not getting distracted.
9	**Student-generated questions** Ss pose questions about what they would like to find out	T/Class: Dialogic	Ss speaking, T writing (their questions).	Prior knowledge of the groups.		Good listening behaviour. Importance of listening and concentrating for learning. T tells Ss that she doesn't know all the answers.
10 (i)	LESSON 2 **Recap** Teacher-guided reporting: talk about what happened last lesson (procedures and knowledge)	T/Class: Dialogic	Spoken by T + S: Ss reconstructing events of past lesson.	Prior knowledge of the groups.	*Classify means putting like ideas together* Science lexis: *attract.*	

10 **(ii)**	**and** **Set up for new task** (to find similarities and differences between different magnets) T gives instructions for task	T/Class: Monologue	Spoken: Context-embedded, language accompanying action. (T is demonstrating with materials.)	
11 **(i)**	**Carrying out the task** Finding similarities and differences between different shaped magnets	Groups: Participatory	Spoken: Context-embedded language accompanying action.	Similarities and differences between magnets.
	T interrupts groups to give instructions for sorting and recording	T/Class: Monologue and IRF	Spoken: T gives further instructions. Ss retells instructions.	*T refers to sitting patiently when you've finished. Listening behaviour. T refers to the rule when sitting on the floor.*
11 **(ii)**	**Sorting small objects, and recording.** Ss sort objects (pin, needle, lid, coin, pasta, plastic lid, etc.) using own criteria, record how they group them	Group: Participatory	Spoken: Context-embedded language accompanying action. Written: Ss record names of objects in each group.	Ss asking each other for names of objects: *What are these called what does mean?* e.g. split pin, thumbtack, pasta, pin.

No.	Teaching/learning processes	HOW		WHAT		
		Dominant participant and interaction structures	Mode/degree of context-embeddedness	Knowledge constructed about science	Knowledge constructed about language	Knowledge constructed about how to be a student
12	**Setting up new task** T gives instructions for next activity	T/Class: Monologue and IRF	Spoken: Context-embedded. T demonstrates using materials.	What objects will attract and what won't attract: magnetic and non-magnetic objects.	Meaning of *predict*. Language for predicting. Ss suggest: *I think, I suppose, my prediction is, maybe.*	How to work in groups. Listening behaviour. Focusing attention on speakers. Cooperating.
13	**Carrying out task and predicting results** Ss predict which objects are magnetic, test predictions and record results	Group: Participatory	Spoken: Context-embedded, language accompanying action; large number of imperatives/action exchanges.	Magnetic and non-magnetic objects.		
14	**Teacher-guided reporting** Ss report results of experiment to class	T/Class: Dialogic	Spoken: Language reconstructing personal experience	Magnetic and non-magnetic objects.	Science lexis: *repel* Reminder from T to use *language we talked about* (re: prediction)	Listening behaviour. Importance of listening. Should look at speaker.

15 (i)	**LESSON 3** **Recap** T recaps on last class	T/Class: Dialogic	Spoken: Language reconstructing personal experience.		
15 (ii)	**and** **Set up for new task** (Language-based task). T models and elicits generalizations based on reports in episode 14.	T/Class: IRF and Dialogic	Spoken T models more *written-like* spoken language. T writes on board Ss's suggestions for starting a generalization: most; all; many; some; magnets; metal.	Properties of magnets.	Meaning of *generalization*. How to begin a generalization. Suggestions from Ss: *all, some, most, many, the thing's name.*
15 (iii)	**Oral rehearsal for writing activity** Ss share one generalization with a partner	Pairs: Participatory	Spoken: Rehearsal for writing, written reconstruction based on previous experiences.	Properties of magnets.	
15 (iv)	**Set up for new task** Language-based task, writing generalizations	T/Class: Monologue and IRF	Spoken: T gives instructions. Ss retell. Ss ask questions about task.		Meaning of generalization S: *do we write sentences?* S: *What is that word you speak?*

No.	Teaching/learning processes	HOW		WHAT		
		Dominant participant and interaction structures	Mode/degree of context-embeddedness	Knowledge constructed about science	Knowledge constructed about language	Knowledge constructed about how to be a student
16	**Writing generalizations**	Individual	Written: Construction based on earlier reconstructions of personal experiences.	Properties of magnets.		
17	**Sharing written generalizations** Ss share individual generalizations with class	T/Class: Dialogic and IRF	Spoken: Construction based on earlier reconstructions of personal experiences.	Properties of magnets.	Joining two sentences with a connective.	Concentrating.
18	**Set up for new task** (finding out about behaviour of two magnets). T gives instructions, referring to written instructions.	T/Class: Monologue	Spoken and written: modeshifting, T. demonstrates written instructions using objects.		Science lexis: (based on written instructions) e.g. *smooth surface, poles, alternating.*	How to work in groups: working collaboratively.
19	**Carrying out task** Doing experiment, finding out how two bar magnets behave	Group: Participatory (T joins group) Dialogic	Spoken: Context-embedded, language accompanying action;	Magnetic attraction and repulsion.	S: *what's that called?*	Taking turns, having a go.

No.	Activity	Interaction	Mode	Content	Notes
20	**Teacher-guided reporting** (about process of group work)	T/Class: Dialogic	large number of imperatives and action exchanges. Spoken: Reconstruction of personal experiences.		What helps group work.
21	**LESSON 4 Recap and set up**	T/Class: Monologue	Spoken: T gives instructions. Ss retell.	Magnetic attraction and repulsion.	T refers to *clear precise language,* and *unpacking language.*
22	**Recounting experiment and guiding results** In groups Ss reflect on findings from episode 19 (rehearsal for teacher-guided reporting)	Group: Participatory	Spoken: Reconstruction of experience, (without concrete referents), a jointly constructed oral report.	Magnetic attraction and repulsion.	
23 (i)	**Teacher-guided reporting**	T/Class: Dialogic	Spoken: Reconstruction of personal experiences.		Listening behaviour.
23 (ii)	**Summarizing findings and making generalizations**	T/Class: IRF	Spoken: Construction based on earlier reconstructions of personal experiences.	Opposite poles attract. Like poles repel.	Revision of science lexis.

No.	Teaching/learning processes	HOW		Knowledge constructed about science	WHAT	
		Dominant participant and interaction structures	Mode/degree of context-embeddedness of discourse		Knowledge constructed about language	Knowledge constructed about how to be a student
23 (iii)	Setting up new task (writing generalizations). Language-based task.	T/Class: Monologue and IRF	Spoken and written: T writes key lexis on board, using suggestions from Ss. T gives instructions. Ss retell.	Opposite poles attract. Like poles repel.	Science lexis revised. Generalizing. S asks *do we have to write in a sentence?*	
24	Writing generalizations In groups Ss write two statements	Group: Participatory	Spoken and written: Ss write about their own experiment, and then about their overall learning.	Various – personal learning.	Spelling (Ss request spelling of some words).	
25	Sharing writing with class	T/Class: Dialogic	Written and spoken: Ss read aloud their writing from previous episode T demonstrates with magnets as Ss are reading.	Opposites poles attract. Like poles repel.	How to write a generalization. Revising how to write for an audience. T talks about *Making language more precise.* S uses *whereas.* T draws attention to this, refers to it as a	

					connective. Revision of Science lexis	
26	**Writing** What Ss have learned so far	Individual	Written	Various – personal learning.		
27	**LESSON 5** **Recap** and **set up for new task** (comparing north and south poles and presenting information on graph). T models how to construct graph.	T/Class: Dialogic T/Class: Monologue	Spoken: Constructing generalizations. Spoken: Mode shifting, T demonstrates written instructions using concrete objects, also referring to graph on board. T models role of Ss: *I might say . . .*	Presenting information as a graph.	Need to read instructions. Language for predicting: suggestions from Ss *it could be, my prediction is, probably.*	Raising hand. Need for concentration.
28	**Carrying out task** Doing experiment, comparing different magnets, and both poles, to find out relative strengths. Information presented as a bar graph.	Group: Participatory	Spoken: context-embedded, language accompanying action.	Relative strength of poles, and relative strength of different magnets. Graphing information.		

No.	Teaching/learning processes	HOW		WHAT		
		Dominant participant and interaction structures	Mode/degree of context-embeddedness of discourse	Knowledge constructed about science	Knowledge constructed about language	Knowledge constructed about how to be a student
29	LESSON 6 Recap	T/Class: Dialogic	Spoken: Reconstruction of experience based on previous episode.	Relative strength of poles, and relative strength of different magnets. Graphing information.	Lexis for graphing: *axis, vertical, horizontal*.	
		Monologue and IRF				Need for concentration.
	and set up for new task (comparing relative strengths of different magnets and of poles)	Monologue and IRF	Mode shifting, T demonstrates written instructions using concrete objects, also referring to graph on board.			
30	**Carrying out task** Doing experiment. Comparing strengths of different magnets, and of each pole.	Group: Participatory	Spoken: Context-embedded, language accompanying action.	Relative strength of poles, and relative strength of different magnets. Graphing information.		
31	**Teacher-guided reporting** Reporting of results from episodes 28 and 30.	T/Class: Dialogic IRF	Spoken: Reconstruction of experiences based on previous episode.	Relative strength of poles, and relative strength of different magnets. Graphing	T explains that when Ss are reporting, listeners should be able to *get a picture in*	

#	Stage	Interaction	Mode	Content	Language focus	Importance
			Construction of generalizations based on reconstructions.	information. (Note – Ss *your mind.* reach incorrect conclusions: *The north pole is stronger than the south pole.*)		
32	**LESSON 7 Recap** (of four experiments in episodes 28 and 30)	T/Class: Monologue Dialogic IRF	Spoken: Reconstruction of experiences.	T refers to *being true scientists, thinking and talking like scientists.* T refers to testing, getting results, making generalizations, generalizing on basis of situations.	Science lexis.	
	and set up for new task (writing generalizations based on all experiments)		Spoken: T refers to words on board (key lexis). T gives instructions. Ss retell.		T refers to need for *clear language.*	Importance of concentration.
33	**Individual writing** Ss write generalizations based on all experiments	Individual	Written.	Various – personal learning around properties of magnets.		
34	**Setting up new task** (to share generalizations)	T/Class: Monologue IRF	Spoken: T gives instructions. Ss retell.	Various – personal learning around properties of magnets.	T models how to make a generalization. Language should *get the message across, be expressed well.*	

No.	Teaching/learning processes	HOW		WHAT		
		Dominant participant and interaction structures	Mode/degree of context-embeddedness of discourse	Knowledge constructed about science	Knowledge constructed about language	Knowledge constructed about how to be a student
35	Sharing individual generalizations	Pairs: Participatory T briefly joins each pair	Spoken: Based on texts students have written.	Various – personal learning around properties of magnets.	Talk by T about language of generalizing versus giving individual results. T tells students they need to *rework the language.* Ss suggest sentence beginnings.	S: *What we have to do is* S: *Miss told us to . . .*
36	LESSON 8 Recap (of process of previous lesson, episodes 32–35) and setting up for new task (pair and group writing task)	T/Class: IRF T/Class: Monologue and IRF	Spoken. T gives instructions. Ss retell.	*thinking like scientists drawing conclusions*	General and particular statements. What a generalization is, and why it is necessary in science.	*Listen if someone's speaking . . . learn from them.* Listening behaviour.
37	Proofing written work (Ss compare each other's generalizations and make suggestions	Pairs: Participatory	Spoken: Based on Ss' individual written texts.	Various – personal learning around properties of magnets.	Particular and general statements.	

	for improvements, first in pairs and then in a group of four)	Group: Participatory Group: Participatory	Spoken: Based on pairs' written texts.	Ss talk about their writing, e.g. *put an 's' on it.* T refers to need for accuracy because final product will be *public.*
38	**LESSON 9** **Recap** Review of process of last lesson (episodes 36–37)	T/Class: IRF	Spoken: Reconstruction (of previous lesson).	
39	**Producing final product for classroom display** Ss write generalizations on large sheet of card	Groups: Participatory		Various – personal learning around properties of magnets.
40	**Preparation for teacher-guided reporting** Ss check generalizations and decide how they will present group display to class	T/Class: Monologue Groups: Participatory	Spoken: T gives instructions Spoken: Ss talk about written texts (content and language).	Various – personal learning around properties of magnets.

		HOW		WHAT		
No.	Teaching/learning processes	Dominant participant and interaction structures	Mode/degree of context-embeddedness	Knowledge constructed about science	Knowledge constructed about language	Knowledge constructed about how to be a student
41	**Teacher-guided reporting.** Ss presents their generalizations	T/Class: Dialogic	Spoken: Oral discussion of written texts.	Various – personal learning around properties of magnets.	T talks about making generalizations; proofreading writing; generalizing versus particularizing. Discussion of wording of Ss' generalizations. Comments from T: *We're talking about the way the language is put together.*	
42	**Set up for new task** (to design a game using magnets) T gives Ss instruction cards. Discussion of how to work in a group	T/Class: IRF T/Class: Dialogic	Written and spoken: Mode shifting. T reads and 'unpacks' instructions. Spoken: T illustrates each of Ss' ideas with	Applying knowledge gained about properties of magnets, attraction and repulsion.	T refers to written instructions for task: *Specifications – what does that mean? Determine modifications and improvements – what does that mean?*	Working in a group: suggestions from T and Ss: about *how we negotiate; take turns; share ideas; communicate with the group; turn taking; quiet voices; making*

			likely wording: *One suggestion I have is*		*What does negotiate mean?*
					suggestions; coming to a decision when every member's idea is different.
43	**Deciding on design for game**	Groups: Participatory T joins group: dialogic	Spoken: Construction of ideas: *we could; it could have.*	Revision and application of science knowledge.	
44	**Game made in craft lesson** *Researcher not present*				
45	**Groups present games to class**	T/Class: Participatory Dialogic	Spoken: Context-embedded as Ss demonstrate. Construction as Ss explain rules.	Revision and application of science knowledge.	

References

Ada, A. (1988), 'The Pajaro Valley experience: working with Spanish-speaking parents to develop children's reading and writing skills in the home through the use of children's literature', in T. Skutnabb-Kangas and J. Cummins (eds), *Minority Education: From Shame to Struggle*. Clevedon: Multilingual Matters, pp. 223–238.

Alijaafreh, A. and Lantolf, J. (1994), 'Negative feedback as regulation and second language learning in the zone of proximal development', *The Modern Language Journal* 78, 465–83.

Allen, P., Swain, M., Harley, B. and Cummins, J. (1990), 'Aspects of classroom treatment: towards a more comprehensive view of second language education', in B. Harley, P. Allen, J. Cummins, and M. Swain (eds), *The Development of Second Language Proficiency*. Cambridge: Cambridge University Press.

Allwright, D. and Bailey, K. (1991), *Focus on the Language Classroom: an Introduction to Classroom Research for Language Teachers*. Cambridge: Cambridge University Press.

Au, K. (1978), 'Participation structures in a reading lesson with Hawaiian children: analysis of a culturally appropriate instructional event', *Anthropology and Education Quarterly*, 11, 91–115.

Au, K., and Mason, J. (1983), 'Cultural congruence in classroom participation structures: achieving a balance of rights', *Discourse Processes*, 6, 145–67.

Austin, J. (1962), *How to Do Things with Words*. London: Oxford University Press.

Baker, K. (1992), Review of *Forked Tongue*. *Bilingual Basics* (Winter, Spring), 6–7.

Bakhtin, M. (1981), *The Dialogic Imagination*. Austin: University of Texas Press.

Barnes, D. (1976), *From Communication to Curriculum*. Harmondsworth: Penguin.

Barnes, D., Britton, J. and Torbe, M. (1986), *Language, the Learner and the School* (3rd edn). Harmondsworth: Penguin.

Baynham, M. (1993), 'Literacy in TESOL and ABE: exploring common themes', *Open Letter*, 2 (2), 4–16.

Baynham, M. and Lobanga Masing, H. (2000), 'Mediators and mediation in multilingual literacy practices', in M. Martin-Jones and K. Jones (eds), *Multilingual Literacies: Comparative Perspectives on Research and Practice*. Amsterdam: John Benjamins.

Bellack, A., Kliebard, H., Hyman, R. and Smith, F. (1966), *The Language of the Classroom*. Columbia: Teachers' College Press.

Berk, L. and Winsler, A. (1995, pub. 2005), *Scaffolding Children's Learning: Vygotsky and Early Childhood Education*. Washington DC: National Association for the Education of Young Children.

Bernstein, B. (1999), 'Vertical and horizontal discourse: an essay', *British Journal of Sociology of Education*, 20(2), 157–73.

Bernstein, B. (1996), *Pedagogy, Symbolic Control and Identity*. London: Taylor and Francis.

Bernstein, B. (1971), *Class, Codes and Control 1: Theoretical Studies towards a Sociology of Language*. London: Routledge and Kegan Paul.

Berry, M. (1981), 'Systemic linguistics and discourse analysis: a multi-layered approach to exchange structure', in M. Coulthard and M. Montgomery (eds), *Studies in Discourse Analysis*. London: Routledge and Kegan.

Biber, D. (1986), 'Spoken and written textual dimensions in English: resolving the contradictory findings', *Language*, 62, 384–414.

Biggs, A. and Edwards, V. (1991). ' "I treat them all the same": teacher-pupil talk in multi-ethnic classrooms', *Language and Education*, 5, 161–76.

Block, D. (1996), 'Not so fast! Some thoughts on theory culling, relativism, accepted findings and the heart and soul of SLA', in *Applied Linguistics*, 17(1), 63–83.

Bourne, J. (2003), 'Vertical discourse: the role of the teacher in the transmission and acquisition of decontextualised language', *European Educational Research Journal*, 2(4), 496–520.

Brilliant-Mills, H. (1993), 'Becoming a mathematician: building a situated definition of mathematics', *Linguistics and Education*, 5, 301–34.

Britton, J. (1970), *Language and Learning*. London: Allen Lane.

Brooks, F., Donato, R. and McGlone, J. (1997), 'When are they going to say "it" right? Understanding learner talk during pair-work activity', *Foreign Language Annals*, 46, 524–41.

Bruner, J. (1986). *Actual Minds, Possible Worlds*. Cambridge, MA: Harvard University Press.

Bruner, J. (1985), 'Vygotsky: a historical and conceptual perspective', in V. Wertsch (ed.), *Culture, Communication and Cognition*. Cambridge: Cambridge University Press.

Bruner, J. (1978), 'The role of dialogue in language acquisition', in A. Sinclair, R. Jarvella, and W. Levelt (eds), *The Child's Conception of Language*. New York: Springer-Verlag.

Bruner, J. (1975), 'Language as an instrument of thought', in A. Davies (ed.), *Problems of Language and Learning*. London: Heinemann.

Butt, D., Fahey, R., Feex, S., Spinks, S. and Yallop, C. (2000), *Using Functional Grammar: An Explorer's Guide*. NCELTR: Macquarie University Sydney.

Canale, M. (1983), 'On some dimensions of language proficiency', in J. Oller (ed.), *Issues in Language Testing Research*, Rowley MA: Bewbury House, pp. 333–342.

Carroll, S. and Swain, M. (1993), 'Explicit and implicit negative feedback: an empirical study of the learning of linguistic generalisations', *Studies in Second Language Acquisition*, 15, 357–86.

Cazden, C. (1990), 'Differential treatment in New Zealand: reflections on research in minority education', *Teaching and Teacher Education*, 6, 291–303.

Cazden, C. (1989), 'Richmond Road: a multilingual/multicultural primary school in Auckland, New Zealand', *Language and Education*, 3, 143–66.

Cazden, C. (1988), *Classroom Discourse: the Language of Teaching and Learning*. Portsmouth, NH: Heinemann.

Chang, G. and Wells, G. (1988), 'The literate potential of collaborative talk', in M. MacLure, T. Phillips and A. Wilkinson (eds), *Oracy Matters*. Milton Keynes: Open University Press.

Chaudron, C. (1988), *Second Language Classrooms: Research on Talking and Learning*. Cambridge: Cambridge University Press.

Chaudron, C. (1985), 'A method for examining the input/intake distinction', in S. Gass and C. Madden (eds), *Input in Second Language Acquisition*. Rowley, MA: Newbury House.

Christie, F. (1995), 'Pedagogic discourse in the primary school', *Linguistics and Education*, 7, 221–42.

Christie, F. (1994), *On Pedagogic Discourse*. Melbourne: Australian Research Council.

Christie, F. (1992a), *Teaching English Literacy: A Project of National Significance on the Preservice Preparation of Teachers for Teaching English Literacy*. Darwin, NT: Report to Department of Employment, Education and Training.

Christie, F. (1992b), 'Literacy in Australia', in W. Grabe *et al* (eds), *Annual Review of Applied Linguistics, 12 Literacy*. New York: Cambridge University Press, pp. 142–155.

Christie, F. (1990), 'The changing face of literacy', in F. Christie (ed.), *Literacy for a changing world*. Victoria: ACER.

Clarke, M. (1995), *Keynote Address*. Paper presented at the Annual Summer Institute of English, Rabat.

Clarke, M. (1994), 'The dysfunctions of the theory/practice discourse', *TESOL Quarterly*, 28(1), 9–21.

Collier, V. (1989), 'How long? A synthesis of research in academic achievement in a second language', *TESOL Quarterly*, 23, 509–31.

Cope, B. and Kalantzis, M. (1995), *The Power of Literacy*. London: Falmer Press.

Corson, D. (1993), *Language, Minority Education and Gender*. Clevedon: Multilingual Matters.

Cummins, J. (2000), *Language, Power and Pedagogy: Bilingual Children in the Crossfire*. Clevedon: Multilingual Matters.

Cummins, J. (1996), *Negotiating Identities: Education for Empowerment in a Diverse Society*. Los Angeles: California Association for Bilingual Education.

Cummins, J. (1994), 'Knowledge, power and identity in teaching English as a second language', in F. Genesee (ed.), *Educating Second Language Children: The whole child, the whole curriculum, the whole community*. New York: Cambridge University Press.

Cummins, J. (1988), 'From multicultural to anti-racist education', in T. Skutnabb-Kangas and J. Cummins (eds), *Minority Education: from Shame to Struggle*. Clevedon: Multilingual Matters.

Cummins, J. (1986), 'Empowering minority students: A framework for intervention', *Harvard Education Review*, 15, 18–36.

Cummins, J. (1984), *Bilingualism and Special Education: Issues in Assessment and Pedagogy*. Clevedon: Multilingual Matters.

Darder, A. (1991), *Culture and Power in the Classroom: A Critical Foundation for Bicultural Education.* New York: Bergin and Garvey.

Davis, K. (1995), 'Qualitative theory and methods in applied linguistics research', *TESOL Quarterly*, 29(3), 427–53.

Davison, C. and Williams, A. (2001), 'Integrating language and content: unresolved issues', in B. Mohan, C. Leung and C. Davison, *English as a Second Language in the Mainstream: Teaching, Learning and Identity.* Harlow: Longman, pp. 51–70.

Delpit, L. (1988), 'The silenced dialogue: power and pedagogy in educating other people's children', *Harvard Educational Review*, 58(3), 280–98.

Derewianka, B. (2003a), 'Grammatical metaphor in the transition to adolescence', in A. Simon-Vandenbergen, M. Taverniers and L. Ravelli (eds), *Grammatical Metaphor: Views from Systemic Functional Linguistics.* Philadelphia: John Benjamins, pp. 185–219.

Derewianka, B. (2003b), 'Making grammar relevant to students' lives', in G. Bull and M. Anstey (eds), *The Literacy Lexicon* (2nd edn). NSW: Pearson, pp. 37–49.

Derewianka, B. (2001), 'Pedagogical grammars: their role in English language teaching', in A. Burns and C. Coffin (eds), *Analysing English in a Global Context: A Reader.* London: Routledge in Association with Macquarie University and The Open University, pp. 24–269.

Derewianka, B. (1990), *Exploring How Texts Work.* Sydney: Primary English Teaching Association.

Dewey, J. (1968 (first published 1916)), *Democracy and Education.* New York: Free Press.

Dewey, J. (1902), *The Child and the Curriculum and the School and the Society.* Chicago: University of Chicago Press.

Dillon, J. (1990), *The Practice of Questioning.* London: Routledge.

Dillon, J. (1988), *Questioning and Teaching.* London: Croom Helm.

Donaldson, M. (1978), *Children's Minds.* Glasgow: Collins.

Donato, R. (2000), 'Sociocultural contributions to understanding the foreign and second language classroom', in J. Lantolf (ed.), *Sociocultural Theory and Second Language Learning.* Oxford: Oxford University Press, pp. 27–50.

Donato, R. (1994), 'Collective scaffolding in second language learning', in J. Lantolf and G. Appel, *Vygotskian Approaches to Second Language Learning.* Norwood, NJ: Ablex Press.

Driver, R. (1994), 'The fallacy of induction in science teaching', in R. Levinson (ed.), *Teaching Science.* London.

Driver, R. (1983), *The Pupil as Scientist?* Milton Keynes: Open University Press.

Driver, R. and Oldham, V. (1986), 'A constructivist approach to curriculum development', *Studies in Science Education*, 13, 105–22.

Duckworth, E. (1987), *'The Having of Wonderful Ideas' and Other Essays on Teaching and Learning.* New York: Teachers' College Press, Columbia University.

Dufficy, P. (2005), 'Becoming in classroom talk', in *Prospect* 20(1) (Special Issue – Rethinking ESL Pedagogy: Sociocultural Approaches to Teaching and Learning), 59–81.

Dunn, L. (1987), *Bilingual Hispanic Children on the US Mainland: A Review of Research on their Cognitive, Linguistic and Scholastic Development*. Circle Pines, MN: American Guidance Service.

Early, M. (1990), 'Enabling first and second language learners in the classroom', *Language Arts*, 67, 567–75.

Early, M. (1985), 'Input and interaction in content classrooms: foreigner talk and teacher talk in classroom discourse'. Unpublished PhD, University of California.

Eckerman, A. (1994), *One Classroom, Many Cultures: Teaching Strategies for Culturally Different Children*. Sydney: Allen and Unwin.

Edelsky, C., Altwerger, B. and Flores, B. (1991), *Whole Language: What's the Difference?* Portsmouth, NH: Heinemann.

Edwards, A. and Furlong, V. (1978), *The Language of Teaching*. London: Heinemann.

Edwards, A. and Westgate, D. (1994), *Investigating Classroom Talk*. Barcombe: Falmer.

Edwards, D. (1990), 'Classroom discourse and classroom knowledge', in C. Rogers and P. Kutnick (eds), *The Social Psychology of the Primary School*. London: Routledge.

Edwards, D. and Mercer, N. (1987), *Common Knowledge: The Development of Understanding in the Classroom*. London: Methuen.

Edwards, T. (1992), 'Teacher-talk and pupil competence', in K. Norman (ed.), *Thinking Voices: The Work of the National Oracy Project*. London: Hodder and Stoughton.

Eggins, S. (2004), *An Introduction to Systemic Functional Linguistics* (2nd edn). London: Continuum.

Eggins, S. (1994), *An Introduction to Systemic Functional Linguistics*. London: Pinter.

Ellis, R. (1994), *The Study of Second Language Acquisition*. Oxford: Oxford University Press.

Ellis, R. (1991), 'The interaction hypothesis: a critical evaluation', in E. Sadtano (ed.), *Language Acquisition and the Second/Foreign Language Classroom*. Singapore: Anthology Series 28, SEAMEO Regional Language Centre.

Ellis, R. and Wells, G. (1980), 'Enabling factors in adult-child discourse', *First Language*, 1, 46–82.

Engerström, Y. and Middleton, D. (eds) (1996), *Cognition and Communication at Work*. Cambridge: Cambridge University Press.

Engeström, Y. (1990), *Learning, Working and Imagining: Twelve Studies in Activity Theory*. Helsinki: Orienta-Konsultit.

Erickson, F. (1984), 'Rhetoric, anecdote and rhapsody: coherence strategies in a conversation among Black American adolescents', in D. Tannen (ed.), *Coherence in Spoken and Written Discourse*. Norwood, NJ: Ablex.

Ernst-Slavit, G. (1997), 'Different words, different worlds', *Linguistics and Education*, 9(1), 25–48.

Faltis, C. and Hudelson, S. (1994), 'Learning English as an additional language in K-12 schools', *TESOL Quarterly*, 28(3), 457–67.

Farrar, M. (1990), 'Discourse and the acquisition of grammatical morphemes', *Journal of Child Language*, 17, 607–24.

Feez, S. (1995), 'Systemic functional linguistics and its applications in Australian Language Education: a short history', *Interchange*, 27, 8–11.

Floriani, A. (1993), 'Negotiating what counts: roles and relationships, texts and contexts, content and meaning', *Linguistics and Education*, 5, 241–73.

Forman, E. and Cazden, C. (1985), 'Exploring Vygotskian perspectives in education: the cognitive value of peer interaction', in J. Wertsch (ed.), *Culture, Communication and Cognition; Vygotskian Perspectives*. Cambridge: Cambridge University Press.

Freebody, P., Ludwig, C. and Gunn, S. (1995), *Everyday Literacy Practices In and Out of Schools in Low Socioeconomic Urban Communities*. Canberra: Department of Emplyment, Education and Training.

Freire, P. (1983), 'Banking education', in H. Giroux and D. Purpel (eds), *The Hidden Curriculum and Moral Education: Deception or Discovery?* Berkeley, CA: McCutcheon Publishing Corporation.

Gallimore, R. and Tharp, R. (1990), 'Teaching mind in society', in L. Moll (ed.), *Vygotsky and Education. Instructional Implications and Applications of Sociohistorical Psychology*. Cambridge: Cambridge University Press, pp. 175–205.

Genesee, F. (ed.) (1994), *Educating Second Language Children: The Whole Child, the Whole Curriculum, The Whole Community*. New York: Cambridge University Press.

Genesee, F. (1987), *Learning Through Two Languages: Studies of Immersion and Bilingual Education*. Cambridge, MA: Newbury House.

Gerot, L. and Wignell, P. (1994), *Making Sense of Functional Grammar*. Sydney: Antipodean Educational Enterprises.

Gibbons, J., White, W. and Gibbons, P. (1994). 'Combating educational disadvantage among Lebanese Australian children', in T. Skutnabb-Kangas and R. Phillipson (eds), *Linguistic Human Rights: Overcoming Linguistic Discrimination*. Berlin: Mouton de Gruyter.

Gibbons, P. (2003), 'Mediating language learning: teacher interactions with ESL students in a content-based classroom', *TESOL Quarterly*, 37(2), 247–73.

Gibbons, P. (2002), *Scaffolding Language, Scaffolding Learning: Teaching Second Language Learners in the Mainstream Classroom*. Portsmouth, NH: Heinemann.

Gibbons, P. (1998), 'Classroom talk and the learning of new registers in a second language', *Language and Education*, 12(2), 99–118.

Gibbons, P. (1991, pub. 1993), *Learning to Learn in a Second Language*. Portsmouth, NH: Heinemann.

Graddol, D., Maybin, J. and Stierer, B. (eds) (1994), *Researching Language and Literacy in Social Context*. Clevedon: Multilingual Matters.

Green, J. and Dixon, C. (1993), 'Talking knowledge into being: Discursive and social practices in classrooms', *Linguistics and Education*, 5 (3–4), 231–9.

Gutierrez, K. and Larson, J. (1994), 'Language borders: Recitation as hegemonic discourse', in *International Journal of Education*, 31, 22–36.

Gutierrez, K. and Stone, L. (2000), 'Synchronic and diachronic dimensions of social practice: An emerging methodology for cultural-historical perspectives on literacy learning', in C. Lee and P. Smagorinsky (eds), *Vygotskian Perspectives on Literacy Research*. Cambridge: Cambridge University Press.

Gutierrez, K., Larson, J. and Kreuter, B. (1995), 'Cultural tensions in the scripted classroom: the value of the subjugated perspective', in *Urban Education*, 29(4), 410–42.

Gutierrez, K., Rhymes, B. and Larson, J. (1995), 'Script, counterscript, and underlife in classrooms: James Brown vs Brown vs. Board of Education', in *Harvard Educational Review*, 65, 445–71.

Hakuta, K., Butler, Y. and Witt, D. (2000), *How Long Does It Take For English Learners To Attain Proficiency?* Santa Barbara: University of California, Linguistic Minorities Project.

Hall, J. (1998), 'Differential teacher attention to student utterances: The construction of different opportunities for learning in the IRF', *Linguistics and Education*, 9(3), 287–311.

Hall, J. (1995), '(Re)creating our worlds with words: A sociohistorical perspective of face-to-face interaction', *Applied Linguistics*, 16, 206–32.

Halliday, M. (2001), 'Literacy and linguistics: relationships between spoken and written language', in A. Burns and C. Coffin (eds), *Analysing English in a Global Context: A Reader*. London: Routledge in Association with Macquarie University and The Open University, pp. 181–93.

Halliday, M. (1993), 'Towards a language-based theory of learning', in *Linguistics and Education*, 5, 93–116.

Halliday, M. (1991), 'The notion of "context" in language education'. Paper presented at *Language Education: Interaction and Development*, Ho Chi Minh, Vietnam.

Halliday, M. (1985a), *Spoken and Written Language*. Geelong, Victoria: Deakin University Press.

Halliday, M. (1985b), *An Introduction to Functional Grammar*. London: Edward Arnold.

Halliday, M. (1984), 'Language as code and language as behaviour: a systemic functional interpretation of the nature and ontogenesis of language', in R. Fawcett, M. Halliday, S. Lamb and A. Makkai (eds), *The Semiotics of Culture and Language* (Vol. 1). London: Pinter.

Halliday, M. (1978), *Language as Social Semiotic: the Social Interpretation of Language and Meaning*. London: Arnold.

Halliday, M. (1975), *Learning How to Mean: Explorations in the Development of Language*. London: Arnold.

Halliday, M. and Hasan, R. (1985), *Language, Context and Text*. Geelong, Victoria: Deakin University Press.

Hammond, J. (1990), 'Is learning to read and write the same as learning to speak?' in F. Christie (ed.), *Literacy for a Changing World*. Victoria: ACER, pp. 26–53.

Hammond, J. and Gibbons, P. (2005), 'Putting scaffolding to work: the contribution of scaffolding in articulating ESL education', *Prospect*, 20(1) (Special Issue – Rethinking ESL Pedagogy: Sociocultural Approaches to Teaching and Learning), 6–30.

Harklau, L. (1994), 'ESL versus mainstream classes: contrasting second language learning environments', *TESOL Quarterly*, 28(2), 241–72.

Hasan, R. (2000), 'The ontogenesis of decontextualised language: some achievements of classification and framing', in A. Morais, B. Davies, H. Daniels and A. Sadovnik (eds), *Towards a Sociology of Pedagogy*. Berlin: Peter Lang.

Hasan, R. and Williams, G. (eds) (1997), *Literacy in Society*. London: Longman.

Hatch, E. (1978), 'Discourse analysis in second language acquisition', in E. Hatch (ed.), *Second Language Acquisition*. Rowley, MA: Newbury House.

Heap, J. (1995), 'The status of claims in "qualitative" educational research', *Curriculum Inquiry*, 25(3), 271–92.

Heath, S. (1983), *Ways With Words: Language, Life and Work in Communities and Classrooms*. Cambridge: Cambridge University Press.

Heath, S. (1982), 'What no bedtime story means: narrative skills at home and school', in *Language and Society*, 11, 49–76.

Heras, A. (1994), 'The construction of understanding in a sixth grade classroom', *Linguistics and Education*, 5, 275–99.

Hill, J. and Irvine, J. (1992), *Responsibility and Evidence in Oral Discourse*. Cambridge: Cambridge University Press.

Hymes, D. (1971), 'On linguistic theory, communicative competence and the education of disadvantaged children', in M. Wax, S. Diamond and F. Gearing (eds), *Anthropological Perspectives on Education*. New York: Basic Books.

Jensen, A. (1969), 'How can we best boost IQ and scholastic achievement?', *Harvard Educational Review*, Reprint Series 2.

John-Steiner, V. (1975), 'The road to competence in an alien land: a Vygotskian perspective on bilingualism', in J. Wertsch (ed.), *Culture, Communication and Cognition*. Cambridge, MA: Cambridge University Press.

Jones, A. (1987), 'Which girls are "learning to lose"?' in S. Middleton (ed.), *Women and Education in Aoteoroa*. Wellington: Bridget Williams Books.

Kalantzis, M. and Cope, B. (1988), 'Why we need multicultural education: a review of the "ethnic disadvantage" debate', *Journal of Intercultural Studies*, 9(1), 39–57.

Kozulin, A. (1998), *Psychological Tools: A Sociocultural Approach to Education*. Cambridge, MA: Harvard University Press.

Kramsch, C. (1995). The applied linguist and the foreign language teacher: Can they talk to each other? *Australian Review of Applied Linguistics 18*, 1–16.

Kramsch, C. (1993), *Context and Culture in Language Teaching*. Oxford: Oxford University Press.

Krashen, S. (1989), *Language Acquisition and Language Education*. New York: Prentice Hall International.

Krashen, S. (1988), 'Five hypotheses about second language acquisition', in T. Quinn and T. McNamara (eds), *Issues in Second Language Learning*. Geelong, Victoria: Deakin University Press.

Krashen, S. (1985), *The Input Hypothesis: Issues and Implications*. London: Longman.

Kress, G. (1987), 'Genre in a social theory of language: a reply to John Dixon', in I. Reid (ed.), *The Place of Genre in Learning: Current Debates*. Geelong, Victoria: Deakin University Press.

Kumaravadivelu, B. (1994), 'The postmethod condition: (E)merging strategies for second/foreign language teaching', *TESOL Quarterly*, 28(1), 27–47.

Lantolf, J. (ed.) (2000a), *Sociocultural Theory and Second Language Learning*. Oxford: Oxford University Press.

Lantolf, J. (2000b), 'Introducing sociocultural theory', in J. Lantolf (ed.), *Sociocultural Theory and Second Language Learning*. Oxford: Oxford University Press, pp. 1–26.

Lantolf, J. (1996), 'SLA theory building: "letting all the flowers bloom"', *Language Learning*, 46(4), 713–49.

Lantolf, J. and Alijaafreh, A. (1995), 'Second language learning in the zone of proximal development: a revolutionary experience', *International Journal of Educational Research*. 23, 619–32.

Larsen-Freeman, D (1990), 'On the need for a theory of language teaching', in J. Atlatis (ed.), *Georgetown Round Table on Languages and Linguistics*. Washington, DC: Georgetown University Press.

Lave, J. and Wenger, E. (1991), *Situated Learning. Legitimate Peripheral Participation*. Cambridge: Cambridge University Press.

Lee, C. and Smagorinsky, P. (2000), *Vygotskian Perspectives On Literacy Research. Constructing Meaning Through Collaborative Enquiry*. Cambridge: Cambridge University Press.

Lemke, J. (1998), 'Multiplying meaning: visual and verbal semiotics in scientific text', in J. Martin and R. Veel (eds), *Reading Science: Critical and Functional Perspectives on Discourses of Science*. London: Routledge.

Lemke, J. (1990), *Talking Science: Language, Learning and Values*. Norwood, NJ: Ablex.

Leont'ev, A. (1981), 'The problem of activity in psychology', in J. Wertsch (ed.), *The Concept of Activity in Soviet Psychology*. Armonk, NY: Sharpe.

Lightbown, P. and Spada, W. (1990), 'Focus on form and corrective feedback in communicative language teaching: effects on second language learning', *Studies in Second Language Acquisition*, 12, 429–48.

Lin, A. (2001), 'Doing-English-lessons in the reproduction or transformation of social worlds?' in C. Candlin and N. Mercer (eds), *English Language Teaching in its Social Context*. London: Routledge, pp. 271–86.

Lin, A. (1993), 'Language of and in the classroom: constructing the patterns of social life', *Linguistics and Education*, 5, 367–409.

Lock, S. (1983), *Second-language Learners in the Classroom*. Canberra: Materials Production Curriculum Branch.

Long, M. (1996), 'The role of the linguistic environment in second language acquisition', in W. Ritchie and T. Bhatia (eds), *Handbook of Language Acquisition: Vol 2 Second Language Acquisition*. New York: Academic Press.

Long, M. (1983), 'Native speaker/non native speaker conversations and the negotiation of comprehensible input', *Applied Linguistics*, 4, 126–41.

Long, M. and Porter, P. (1985), 'Group work, interlanguage talk, and second language acquisition', *TESOL Quarterly*, 19, 207–8.

Long, M. (1981), 'Input, interaction and second language acquisition', in H. Winitz (ed.), *Native Language and Foreign Language Acquisition*. New York: Annals of the New York Academy of Sciences, 379.

Lotman, Y. M. (1988), 'Text within a text', *Soviet Psychology*, 24(3), 32–51.

Lyster, R. (1998), 'Recasts, repetition and ambiguity in second language classroom discourse', *Studies in Second Language Acquisition*, 20(1), 51–8.

Lyster, R. and Ranta, L. (1997), 'Corrective feedback and learner uptake: negotiation of form in communicative classrooms', *Studies in Second Language Acquisition*, 19, 37–66.

Macken, M. and Rothery, J. (1991), *A Model for Literacy in Subject Learning*. Sydney: Disadvantaged Schools Program.

Malcolm, I. (1982), 'Speech events of the aboriginal classroom', *International Journal of the Sociology of Language*, 36, 115–34.

Maley, Y., Candlin, C., Crichton, J., and Koster, P. (1995), 'Orientations in lawyer–client interviews', *Forensic Linguistics*, 2(1), 42–5.

Martin, J. (1993a), 'A contextual theory of language', in B. Cope and M. Kalantzis (eds), *The Powers of Literacy*. London: Falmer.

Martin, J. (1993b), 'Genre and literacy: modelling context in educational linguistics', *Annual Review of Applied Linguistics*, 13, 141–72.

Martin, J. (1990), 'Literacy in science: learning to handle text as technology', in F. Christie (ed.), *Literacy for a Changing World*. Hawthorn, Australia: ACER, pp. 79–117.

Martin, J. (1984), 'Language, register and genre', in F. Christie (ed.), *Children Writing, Study Guide*. Geelong, Victoria: Deakin University Press.

Martin, J. and Veel, R. (1998), *Reading Science*. London: Routledge.

Martin, J., Christie, F. and Rothery, J. (1987), 'Social processes in education: a reply to Sawyer and Watson (and others)', in I. Reid (ed.), *The Place of Genre in Learning: Current Debates*. Geelong, Victoria: Centre for Studies in Literary Education, Deakin University Press, pp. 46–57.

Maybin, J. (1994), 'Children's voices: talk, knowledge and identity', in D. Graddol, J. Maybin and B. Stierer (eds), *Researching Language and Literacy in Social Context*. Clevedon: Multilingual Matters, pp. 131–50.

Maybin, J., Mercer, N. and Stierer, B. (1992), 'Scaffolding learning in the classroom', in K. Norman (ed.), *Thinking Voices, The Work of the National Oracy Project*. London: Hodder and Stoughton.

McCafferty, S. (1998), 'Non-verbal expression and L2 private speech', *Applied Linguistics*, 19 (1), 73–96.

McCafferty, S. (1996), 'The use of non-verbal forms of expression in relation to L2 private speech', *Applied Linguistics*, 19(1), 73–96.

McDermott, R. (1993), 'The acquisition of a child by a learning disability', in S. Chaiklin and J. Lave (eds), *Understanding practice: Perspectives on activity and context*. Cambridge: Cambridge University Press, pp. 269–305.

McGroarty, M. (1993), 'Cooperative learning and language acquisition', in D. Holt (ed.), *Cooperative Learning: A Response to Linguistic and Cultural Diversity*. Washington DC: Centre for Applied Linguistics.

McKay, P., Davies, A., Devlin, B., Clayton, J., Oliver, R. and Zammit, S. (1997), *The Bilingual Interface Report*. Canberra: Department of Employment, Education, Training and Youth Affairs.

McLaren, P. (1994), *Life in Schools: An Introduction to Critical Pedagogy*. New York: Longman.

McNally, D. (1973), *Piaget, Education and Teaching*. Sydney: Hodder and Stoughton.

Mehan, B. (1979), *Learning Lessons*. Cambridge, MA: Harvard University Press.

Mercer, N. (2002), 'Developing dialogues', in G. Wells and G. Claxton (eds), *Learning for Life in the 21st Century*. Oxford: Blackwell, pp. 141–153.

Mercer, N. (2000), *Words and Minds, How We Use Language to Think Together*. London: Routledge.

Mercer, N. (1995), *The Guided Construction of Knowledge: Talk Amongst Teachers and Learners*. Clevedon: Multilingual Matters.

Met, M. (1994), 'Teaching content through a second language', in F. Genesee (ed.), *Educating Second Language Children: the Whole Child, the Whole Curriculum, the Whole Community*. New York: Cambridge University Press.

Michaels, S. (1981), ' "Sharing time": children's narrative styles and differential access to literacy', *Language in Society*, 10, 423–42.

Michaels, S. and Cazden, C. (1986). 'Teacher/child collaboration as oral preparation for literacy', in B. Schiefflein and P. Gilmore (eds), *The Acquisition of Literacy: Ethnographic Perspectives*. Norwood, NJ: Ablex.

Michell, M. and Sharpe, T. (2005), 'Collective instructional scaffolding in English as a second language classrooms', *Prospect*, 20(1), (Special Issue – Rethinking ESL Pedagogy: Sociocultural Approaches to Teaching and Learning), 31–58.

Mohan, B. (2002), 'The second language as a medium of learning', in B. Mohan, C. Leung and C. Davison, *English as a Second Language in the Mainstream: Teaching, Learning and Identity*. Harlow: Longman, pp. 107–26.

Mohan, B. (1986), *Language and Content*. Reading, MA: Addison-Wesley.

Moll, L. (1994), *Vygotsky and Education. Instructional Implications and Applications of Sociohistorical Psychology*. Cambridge: Cambridge University Press.

Morgan, J., Bonamo, K. and Travis, L. (1995), 'Negative evidence on negative evidence', in *Developmental Psychology*, 31, 180–97.

Newman, D., Griffin, P. and Cole, M. (1989), *The Construction Zone: Working for Cognitive Change in School*. Cambridge: Cambridge University Press.

Newmann, F. and Associates (1996), *Authentic Achievement: Restructuring Schools for Intellectual Quality*. San Francisco: Josey Bass.

Nieto, P. (1999), *The Light in their Eyes: Creating Multicultural Learning Communities*. New York: Teachers' College Press.

Nieto, S. (1996), *Affirming Diversity: The Sociopolitical Context of Multicultural Education*. White Plains, NY: Longman.

Norton Pierce, B. (1995), 'The theory of methodology in qualitative research', *TESOL Quarterly*, 29(3), 569–76.

Nunan, D. (1992), *Research Methods in Language Learning*. Cambridge: Cambridge University Press.

Oakes, J. (1985), *Keeping Track: How High Schools Structure Inequality*. New Haven: Yale University Press.

Ochs, E. (1979), 'Transcription as theory', in E. Ochs and B. Schieffelin (eds), *Developmental Pragmatics*. London: Academic Press.

Ohta, A. (2000), 'Rethinking interaction in SLA: developmentally appropriate assistance in the zone of proximal development and the acquisition of L2 grammar', in J. Lantolf (ed.), *Sociocultural Theory and Second Language Learning*. Oxford: Oxford University Press, pp. 51–78.

Ohta, A. (1999), 'Interactional routines and the socialization of interactional style in adult learners of Japanese', *Journal of Pragmatics*, 31, 1493–1512.

Ohta, A. (1995), 'Applying sociocultural theory to an analysis of learner discourse: learner-learner collaborative interaction in the zone of proximal development', *Issues in Applied Linguistics*, 6, 93–121.

Oliver, R. (1995), 'Negative feedback in child NS-NNS conversation', *Studies in Second Language Acquisition*, 17, 459–81.

Olson, D. (1977), 'From utterance to text: the bias in speech and writing', *Harvard Educational Review*, 47, 257–81.

Painter, C. (2004), 'The development of language as a resource for learning', in C. Coffin, A. Hewings and K. O'Halloran (eds), *Applying English Grammar: Functional and Corpus Approaches*. London: Arnold and Open University, pp. 155–71.

Painter, C. (2001), 'Understanding register and genre: implications for language teaching', in A. Burns and C. Coffin (eds), *Analysing English in a Global Context: A Reader*. London: Routledge in Association with Macquarie University and The Open University, pp. 167–80.

Painter, C. (1985), *Learning the Mother Tongue*. Geelong Victoria: Deakin University Press.

Painter, C. (1984), *Into the Mother Tongue; A Case Study in Early Language Development*. London: Pinter.

Parker, K. and Chaudron, C. (1987), *The Effects of Linguistic Simplifications and Elaborative Modifications on Second Language Acquisition*. Hawaii: University of Hawaii, Working Papers in ESL 6.

Pavlenko, A. and Lantolf, J. (2000), 'Second language learning as participation and the (re)construction of selves', in J. Lantolf (ed.), *Sociocultural Theory and Second Language Learning*. Oxford: Oxford University Press, pp. 155–78.

Philips, S. (1983), *The Invisible Culture: Communication in Classroom and Community on the Warm Springs Indian Reservation*. New York: Longman.

Philips, S. (1972), 'Participant structure and communicative competence: Warm Springs children in community and classroom', in C. Cazden, V. John, and D. Hymes (eds), *Functions of Language in the Classroom*. New York: Teachers' College Press.

Phillips, T. (1985), 'Beyond lip-service: discourse development after the age of nine', in G. Wells and J. Nicholls (eds), *Language and Learning: An Interactional Perspective*. East Sussex: Falmer Press, pp. 59–82.

Piaget, J. (1971), *Science of Education and the Psychology of the Child*. London: Longman.

Piaget, J. (1970), 'Piaget's Theory', in P. Mussen (ed.), *Handbook of Child Psychology: formally Carmichael's Manuel of Child Psychology* (4th edn). New York: Wiley.

Pica, T. (1994), 'Research on negotiation: what does it reveal about second language learning conditions, processes and outcomes?' *Language Learning*, 44, 493–527.

Pica, T. (1988), 'Interlanguage adjustments as an outcome of NS-NNS negotiated interaction', *Language Learning*, 38, 45–73.

Pica, T. (1987), 'Second language acquisition, social interaction in the classroom', *Applied Linguistics*, 7, 1–25.

Pica, T., Young, R. and Doughty, C. (1987), 'The impact of interaction on comprehension', *TESOL Quarterly*, 21(4), 737–58.

Pica, T., Holliday, L., Lewis, N. and Morgenthaler, L. (1989), 'Comprehensible output as an outcome of linguistic demands on the learner', *Studies in Second Language Acquisition*, 11, 63–90.

Pica, T., Lincoln-Porter, F., Paninos, D. and Linnel, J. (1996), 'Language learners' interaction: how does it address the input, output and feedback needs of second language learners', *TESOL Quarterly*, 30(1), 59–84.

Porter, P. (1986), 'How learners talk to each other: input and interaction in task-centred discussions', in R. Day (ed.), *Talking to Learn: Conversations in Second Language Acquisition*. Rowley, MA: Newbury House.

Prabhu, N. (1990), 'There is no best method – why?' *TESOL Quarterly*, 24(2), 161–76.

Prabhu, N. (1987), *Second Language Pedagogy: A Perspective*. Oxford: Oxford University Press.

Reddy, M. (1970), 'The conduit metaphor – a case of frame conflict in our language about language', in A. Ortony (ed.), *Metaphor and Thought*. Cambridge: Cambridge University Press.

Reid, J., Forrestal, P. and Cook, J. (1989), *Small Group Learning in the Classroom*. Perth: Chalkface Press.

Richards, J. (1990), *The Language Teaching Matrix*. New York: Cambridge University Press.

Rowe, M. (1986), 'Wait time: slowing down may be a way of speeding up', *Journal of Teacher Education*, 37, 43–50.

Saville-Troike, M. (1984), 'What really matters in second language learning for academic achievement', *TESOL Quarterly*, 18, 199–219.

School Reform Longitudinal Study: Theoretical Rationale for the Development of Productive Pedagogies, A Literature Review. The School Reform Longitudinal Study Research Team, Graduate School of Education, The University of Queensland Australia, 1997–2001.

Schratz, M. and Walker, R. (1995), *Research as Social Change: New Opportunities for Qualitative Research*. London: Routledge.

Sharpe, M. (2006), '"Unpacking" scaffolding: identifying discourse and multimodal strategies that support learning', *Language and Education* 20(3).

Short, D. (1993), 'Assessing integrating language and content', *TESOL Quarterly*, 27(4).

Shuy, R. (1991), 'Secretary Bennet's teaching: an argument for responsive teaching', in E. Eisner (ed.), *The Enlightened Eye: Qualitative Inquiry and the Enhancement of Educational Practice*. New York: Macmillan, 135–49.

Simon, R. and Dippo, D. (1986), 'On critical ethnographic work', *Anthropology and Education Quarterly*, 17, pp. 198–201.

Sinclair, J. and Coulthard, R. (1975), *Towards an Analysis of Discourse: the English Used by Teachers and Pupils*. London: Oxford University Press.

Smagorinksky, P. and O'Donnell-Allen, C. (2000), 'Idiocultural diversity in small groups: the role of the relational framework in collaborative learning', in C. Lee and P. Smagorinsky (eds), *Vygotskian Perspectives on Literacy Research*. Cambridge: Cambridge University Press, pp. 165–90.

Snow, C. (1986), 'Conversations with children', in P. Fletcher and M. Garman (eds), *Language Acquisition: Studies in First Language Development* (2nd edn). Cambridge: Cambridge University Press.

Snow, M., Met, M. and Genesee, F. (1989), 'A conceptual framework for the integration of language and content in second/foreign language instruction', *TESOL Quarterly*, 23(2), 201–17.

Stetsenko, A. and Arievitch, I. (2002), 'Teaching, learning and development: a post-Vygotskian perspective', in G. Wells and G. Claxton (eds), *Learning for Life in the 21st Century*. Oxford: Blackwell, pp. 84–96.

Stierer, B. and Maybin, J. (1994), *Language, Literacy and Learning in Educational Practice*. Clevedon: Multilingual Matters.

Stubbs, M. (1986), *Educational Linguistics*. Oxford: Blackwell.

Swain, M. (2000), 'The output hypothesis and beyond: mediating acquisition through collaborative dialogue', in J. Lantolf (ed.), *Sociocultural Theory and Second Language Learning*. Oxford: Oxford University Press, pp. 97–114.

Swain, M. (1996), 'Integrating language and content in immersion classrooms: research perspectives', *The Canadian Modern Language Review*, 52, 529–48.

Swain, M. (1995a), 'Three functions of output in second language learning', in G. Cook and B. Seidlehofer (eds), *Principle and Practice in Applied Linguistics: Studies in Honour of H. G. Widdowson*. Oxford: Oxford University Press.

Swain, M. (1995b), *Collaborative Dialogue: its contribution to second language learning*. Plenary paper presented at AAAL Conference, Long Beach, California.

Swain, M. (1985), 'Communicative competence: some roles of comprehensible input and comprehensible output in its development', in S. Gass and C. Madden (eds), *Input in Second Language Acquisition*. Cambridge, MA: Newbury House.

Swain, M. and Lapkin, S. (1998), 'Interaction and second language learning: two adolescent French immersion students working together', *The Modern Language Journal*, 83, 320–8.

Swain, M. and Lapkin, S. (1990), 'Aspects of the sociolinguistic performance of early and late French immersion students', in R. Scarcella, E. Andersen and S. Krashen (eds), *Developing Communicative Competence in a Second Language*. New York: Newbury House.

Tabak, I. (2004), 'Synergy: a complement to emerging patterns of distributed scaffolding', *The Journal of the Learning Sciences*, 13(3), 305–35.

Tharp, R. and Gallimore, R. (1988), *Rousing Minds to Life*. Cambridge: Cambridge University Press.

Thorne, S. (2004), 'Cultural historical activity theory and the object of innovation', in O. St John, K. van Esch and E. Schalkwijk (eds), *New Insights into Foreign Language Learning and Teaching.* Frankfurt: Peter Lang Verlag, pp. 51–70.

Toohey, K. (2000), *Learning English at school: Identity, social relations and classroom practice.* Clevedon: Multilingual Matters.

Torr, J. (1993), 'Classroom discourse: children from English speaking and non-English speaking backgrounds', *Australian Review of Applied Linguistics,* 16(1), 37–56.

Tough, J. (1979), *Talk for Teaching and Learning, Schools Council Communication Skills Project 7–13.* London: Ward Lock Educational in association with Drake Educational Associates.

Tough, J. (1977), *Talking and Learning, Schools Council Communication Skills in Early Childhood Project.* London: Ward Lock Educational in association with Drake Educational Associates.

Unsworth, L. (ed.) (2000), *Researching Language in Schools and Communities: Functional Linguistics Perspectives.* London: Cassell.

van Lier (2001), 'Constraints and resources in classroom talk: issues of equality and symmetry', in C. Candlin and N. Mercer (eds), *English Language Teaching in its Social Context.* Open University and London: Routledge, pp. 90–107.

van Lier (2000), 'From input to affordance: social-interactive learning from an ecological perspective', in J. Lantolf (ed.), *Sociocultural Theory and Second Language Learning.* Oxford: Oxford University Press.

van Lier, L. (1996), *Interaction in the Language Curriculum: Awareness, Autonomy and Authenticity.* London: Longman.

van Lier, L. (1994), 'Forks and hope: pursuing understanding in different ways', *Applied Linguistics,* 15(3), 328–46.

van Lier, L. (1988), *The Classroom and the Language Learner.* Harlow: Longman.

van Lier, L. and Matsuo, N. (2000), 'Varieties of conversational experience: looking for learning opportunities', *Applied Language Learning,* 11(2).

Varonis, E. and Gass, S. (1985), 'Native/non-native conversation: a model for the negotiation of meaning', *Applied Linguistics,* 6, 71–90.

Vogt, L., Jordan, C. and Tharp, R. (1987), 'Explaining school failure, producing school success: two cases', *Anthropology and Education Quarterly,* 19, 276–86.

Vygotsky, L. (1986), *Thought and Language.* (ed. and trans. Kozulin, A.) Cambridge, MA: Harvard University Press.

Vygotsky, L. (1981), 'The Genesis of Higher Mental Functions', in J. Wertsch (ed.), *The Concept of Activity in Soviet Psychology.* Armonk, NY: M. E. Sharpe.

Vygotsky, L. (1978), *Mind in Society: The Development of Higher Psychological Processes.* London: Harvard University Press.

Walsh, C. (1991), *Issues of Language, Power and Schooling for Puerto Ricans.* Toronto: Oise Press.

Webster, A., Beveridge, M. and Reed, M. (1996), *Managing the Literacy Curriculum.* London: Routledge.

Wegerif, R. and Mercer, N. (1996), 'Computers and reasoning through talk in the classroom', *Language and Education*, 10(1), 47–64.

Wells, G. (2000), 'Dialogic inquiry in the classroom: building on the legacy of Vygotsky', in C. Lee and P. Smagorinsky (eds), *Vygotskian Perspectives on Literacy Research*. New York: Cambridge University Press, pp. 51–85.

Wells, G. (1999a), 'Language and education: reconceptualising education as dialogue', in *Annual Review of Applied Linguistics*, 19, 135–55

Wells, G. (1999b), *Dialogic Inquiry: Towards a Sociocultural Practice and Theory of Education*. New York: Cambridge University Press.

Wells, G. (1996), 'Using the tool-kit of discourse in the activity of learning and teaching', *Mind, Culture and Language*, 3(2), 74–101.

Wells, G. (1995), 'Language and the inquiry-oriented curriculum', *Curriculum Inquiry*, 25(3), 233–69.

Wells, G. (1994), 'The Complementary Contributions of Halliday and Vygotsky to a language based-theory of learning', *Linguistics and Education*, 6, 41–90.

Wells, G. (1992), 'The centrality of talk in education', in K. Norman (ed.), *Thinking Voices, the Work of the National Oracy Project*. London: Hodder and Stoughton.

Wells, G. (1986), *The Meaning Makers: Children Learning Language and Using Language to Learn*. Portsmouth, NH: Heinemann.

Wells, G. (1981), *Learning Through Interaction: The Study of Language Development*. Cambridge: Cambridge University Press.

Wells, G. and Claxton, G. (eds) (2002), *Learning for Life in the 21st Century*. Oxford: Blackwell.

Wells, G. and Chang-Wells, G. (1992), *Constructing Knowledge Together: Classrooms as Centers of Inquiry and Literacy*. Portstmouth, NH: Heinemann.

Wertsch, J. and Toma, C. (1991), 'Discourse and learning in the classroom: a sociocultural approach', in L. Steffe (ed.), *Constructivism in Education*. Hillsdale, NJ: Lawrence Erlbaum Associates.

Wertsch, V. (ed.) (1985), *Culture, Communication and Cognition: Vygotskian Perspectives*. Cambridge, MA: Cambridge University Press.

Wertsch, V. and Cole, M. Virtual Seminar on Vygotsky, <http:/www.massey.ac.nz/~alock/virtual/project2.htm>, accessed January 1996.

Widdowson, H. (1990), 'Pedagogic research and teacher education', in H. Widdowson (ed.), *Aspects of Language Teaching*. Oxford: Oxford University Press.

Wilkinson, A. M. (1965), *Spoken English*. Birmingham: University of Birmingham School of Education.

Williams, G. and Lukin, A. (2003), *The Development of Language. Functional Perspectives on Species and Individuals*. London: Continuum.

Wong-Fillmore, L. (1985), 'When does teacher talk work as input?' in S. Gass and C. Madden (eds), *Input in Second Language Acquisition*. Rowley, MA: Newbury House.

Wood, D. (1986), 'Aspects of teaching and learning', in M. Richards and P. Light (eds), *Children of Social Worlds*. Cambridge: Polity Press.

Wood, D., Bruner, J. and Ross, G. (1976), 'The role of tutoring in problem solving', *Journal of Child Psychology and Psychiatry*, 17(2), 89–100.

Young, R. (1992), *Critical Theory and Classroom Talk*. Clevedon: Multilingual Matters.

Zimmerman, C. (1997), 'Do reading and interactive vocabulary instruction make a difference? An empirical study', *TESOL Quarterly*, 31(1), 121–38.

Index

Allwright, D. and Bailey, K. 51
artefacts, cultural practices and 24–5
Australia, Queensland School Reform
    Longitudinal Study 252
Australian study
  approaches to analysis 80–93
  children 73, 76–7
  data sources 86–7
  field notes 89
  interpretation 80–93
  observation 83–5
  school community 73–5
  teachers 75–6
  teaching programme (magnetism)
    77–80
  telling the story 93
  transcription issues 87–9, 90–3

Bernstein, B. 6, 67, 104, 169
Berry, M. 38, 128, 149
Block, D. 10, 81
boundaries, lesson characteristics 54
Bourne, J. 6, 19–20
Bruner, J. 26, 49

categories, rationale and explanation of
    95–100
Cazden, C. 149
Chang, G. and Wells, G. 158, 169
Chomsky, N. 28–9
Christie, F. 85, 100–1, 104–5, 111
Clarke, M. 9, 10, 43, 82–3
classroom-based issues 53–6
'communicative consensus' 47
comprehensible input 45–6, 170
conduit metaphor of language 15–18
consistency of lesson formats 54
content-based language teaching 59–63
context 30–2
contextual dependency 35–6, 123
contingently responsive speech
    (semantically contingent
    responsiveness) 49, 50, 116, 231–3

critical perspectives 63–70
'cultural capital' 69
culture
  as context for language as system 28
  practices and artefacts 24–5
  see also sociocultural theory
Cummins, J. 5, 17–18, 32, 61, 62, 63–4,
    66, 67, 226
curriculum macrogenre 100–4

Davis, K. 81
deficit/deprivation theories 66–7
Delpit, L. 56, 69, 105, 110
developmental (genetic) method 22
dialogue see exchanges (dialogue)
disciplines/subjects
  boundaries 54
  language teaching across 7–9
discourse
  of deficit/deprivation theories 66–7
  and identity 63–5
  as learning 48–52
  mode 30
  proleptic 236–7
  three 'fields' within 104–13
dominant participation and interaction
    structures 98
Donato, R. 244–5
Driver, R. 80, 102–3, 148
  and Oldham, V. 100

Early, M. 56, 62
Eckermann, A. 66
'ecological approach' to research 236
Edwards, A. and Furlong, V. 169–70
Edwards, A. and Westgate, D. 8, 11, 84–5,
    92, 118
Edwards, D. and Mercer, N. 6, 24, 96, 115,
    142, 164, 174, 181, 224, 228
Edwards, T. 196
Eggins, S. 30–1, 33
egocentric speech see 'inner speech'
Ellis, R. 47, 48, 50

English, as medium of education 55
episode summaries 95–100
exchanges (dialogue) 115–17
    extended 251–62
    participatory 117–19
    types of 36–8
experiential meanings 31, 32
explicitness, notion of 56

Faltis, C. and Hudelson, S. 62
Feez, S. 19
'filtering' 232
Floriani, A. 85, 170
form, negotiation of 51–2
Freire, P. 16

genetic (developmental) method 22
Gibbons, P. 55, 60, 62, 217
grammar 27–30
    see also systemic functional grammar
        (SFG)
group(s)
    behaviour, appropriate and
        inappropriate 111–13
    learning, 'intermental development
        zone' (IDZ) 26–7
    talk and group tasks 57–9
Gutierrez, K.
    Larson, J. and Kreuter, B. 64
    and Stone, 65

Hall, J. 64–5
Halliday, M. 27–8, 29, 31, 32, 37, 40, 63,
    123, 148, 194, 203, 228, 232
Hasan, R. 6
Hatch, E. 48–9
'here and now' *see* contextual
    dependency
hypothesis testing 47

ideational meanings 31
identity, discourse and 63–5
immersion model, content-teaching
    within 61–3
individual and whole-class work,
    boundaries 54
initiation-response-feedback (IRF) 83, 85,
    115
    and dialogue exchanges 115–17
'inner speech', social origins of 22–4
input, comprehensible 45–6, 170
interactants
    'communicative consensus' between
        47

discourse and identity 63–5
    status of 58, 59
interaction(s) 62
    contingent, mediation through
        231–3
    patterns 113–19
    power relations 64, 67–8, 69–70
    structures, dominant participation and
        98
    transcribed 87–9
    see also participation
'intermental development zone' (IDZ)
    26–7
interpersonal meanings 31, 32
interpretive approach 80–3

knowledge
    Australian study teaching programme
        78
    as commodity 15–18
    constructions 99–100
'knowledge framework' 123
Krashen, S. 26, 45, 151

Lantolf, J. 43, 137, 235
Lave, J. and Wenger, E. 21
learners (students)
    Australian study 73, 76–7
    knowledge constructed about 100
    output 46–8
    as passive recipients 16
    proleptic discourse 236–7
    reformulation 265–6
    reviews 237–8
    speaker rights 263–5
    talking about 110–11
    and teachers 2–7
        engagement in instructions 239–42
        extended dialogue 251–62
    see also interactants; minority learners;
        peer(s)
Lemke, J. 95–6, 117, 126, 129, 131, 133,
    141, 148–9, 199, 210, 213, 220, 226,
    230, 231, 262
Leont'ev, A. 40
'literate talk' 158, 169, 244
Long, M. 50
Lyster, R. 52
    and Ratna, L. 51–2

McGroaty, M. 57, 59, 60
McKay, P. *et al* 2
McLaren, P. 66
McNally, D. 19

magnetism 34–6, 99–100, 107–12
  see also Australian study; science
Martin, J. 4, 30, 32, 33, 34–6
Maybin, J. 244
  et al 173, 175
meaning
  and context 31–2
  'provisional meaning' 244
mediation
  contingent interactions 231–3
  notion of 24–5
  recontextualization: 'rewriting history'
    227–31
  teaching as 223–4
  technicalizing talk 210–23
  as theory of teaching-and-learning
    224–7
  of thinking 200–10
  see also scaffolding
Mercer, N. 24, 26–7, 39, 142–3, 169, 175,
  179, 225, 233
'message abundancy' 55–6, 141, 169
metafunctions of language 31, 32
metalinguistic talk 47–8, 99–100,
  107–12
metaphors 43–5
  language as conduit 15–18
micro-mode shifting 125–6
minority learners
  Australian study 73
  critical perspectives 63–70
  redefining 65–6
mode of context-embeddedness 98–9
mode continuum (spoken and written
    language) 32–6
mode shifting 119–20, 142–3
  examples from classroom 1 144–53,
    277–83
  examples from classroom 2 153–68,
    284–99
  implications for pedagogy 168–72
  micro-mode shifting 125–6
Mohan, B. 5, 17, 62, 63, 123, 124

negotiation of form 51–2
Newman, F. Griffiths, P. and Cole, M. 26
'noticing' 47

Oakes, J. 66
Ochs, E. 90
Oliver, R. 51
organizational structures, participant and
    53–6
output of learners 46–8

paraphrasing 55
Parker, K. and Chaudron, C. 55–6
participant and organizational structures
    53–6
participation 64–5
  dominant, and interaction structures 98
  exchanges 117–19
  metaphor 44
  in reviews 237–8
  see also interaction(s)
pedagogy
  challenging 67–70
  theory and practice 82–3
peer(s)
  collaboration with 242–51
  status of interactants 58, 59
Phillips, T. 20
'philosophical grammars' 29
Piaget, J. 18–19, 23, 25
Pica, T. 45–6, 58–9
Plowden Report 20
power relations 64, 67–8, 69–70
'private speech', social origins of 22–4
process-oriented approaches 106–7
progressive approaches 19–20
proleptic discourse 236–7
'provisional meaning' 244

'recasts' 50–3, 125, 126–31
recontextualization 227–31
reformulation 265–6
register
  instructional and regulative 104–6
  linguistic, of text 30–2, 97
reminding and handing over 125–6,
    137–9
repetition 55–6, 141, 169
researchers and teachers 9–12
'retroactive contextualization' 230
reviews, participating in 237–8

scaffolding 175–6
  examples
    stage 1: review and orientation
      177–81
    stage 2: setting up new task 181–96
    stage 3: doing task 196–8
    stage 4: reflection on task 198–200
school community, Australian study
    73–5
Schratz, M. and Walker, R. 10, 11
science 99, 106–7
  see also magnetism
SFG *see* systemic functional grammar

semantically contingent responsiveness
see contingently responsive
speech
semiotic interpretation of language 30
Simon, R. and Dippo, D. 80
skills, Australian study teaching
programme 78
social interaction *see* group(s);
interactants; interaction(s)
social origins of 'inner speech' 22–4
social view of language 27–38
sociocultural theory of learning 20–1,
39–41, 43–4
sociolinguistic differences 67–8
speaker rights 263–5
speaker roles 38
speech act theory 36–7
status of interactants 58, 59
Stierer, B. and Maybin, J. 225–6
students *see* interactants; learners
(students); minority learners;
peer(s)
subjects *see* disciplines/subjects
Swain, M. 44, 46–8, 59, 61, 137, 235
and Lapkin, S. 251–2
systemic functional grammar (SFG) 27–8,
29–30, 32
relevance to sociocultural theory of
learning 39–41, 63
and transformational grammar 28–9

'talk curriculum' 24
talk(ing)
about 'being a student' 110–11
about language (metalinguistic talk)
47–8, 99–100, 107–12
about talk 125, 132–6, 266–71
as experts 251
group, and group tasks 57–9
teacher-talk 54–5
technicalizing 210–23
target language, learning through medium
of 17
see also content-based language
teaching
teacher- vs. student-centred classes 53–6
teacher-talk 54–5

teacher(s)
Australian study 75–6
monologue 114–15
questions 56–7
and researchers 9–12
role 16
see also learners (students), and
teachers
teaching as 'facilitation' 18–19
teaching/learning cycle 100–4
teaching/learning processes 98
technicalizing talk 210–23
technology, written and spoken language
34
text 30
linguistic register of 30–2, 97
situation as context for language as 28
textual meanings 31
Thorne, S. 173
Torr, J. 56–7
Tough, J. 20
traditional language instruction 17, 58
transformational grammar 28–9
turn allocation 54

van Lier, L. 8, 9, 10–11, 49, 51, 70, 81, 82,
87, 106–7, 113, 114, 117, 150,
180–1, 220, 232, 235, 236, 252, 255,
274
'vertical constructions' 49
Vygotsky, L. 4–5, 20–1, 21–7, 40, 47, 57–8,
68–9, 128, 150, 235, 245, 248, 266

Webster, A. *et al* 16, 24, 110, 174, 175, 200
Wegerif, R. and Mercer, N. 148, 149, 155
Wells, G. 15, 23, 25, 40, 49, 80, 82, 128,
168, 174, 177, 252, 256–7, 264
Wertsch, V. and Cole, M. 25
Widdowson, H. 10
Wong-Fillmore, L. 53–4, 177, 237
written language 34, 103–4, 126, 139–42

Young, R. 64

zone of proximal development (ZPD)
25–7, 47, 68–9, 128, 131, 132, 266
see also scaffolding

LaVergne, TN USA
04 January 2010
168882LV00002B/7/P